QUALITATIVE EVALUATION

INTRODUCING QUALITATIVE METHODS provides a series of volumes which introduce qualitative research to the student and beginning researcher. The approach is interdisciplinary and international. A distinctive feature of these volumes is the helpful student exercises.

One stream of the series provides texts on the key methodologies used in qualitative research. The other stream contains books on qualitative research for different disciplines or occupations. Both streams cover the basic literature in a clear and accessible style, but also cover the 'cutting edge' issues in the area.

SERIES EDITOR
David Silverman (Goldsmiths College)

EDITORIAL BOARD
Michael Bloor (University of Wales, Cardiff)
Barbara Czarniawska-Joerges (University of Gothenburg)
Norman Denzin (University of Illinois, Champagne)
Barry Glassner (University of Southern California)
Jaber Gubrium (University of Florida, Gainesville)
Anne Murcott (South Bank University)
Jonathan Potter (Loughborough University)

TITLES IN SERIES
Doing Conversational Analysis: A Practical Guide
Paul ten Have

Using Foucault's Methods
Gavin Kendall and Gary Wickham

The Quality of Qualitative Research
Clive Seale

Qualitative Evaluation
Ian Shaw

Research Life Stories and Family Histories
Robert L. Miller

QUALITATIVE EVALUATION

Ian Shaw

SAGE Publications
London · Thousand Oaks · New Delhi

SAGE Publications Ltd
6 Bonhill Street
London EC2A 4PU

SAGE Publications Inc
2455 Teller Road
Thousand Oaks, California 91320

SAGE Publications India Pvt Ltd
32, M-Block Market
Greater Kailash - I
New Delhi 110 048

British Library Cataloguing in Publication data

A catalogue record for this book is
available from the British Library

ISBN 0 7619 5689 1
ISBN 0 7619 5690 5 (pbk)

Library of Congress catalog record available

Typeset by Type Study, Scarborough, North Yorkshire
Printed in Great Britain by Redwood Books, Trowbridge, Wiltshire

To my parents

Contents

Acknowledgements

Jonathan Scourfield, Nicki Barnes, Paula Harris, Colin Lewis and, once more, Nick Evans, for softening some of the day to day demands of life in ways which had a major impact on the writing of this book. Anthea, for the caravan.

1

Encountering qualitative evaluation

CONTENTS

'What the evaluation field needs is a good social anthropologist.'

Lee Cronbach

Well over thirty years have passed since Robert Stake heard Lee Cronbach make the remark above. What was far-sighted and radical in the early 1960s is unnervingly telling and apposite near the turn of the millennium. Triumphalist acclaim of the successes of evidence-based action and inquiry is heard everywhere in public life, from prisons to pharmacy, policing to social welfare. Controlled evaluations of social interventions measured against behavioural outcomes are believed to hold promise of verifying what works and what doesn't. If professionals and practitioners cannot read the results, see the obvious implications, and act on them, so much the worse for them. Yet, truth to tell, quantitative, outcome-oriented measures of accountability are typically bereft of the intensity, subtlety, particularity, ethical judgement and relevance that potentially character-ize evaluation born of ethnography.

In deliberate counterpoint, the appearance of this book within a series introducing qualitative methodology asserts that the relationship between evaluative purposes and qualitative social science is a – possibly *the* – fulcrum for generating good evaluation inquiry.

Writing this book has been a disconcerting experience – a steady path in its early stages from 'knowledge' to ignorance. Perhaps this is as it should be. I thought I knew something about evaluation. After all, I had written about and practised it. Yet it was an early discovery that, to all intents and purposes, I had never previously thought about it. I did not start from the thematic 'strands of qualitative evaluation', elucidated later in this introductory chapter. I ended with them, as persuasions.

Wrong turnings, border posts and friendly fire

There are exciting challenges, issues and innovations within evaluation. Yet it would be blinkered naïvety if I were to give the impression that all we need to do is apply qualitative methodology to evaluation and all will be light and maybe sweetness as well. There are major ambiguities about both the subject and object of such application – about the influence of the evaluation establishment, the terms under which debates are developed, the relationship between evaluation and social science, the standing of qualitative evaluation, and the response of mainstream ethnography to the evaluation enterprise. I will explore these more fully, as a backdrop to subsequently explaining the emphases which distinguish the chapters ahead.

The evaluation establishment persistently locates qualitative evaluation as, at best, part of a horses-for-courses solution to evaluation methodology, and at worst as the Morris Minor to the evaluation family Rolls-Royce. Few like to raise their hands and admit to being part of an establishment. Yet evaluation indubitably has one. It includes those who carry the mantle of first generation evaluation theorists, produce respected texts on the foundations of programme evaluation, shape the evaluation agenda of governments, or become presidents of the American Evaluation Association. Proponents of the horses-for-courses approach to evaluation believe – to extend the metaphor – that, when the ground is hard or firm, outcome-oriented evaluation designs can safely be jockeyed into position, whereas when the ground is soft we should opt for mounts which can safely negotiate an understanding of sticky institutional processes.

The lurking suspicion remains, however, that in a world of sunny days and dry evaluation race courses the methods of choice are those which will promise us firm information about outcomes, effects and efficiency. While qualitative evaluation will do when the course is soft, the ground will sooner or later dry out and it will become possible and desirable to find out whether programmes, policies or projects have had any measurable effect. For such questions the randomized, controlled, clinical trial provides the 'gold standard, the Rolls Royce of evaluation approaches' (Chelimsky, 1997: 101). Unfortunately, neither the elitism of quasi-experimentation nor the eclectic pluralism of horses-for-courses, with its tacit assumption of 'live and let live', can deliver relevant and rigorous evaluation.

The everyday world of evaluation practice continues to be led by preoccupations with measurement, traditional worries regarding reliability and validity, and other concerns captured within quantitative methodology. These concerns have been given a new lease of life and purposefulness in the wake of the enthusiasm for evidence-based approaches to a range of social interventions and their evaluation. There are both broad-stream and more narrow-stream versions of evidence-based practice. The broad-stream version is mainly practice-driven. It includes an emphasis on accountability, close working relationships between researchers and practitioners, a general obligation to ground practice judgements in evidence, and an explicit drawing on research findings to support decisions. It also includes a programme to ease access to data, and to promote the dissemination of research findings in understandable form, an orientation to outcome issues in practice, and a twin stress on feasible and incremental professional development.

The more focused, narrow-stream version of evidence-based practice is often academic-driven. This more restricted use of the term includes the features of the broader stream, but in addition typically entails a confidence in measurement, instrumentation, the objectivity of evidence, behavioural indices of good professional practice, quasi-experimentation, and on occasion negativity towards qualitative evaluation methodology.

My reservations are primarily about the narrow-stream version. The phrase is something of a give-away. What do we mean by 'evidence'? What do we mean by 'practice'? How is one 'based' on the other? Far too much is assumed. But of course, one does not describe a holy grail – one simply searches.

The confidence in measurement within evidence-based practice betrays a naïve view of how easy it is to grasp an understanding of reality. The failure to problematize the evidence/practice relationship is the Achilles heel of evidence-based practice. The assumption found in most writers of this persuasion is that utilization of evaluation findings is a relatively straightforward matter. Where it is a problem, it is typically put down to a breakdown in communication or the self-interested resistance of professionals (Sheldon and Macdonald, 1989–90). To regard theory and practice problems in this way is to relegate 'practice' to the subordinate, the acted-upon, and to fail to recognize that practical problems of this kind occur in the course of *any* undertaking. To assume that difficulties of this kind can somehow be identified and tackled in theory and then applied in practice tends to conceal how they are in fact generated out of practice. Evidence-based practice thus has an inept understanding of how research is used. It is married, for better or worse, to strong accountability models of evaluation, and its advocates typically fail to take issues of power seriously. Almost all forms of evidence-based practice are non-participatory. Issues of gender and race tend to be treated as technical problems that can be mitigated if not completely resolved. Unfortunately, tight designs do not lead to truth, and 'unexamined technicalism in evaluation research is worse than no evaluation at all' (Palumbo, 1987: 31).

If reluctance to abandon confidence in technical design solutions is the first major problem, the second springs from misguided attempts to carve out a territory for evaluation which distances it from mainstream social science methodology. We will discover that on most issues it is difficult to find evaluation theorists more different from each other than Michael Scriven on the one hand and Yvonna Lincoln and Egon Guba on the other. Yet they are one in their unreserved belief that research and evaluation are different enterprises, and that to take a contrary view is misguided and deeply damaging. We return to the relation between evaluation and research later in this chapter. Here I simply assert that I regard this demand for divorce or at least separation as bad news for evaluation. I may be mistaken, but I wonder if it stems in part from an American ethnocentrism which promotes the separate occupational identity of evaluators.

There are other taken-for-granted boundaries that artificially limit and constrain the development of evaluation. It has been at once the strength and weakness of evaluation that it draws predominantly on the work of education theorists and researchers. The advantages of a shared vocabulary and practical concerns within education have provided the basis for some of the best writing on evaluation, especially qualitative evaluation. Yet it breeds myopia, and an insularity that has long outlived its usefulness. Sadly the problem is scarcely recognized let alone addressed. Cronbach is almost the only theorist from an educational perspective who has identified and lamented the damage done by the almost complete absence of cross-border work between those who address evaluation-related problems in health, law, social welfare and education. Professional ethnocentrism is as debilitating and potentially discriminatory as national ethnocentrism.

There is one more intellectual border post that needs dismantling. In much evaluation writing, for 'evaluation' one can read 'programme evaluation'. Theorizing about evaluation, the location of evaluation within the processes of political and social change, and debates about how evaluation is and should be used, all tend to be seen as problems about understanding and evaluating relatively large-scale *programmes*. Carol Weiss's work on *policy* evaluation is well known, but too frequently ignored in the evaluation literature. Again, the work of theorists like Robert Stake and Elliot Eisner is widely discussed, yet too little understood in terms of its consequences for the evaluation of direct, local *practice*. There has been some dilution of the hegemony of programme evaluation. For example, mainly through the influence of Scriven, the American Evaluation Association has separate standards for programme evaluation and personnel evaluation. Yet while this may serve claims to occupational territory it does little to promote the concerns which are more central to qualitative evaluation.

There are two further important challenges facing evaluation which thus far have not been met. One of the most significant developments of the last decade has been the gradual emergence of openly ideological forms of research and evaluation. Most evaluation theory – including some of that which helpfully acknowledges the centrality of political issues – pre-dates this development. In consequence, the evaluation establishment has held ranks and appealed to the majority position within evaluation practice as grounds to exclude advocacy evaluation. Chelimsky represents this position. She confesses that evaluation does need standards of quality and practice that make sense for the entire field, not just one segment of it: 'It will be critical for the standards to be inclusive of all legitimate purposes of evaluation, and not merely serve to sanctify one perspective at the expense of another' (Chelimsky, 1997: 108). Yet she concludes that 'honesty is critical and advocacy is not really an option' (p. 109) and probably cannot be incorporated into common standards. The openly ideological evaluator would of course say that this misreads the problem and that mainstream standards are not an option.

The final problem for qualitative evaluation comes from a less expected corner. Mainstream ethnography and significant interests within British sociology have shown a critical disdain for qualitative evaluation. The origins of this lie in the development of social science disciplines (Finch, 1986). But whatever the reason, friendly fire has been one of the most important factors in the weakening of qualitative evaluation, and the stimulation of new artificial boundaries between qualitative research and qualitative evaluation.

Strands of qualitative evaluation

My intention in this book is to argue for a qualitative evaluation that counters each of these challenges, constraints and wrong turnings. The guiding *motifs* of this book can be expressed as a series of propositions:

- Evaluation is distinguished by a cluster of evaluative purposes. This will enable plausible and productive responses to questions of methodological choice, evaluation theorizing, evaluation ethics and advocacy evaluation.
- Evaluation is best understood as entailing the conduct of evaluative *research* rather than a discrete set of evaluation axioms or methodology separate from the wider research enterprise.
- The particular challenges and constraints facing evaluation will usually require qualitative evaluation as the methodology of choice.
- A relevant and rigorous evaluation requires the development of inter-professional evaluation theorizing and strategies.
- Evaluation theory and methodology owes as much to work undertaken by writers and researchers who would not regard themselves as evaluation theorists, as it does to confessedly evaluation theorists.
- Qualitative evaluation promises distinct but coherent perspectives on policy, programme and practice evaluation.

- Qualitative evaluation offers credible partial solutions to problems of causal analysis and outcome evaluation.
- Qualitative evaluation is able to avoid sentimental failures to problematize its own analysis and solutions.

The exposition of these propositions lies in the whole of what follows. For the moment I wish only to underline the first and last. The argument about *evaluative purpose* is perhaps the most pervasive claim in this book: 'Some vision of purpose is, at root, what guides all evaluation practice' (Greene, 1994: 539). The point is not, as such, especially novel. Silverman says of qualitative research in general that 'the multiple logics of qualitative research emerge from their relationships with the general purposes of research projects' (1997b: 25).

There is not one evaluative purpose but many. These include traditional evaluation agendas of accounting for the results of public programmes and policies, and seeking to determine their efficiency. Yet evaluative purposes also include gaining insight into public problems and into past and present efforts to address them. This will include normative explanations in terms of injustice. Evaluation also seeks understanding of how organizations work and how they change, and may develop and assess means of strengthening institutions and improving performance. Increasing agency responsiveness to the public and service users, and working to reform government through the free flow of evaluation information are also central evaluation purposes (Chelimsky, 1997).

Chelimsky links this diversity of purpose to three different conceptual perspectives that she plausibly detects within evaluation. She describes these as:

1 Evaluation for *accountability* (e.g. measuring results or efficiency).
2 Evaluation for *development* (e.g. providing evaluative help to strengthen institutions).
3 Evaluation for *knowledge* (e.g. obtaining a deeper understanding in some specific area or policy field).

We do not need to accept all the implications that Chelimsky believes follow from this analysis. For example, we have seen that she favours a 'horses-for-courses' view of the evaluation enterprise. In doing so she warns against using qualitative strategies (for instance, case studies) to tackle questions and problems which she believes should remain the province of quantitatively-oriented methods which seek control through design. She also excludes advocacy methods in the interests of preserving common standards and views of evaluation quality. Neither of these positions is helpful. Yet the basic idea *is* valuable, especially if we underline the coherence yet diversity which the extended family of evaluative purposes permits: 'Evaluation is not monolithic, but we have behaved as if it were' (Chelimsky, 1997: 104). Let me suggest, by way of illustration, points at which this perspective is fruitful.

First, it prevents the pitfall of assuming that there is a single body of evaluation theory providing the basis for all evaluation practice. Throughout this book we draw on four different literatures: evaluation theory, educational evaluation, social work evaluation and qualitative research methodology. My coverage is not exhaustive but is, I hope, reasonably comprehensive. Its scope is the main evidence I give for the proposition that evaluation theory and methodology owes as much to work undertaken by writers and researchers who would not regard themselves as evaluation theorists, as it does to confessedly evaluation theorists.

Second, it affords breadth yet distinctiveness to decisions regarding evaluation methods. In Chelimsky's words, 'although all three perspectives *may* use any and all methods, because the purposes are different, the methods are typically employed differently as well' (1997: 103). There will be distinguishing uses of methods between conventional researchers and evaluators, and also, as Chelimsky suggests, within evaluation. We will have occasion to recognize and illustrate this point time and again through this book. The close articulation of methodology and purpose avoids the tendency often present in debate about evaluation to set methodology against ideology. Qualitative evaluation divorced from purpose becomes a mere reinvention of the technicalism of which quantitative evaluation has too often been guilty. We should not name qualitative evaluation by methods. On the other hand, evaluation defined exclusively in terms of ideology leaves us without strategy and short- or medium-term direction, and at risk of our own passions.

Third, the argument about purpose allows the difficult issue of openly ideological evaluation to be placed 'on hold' without resorting to either excommunication or beatification.

The last item in the list of propositions is also pervasive in its influence on this book. *Sentimentality* is a recurring risk for all who become involved in one form or another of disciplined inquiry (Shaw, 1999). When it comes to matters of research and evaluation practitioners and theorizers alike are vulnerable to sentimentality, marked by a nurturing of myths and a tendency to superstitious practices.

We are guilty of sentimentality, says Howard Becker,

> when we refuse, for whatever reason, to investigate some matter that should properly be regarded as problematic. We are sentimental especially, when our reason is that we would prefer not to know what is going on, if to know would be to violate some sympathy whose existence we may not even be aware of. (1970, 132–133)

The sentimentalities and superstitious practices that specially concern me are those most closely associated with commitments that I myself share. If there is a debunking note from time to time through this book then this is only as it should be. I believe it was Phillip of Macedon who employed a man with a stick, atop of which was a pig's bladder. The sole function this man fulfilled was to exercise the freedom to wake Phillip at any time of the night, and beat him about the head with the bladder, as a reminder that he was mortal. I have tried to include a few pigs' bladders scattered through the text.

Two questions have been left partly unanswered so far. First, what, if any, are the differences between research and evaluation? Second, what do we assert when we claim that an evaluation is qualitative? I have given away my answer to the first question, but have not acknowledged the counterarguments for a more radical disjuncture between research and evaluation. I have said nothing about the second question. We turn to them now.

Qualitative *evaluation*

No one, to my knowledge, wishes to stand up and say that the terms 'evaluation' and 'research' represent a distinction without a difference. But that is where the agreement almost ends. Table 1.1 assembles several of the ways in which evaluation and research have been distinguished.

Before we comment on these possibilities for distinguishing evaluation from research, a brief clarification of the question is necessary. By asking whether evaluation and research are different, we are compressing three different questions:

1 *Can* research and evaluation be similar/different?
2 *Is* research different from evaluation?
3 *Should* research and evaluation be different or similar?

The first question is theoretical, the second empirical and the third is normative. Part of the problem of this debate stems from the fact that the question is treated as if it were empirical when in fact it is usually normative or theoretical.

Consider for a moment some questions arising from the empirical version of the question. Do funders believe there is a difference between evaluation and research? If so, how are funding decisions affected by that distinction? Government research funders may distinguish, for example,

TABLE 1.1 *Evaluation and research*

Evaluation	Research
Addresses practical problems	Addresses theoretical problems
Culminates in action	Culminates in description
Makes judgements of merit/worth	Describes
Addresses short-term issues	Addresses long-term issues
Evaluation methods	Research methods
Is non-disciplinary	Is disciplinary
Includes insider evaluation	Is always conducted by outsiders

basic research, strategic research and applied research. Whether they 'count' any of these as evaluation is not certain. What do end-users think about the distinction? I suspect, for example, it may matter little to senior managers of a major national voluntary children's agency whether something is counted as evaluation or research, so long as it appears to have a clear 'use'. Again, what do evaluation/research practitioners believe? If we could conceive some hypothetical double blind test, could the inquirers empirically distinguish the processes and products of evaluation on the one hand and research on the other? Similarly, how about respondents? Empirical work in this field may be salutary – though it may resolve few disagreements, because these disagreements are not at the level of substance but of axioms or aims. Axiological disagreements are intransigent (Witkin and Gottschalk, 1988).

The question is also complicated by the fact that little consensus exists on how to define research or evaluation. This sometimes leads to protagonists predefining each in such a way as it telegraphs the solution.

So what about Table 1.1? It is certainly feasible to find respected advocates of each position. For example, Ernest House, one of the most lucid commentators and theorizers in the evaluation field, accepts a version of the short-term/long-term distinction because he believes that science aims for long-term generalizations to universal audiences, whereas evaluation aims for context-bound conclusions for a particular audience (House, 1980). He is seeking to distance himself from Donald Campbell, who appears to argue that evaluation is part of scientific inquiry and subject to similar epistemological concerns. The distinction House draws is an important one, but I find little in it to serve as a plausible basis for distinguishing evaluation from research. We will see in Chapter 4 that research carried out on the uses of evaluation and policy research demonstrates that many officials and politicians are influenced by evidence over a longer term rather than by single studies in the short term.

The practical/theoretical distinction is scarcely any more persuasive. However, it has had influential advocates. Several leaders of the democratic evaluation movement within education, and the teacher-as-researcher movement, have accepted some form of this distinction. Elliott recalls the emergence of democratic evaluation in British education in the 1960s and 1970s. Part of the agenda of this movement was to exclude empiricist methods from the evaluation field. For some, this went as far as to challenge the continuity between any group of research methods and the evaluation enterprise, and to challenge 'the assumption that evaluation expertise can primarily be defined in terms of the mastery of a group of methods at all' (Elliott, 1991: 218). The counterargument of Elliott and others is that the *audience* is the key that distinguishes naturalistic research from naturalistic evaluation. In the latter case the audience is individuals and groups who have a practical interest in the study as opposed to academic peers.

The practical/theoretical distinction certainly raises material issues. The argument that evaluation should not serve academic interests but those of the reference group whose interests are being considered by the evaluation, has rightly been given weight. We will give close attention to this issue through the book. My problem is twofold. First, it seems unnecessary to accept the assumption that ideas, concepts, and theories are inimical to committed action. Mainstream ethnographers and openly ideological evaluators are only two groups who would blanche at the very thought. Second, democratic evaluators seem to accept the associated position that the evaluator has a political stance, whereas 'no such stance is required of the researcher. He stands outside the political process, and values his detachment from it' (Elliott, 1991: 219). Once again, this is far too simplistic, and Elliott has shifted his position to resolve this dualism.

Lincoln and Guba have proposed perhaps the most powerful case for a strong distinction between evaluation and research. In a retrospective essay, Lincoln recalls that they came to the position that there are different forms of 'disciplined inquiry'. They adopted this useful term from Cronbach, to refer to an inquiry that has a texture that displays the raw material entering the argument and the logical processes by which they were compressed and rearranged to make the conclusion credible. They concluded that research, evaluation and policy analysis are different forms of disciplined inquiry. Hence, 'it made no sense to refer to "evaluation research", save as research *on* evaluation methods or models' (Lincoln, 1990: 76).

Lincoln and Guba define research as 'a type of disciplined inquiry undertaken to resolve some problem in order to achieve understanding or to facilitate action' (1986b: 549). In constructing their definition of evaluation they propose several distinctions. First, they accept a familiar distinction from Scriven between summative and formative evaluation. They utilize the American term 'evaluand' to refer to the entity being evaluated:

> The aim of formative evaluation is to provide descriptive and judgmental information, leading to refinement, improvement, alterations, and/or modification in the evaluand, while the aim of summative evaluation is to determine its impacts, outcomes, or results. (1986b: 550)

Second, they distinguish two aspects of value that an evaluator may seek to establish, *merit* and *worth*. 'Merit', as they use the term, refers to the intrinsic, context-free qualities that accompany the evaluand from place to place and are relatively invariant. For example, a curriculum may have a value independent of any local application. 'Worth' refers to the context-determined value, which varies from one context to another. For example, a curriculum may have a certain value for teaching a particular child in a given setting. Based on these distinctions they define evaluation as:

> a type of disciplined inquiry undertaken to determine the value (merit and/or worth) of some entity – the evaluand – such as a treatment, program, facility, performance, and the like – in order to improve or refine the evaluand (formative evaluation) or to assess its impact (summative evaluation). (1986b: 550)

These distinguishing definitions have much in their favour. They safely steer through the tendency to stereotyping and special pleading that mark most efforts at distinctions. They avoid making methodology the distinguishing criterion, and also make difference of purpose the first and foremost issue: 'Research is undertaken to resolve some problem, while evaluation is undertaken to establish value' (1986b: 551).

There are, however, lingering and unhelpful echoes of rhetorical intent. Despite the comparative care with which the definitions are formed, their accompanying comments reinstate several ways of distinguishing research and evaluation which should not be accepted. It is not the case, for example, that 'the expected outcome or use of research is simply the expansion of understanding' (1986b: 551) through what Lincoln and Guba call 'technical reports'. Nor is it sufficient for them to suggest that the audiences for evaluation are more likely to be multiple and heterogeneous and involve stakeholders, while research audiences are relatively homogeneous. In addition, it is gross oversimplification to argue that evaluation reporting 'introduces political considerations to an extent simply not found in research' (1986b: 552). The benefits of having avoided methodological distinctions within their basic definitions are forfeited when they later appear to claim that correspondences between research, evaluation and policy analysis only occur when techniques used to arrive at data, and to draw conclusions from them only 'occasionally overlap' (1986b: 560). More generally, it is a recurrent weakness in all Lincoln and Guba's writing that they convey the false impression that the majority of conventional researchers hold what they describe as the 'traditional paradigm' (1986b: 555).

In sum, there are important differences between evaluation and research which follow from the differing clusters of purposes that direct each form of inquiry. But over-simple generalizations about homogeneous entities of 'research' and 'evaluation' provide bases for rhetoric rather than practice. In my view to talk of 'evaluation research' or 'policy research' does make good sense, and involves no confusion of categories.

Qualitative evaluation

What do we assert when we claim that an evaluation is qualitative? What are the identifying characteristics of a qualitative approach? In what evaluation circumstances might we use qualitative inquiry? What are its strengths over against quantitative methods? Before committing ourselves to some answers, I should say that this book does not simply aim to describe qualitative evaluation methods but also, and in the first instance, to set out and explore the nature of qualitative evaluation methodology. I use the term methodology very broadly in this context to include the interplay between the practice of qualitative methods, the epistemological underpinnings of qualitative evaluation, and evaluative purpose. Hence, 'what importantly distinguishes one evaluation methodology from another is not methods, but rather whose questions are addressed and which values are promoted' (Greene, 1994: 533).

By way of preamble, we should acknowledge that there is a close – if exceedingly tricky – relationship between qualitative understanding and common sense knowledge. By common sense knowledge I do not mean what Geertz calls 'mere matter-of-fact apprehension of reality' (1983: 75). Geertz's influential essay persuades the reader with several reasons why treating common sense as a 'relatively organized body of considered thought' – 'in short, a cultural system' – rather than just 'what anyone clothed and in his right mind knows', should lead on to some useful conclusions (1983: 75, 76).

Once we accept this view of everyday things, there are immediate and extensive consequences for how we envisage qualitative evaluation. We have spent some time considering the relationship between research and evaluation, and have noted how Lincoln and Guba set the question in a wider context by talking of various forms of disciplined inquiry. But once we include common sense knowledge the context is much larger. Campbell, for example, insists 'we must not suppose that scientific knowing replaces common-sense knowing. Rather, science depends upon common sense even though at best it goes beyond it' (1978: 186). He suggests that ordinary knowing and most forms of science share a position somewhere between the extremes of total scepticism (in which we give up 'knowing' or science) and total credulity. They 'somehow combine a capacity for focused distrust and revision with a belief in a common body of knowledge claims' (1978: 187).

Eisner (1991a: 15) draws a useful distinction between qualitative research, qualitative inquiry and qualitative thinking. This is helpful in that it implicitly poses the question of how we ought to understand the relationship between research, evaluation and professional purpose and practice, and ways in which the significance of ideas about qualitative knowing spreads out into everyday life.

The characteristics of qualitative inquiry

Any attempt to list what is common to qualitative evaluation will fall short of universal or even majority agreement. Indeed, there is a widely held view that any attempt to characterize qualitative research as a whole is open to severe criticism (Silverman, 1997b). I hope to steer clear of that debate. I do not set out to provide a list that is either generic to all qualitative research or even exhaustive of qualitative evaluation. Rather, I am suggesting that these characteristics are of core relevance to qualitative evaluation. They will not be accepted by everyone. For instance, we will see in Chapter 3 that disputes about whether qualitative evaluation has a realist or relativist base resonate through apparently more mundane issues about the specific aspects of evaluation research. The list here has realist undertones. It takes Miles and Huberman's work as a starting point.

- Qualitative evaluation is conducted through intense or long-term contact with the field: 'These situations are typically "banal" or normal ones, reflective of the everyday life of individuals, groups, societies and organizations' (Miles and Huberman, 1994: 6). It involves 'looking at the ordinary in places where it takes unaccustomed forms, so that 'understanding a people's culture exposes their normalness without reducing their particularity' (Geertz, 1973: 14).
- The researcher's role is to gain a *'holistic'* overview of the culture and context under study.
- Holism is pursued through inquiry into the *particular*: 'The anthropologist characteristically approaches ... broader interpretations ... from the direction of exceedingly extended acquaintance with extremely small matters'. Grand realities of Power, Faith, Prestige, Love, and so on are confronted 'in contexts obscure enough ... to take the capital letters off' (Geertz, 1973: 21). Qualitative evaluations 'make the case palpable' (Eisner, 1991a: 39).
- The whole and the particular are held in tension. 'Small facts speak to large issues' (Geertz, 1973: 23), and 'in the particular is located a general theme' (Eisner, 1991a: 39). However, we are sometimes left with the impression that this process is fairly obvious – that what we understand about individual classrooms, particular social workers, local clinics, and so on, will be immediately useful for understanding other classrooms, social workers and doctors' clinics. Qualitative evaluators have, however, been weak at this point. Greene complains that:

> the potential contributions of the story to more general social scientific understanding are muted by qualitative evaluators' rejection of formal, propositional explanations for social phenomena. Concomitantly, qualitative evaluators' voice in the policy arena has also been muted, and the stories we tell are only locally powerful. (1996: 281)

- 'The researcher attempts to capture data on the perceptions of local actors "from the inside", through a process of deep attentiveness, of empathic understanding (*verstehen*), and of suspending or "bracketing" preconceptions about the topics under discussion' (Miles and Huberman, 1994: 6). A caveat is in order. This stance does not preclude a normative position. Indeed, qualitative approaches 'can effectively give voice to the normally silenced and can poignantly illuminate what is typically masked' (Greene, 1994: 541).
- Respondent or member categories are kept to the foreground throughout the evaluation.
- Qualitative evaluation is interpretative: 'A main task is to explicate the ways people in particular settings come to understand, account for,

take action, and otherwise manage their day-to-day situations' (Miles and Huberman, 1994: 7). Hence, 'qualitative data are not so much about "behaviour" as they are about *actions* (which carry with them intentions and meanings, and lead to consequences)' (1994: 10). This does not mean that behaviour is not important: 'Behaviour must be attended to, and with some exactness, because it is through the flow of behaviour – or more precisely, social action – that cultural forms find articulation' (Geertz, 1973: 17).

- Relatively little standardized instrumentation is used, especially at the outset. The researcher is essentially the main instrument in the study. Qualitative fieldwork is not straightforward: 'The features that count in a setting do not wear their labels on their sleeve' (Eisner, 1991a: 33).
- Finally, 'most analysis is done in words' (Miles and Huberman, 1994: 7). Judgement and persuasion by reason are deeply involved, and in qualitative evaluation the facts never speak for themselves. Qualitative evaluators have often held the view that we tell a good evaluation account – in part at least – by its coherence. Geertz dissents with vigour, and calls for a more realist view of qualitative accounts. We share his dissent, without wishing to deny the pervasiveness of aesthetics in qualitative accounts of evaluations.

> There is nothing so coherent as a paranoid's delusion or a swindler's story. The force of our interpretations cannot rest, as they are now so often made to do, on the tightness with which they hold together. (Geertz, 1973: 18)

The case for the strengths which qualitative inquiry brings to evaluation has to be exemplified rather than asserted. However, the focus on naturally occurring events, the local groundedness and contextualization of evaluation, the flexibility of study design, and potential for disclosing complexity through holistic approaches, have some degree of self-evident value. In addition, qualitative data have some strengths on which evaluators do not always capitalize. For example, it will be a recurring theme of this book that qualitative evaluations can assess causality 'as it actually plays out in particular settings' (Miles and Huberman, 1994: 10).

Williams (1986) collates the criteria by which we may decide if a qualitative or naturalistic evaluation is appropriate. It will be appropriate in circumstances when:

- Evaluation issues are not clear in advance.
- Official definitions of the evaluand are not sufficient, and insider ('emic') perspectives are needed.
- 'Thick description' (Geertz's phrase) is required.
- It is desirable to convey the potential for vicarious experience of the evaluand on the part of the reader.
- Formative evaluation, aimed at improving the programme, policy or practice, is appropriate.

- The outcome includes complex actions in natural settings.
- Evaluation recipients want to know how the evaluand is operating in its natural state.
- There is time to study the evaluand through its natural cycle. The true power of naturalistic evaluation is dissipated if there is not time to observe the natural functions of the evaluand in their various forms.
- The situation permits intensive inquiry, without posing serious ethical obstacles.
- The evaluand can be studied unobtrusively, as it operates, and in an ethical way.
- Diverse data sources are available.
- There are resources and consent to search for negative instances and counterevidence.
- There is sufficient customer and end-user agreement on methodological strategy.

One may be forgiven for thinking that this provides a powerful battery of reasons for qualitative evaluation. Indeed, the tone of this book is along the lines that qualitative evaluation will usually be the methodology of choice. This is a further reason why the pluralist, horses-for-courses approach is not adequate. An influential early study examined an instance where the analysis of qualitative data produced an explanation that could not be reconciled with quantitative data from the same study. Trend reflects on the case in the hope that it 'may help to dispel the notion that using multiple methods will lead to sounder explanations in an easy, additive fashion' (1979: 68). He notes the common view that observational data are to be used for generating hypotheses or describing processes, while quantitative data are to be used to analyze outcomes and verify hypotheses. Trend concludes,

> I feel that this division of labour is rigid and limiting . . . [The] complementarity is not always apparent. Simply using different perspectives, with the expectation that they will validate each other, does not tell what to do if the pieces do not fit. (1979: 83)

The case made for qualitative in preference to quantitative evaluation should not be lifted from its context. It will be clear from my criticisms of paradigm talk in Chapter 3 that I reject the idea that quantitative and qualitative inquiry are incommensurable. In that sense I agree with Silverman when he says 'there are no principled grounds to be either qualitative or quantitative in approach. It all depends on what you are trying to do' (1997b: 14). My argument throughout is that what we are trying to do – evaluative purpose – will likely as not demand a qualitative approach, and that this is reinforced by the need for a corrective redistribution in the light of the enthusiasms for outcomes, evidence and accountability.

A synopsis

I started the previous section by saying that by methodology I meant the interplay between the practice of qualitative methods, the epistemological underpinnings of qualitative evaluation, and evaluative purpose. In considering beliefs about the nature of knowledge and science that inform qualitative inquiry, I will consider (Chapter 3) three positions, namely, postpositivist realism, relativist constructivism and critical evaluation. The threefold distinction is somewhat idealized. For instance, all three positions accept in different ways that data are socially constructed, but that constructivists foreground this argument. Critical evaluators and many constructivists are also realists, but they doubt (although for very different reasons) the feasibility of achieving a close approximation to reality through their evaluation. Structural issues are present in constructivist explanations, but critical evaluators foreground them along with a strong view about the moral nature of the evaluative task, and usually a strongly partisan position on the use of knowledge. It will become clear that I am unhappy with the rhetoric of paradigms, although I am equally, perhaps more, dismayed whenever naïve methodological pragmatism surfaces in evaluation.

In Chapter 4 we will turn our attention to more 'use-oriented' questions:

- How do we know if we are doing evaluation right?
- Are the results of evaluation research used through direct application to problems or through a more general process of enlightenment?
- What ethical principles and decision rules should guide qualitative evaluation?
- How should our answers to these questions shape the methodology we use?

These are no less thorny questions than the ones considered in Chapter 3. In each case they are shaped, constrained or enriched by virtue of their evaluative purpose. Questions of the validity of inquiry, the uses to which evaluative inquiry may be put, the general approach to methods of inquiry, and even, to some extent, questions of evaluation ethics, are all given a distinctive twist by their evaluative purpose. No territorial elitism is intended by this point. I am not arguing that evaluation issues are more complex, important or even more interesting than the corresponding issues within qualitative research. But they are *different*.

Having surveyed the preoccupations of what Becker calls philosophical and methodological worry as a profession, we change tack in Chapters 5 and 6, to reflect the position that the embodiment of evaluative purpose should not be regarded as much the same whether we are concerned with policies, programmes or individual practitioners. In Chapter 5 we will reflect on some of the issues that surface when we embark on qualitative strategies of programme evaluation. In the second half of that chapter we spell out the alternative views on how information from policy research may be used. In particular, we examine the debate about instrumental *versus* enlightenment models of information use. Chapter 6 addresses some of the interesting questions posed by the vigorous recent growth of interest and practice in the field of direct practice evaluation. We will consider four areas of evaluation practice that can be subsumed under the broad title of practitioner evaluation.

1   Research and evaluation carried out by practitioners.
2   Participatory research.
3   Evaluation as a dimension of direct practice, through, for example, reflective inquiry.
4   Evaluation *for* practitioners carried out usually by academic researchers.

Having explored the special considerations that arise in the conduct of qualitative evaluation of programmes, policies and individual practice, we can safely conclude that the differences between them are far from superficial or marginal. Yet these differences provide no grounds for fragmenting evaluation and policy research into multiple discrete forms of inquiry, each with its own axioms and methodology. From Chapter 7 to the end of the book I aim to illuminate how evaluative purposes undergird differentiated but coherent approaches to decisions of design, fieldwork and qualitative evaluation analysis. Qualitative design decisions entail:

• The assessment of the evaluability of an evaluand.
• Questions of design ethics and social justice.
• Designing qualitative evaluation for understanding outcomes.
• The utilization of qualitative case study designs.
• Designing participatory evaluation.

My aim in Chapter 8 is to provide an illustrated introduction to an evaluative perspective on fieldwork, rather than a potted inventory of fieldwork methods covered with greater depth elsewhere in the literature. In the main part of the chapter we will consider how evaluative purposes shape decisions to use interviews, observation methods, life stories, documents, focus group interviews and simulations. Whatever the method(s), there are recurring methodological fieldwork issues, and we turn to these in the later stages of the chapter. These include ongoing access issues, evaluating sensitive groups, evaluation of stakeholder and service user satisfaction, practitioner evaluation, and participatory evaluation for empowerment. We conclude that chapter with a reminder of how ethical issues are raised not only at the commencement of qualitative evaluation, but throughout the fieldwork.

The major part of the final chapter deals with the themes and issues posed by qualitative evaluation analysis. We pick up a thread from Chapter 6 and note ways that practitioner and participatory evaluation shape the approach to analysis. Participatory analysis raises important questions of analysis ethics, and we consider these and other ethical considerations posed by analyzing and reporting on evaluation. This provides the context for considering the core question of the chapter – how evaluative claims may be grounded and supported. We take up the argument from Chapter 7 regarding the relevance of qualitative evaluation for tackling thorny questions of causes. We move from there to consider several claims that have been made for ways in which qualitative analysis can be made more plausible. These include the use of methods of member validation, triangulation, and methods of synthesizing and meta-analysis. Important and difficult as these questions may be, issues of generalization and the external validity of evaluation are probably more so. We outline and review the more widely canvassed options and approaches to these two issues. We close with a final visit to some of the issues of evaluation authorship, reporting and use that we consider in more general terms in Chapter 4. But before we embark on the main argument of the book a preamble is in order. The case for qualitative evaluation emerges in the context of animated and continuing work by evaluation theorizers. The main outlines of this theorizing are sketched in Chapter 2.

2

Evaluation theorists and qualitative evaluation: persuasions and persuaders

CONTENTS

This chapter is about the 'big names' in evaluation theory. Listing who should be 'in' and who 'out' is a risky business. My linchpin may be your spare screw. The choice is made slightly easier by the fact that my main purpose is to elucidate how the agenda for qualitative evaluation has been developed and shaped through the work of evaluation theorists. My secondary purpose is to sketch a map of issues and developments in wider evaluation theory. Two health warnings are in order, First, this will not portray an 'onward and upward' view of evaluation history. More recent theorists have come to entertain serious doubts about the picture of science as cumulative and progressive development. We share those doubts. Particular developments may prove enriching or impoverishing, enlarging or diminishing. Second, the narrative has little detailed comment. I do not evaluate the evaluators. The issues they raise are put 'on hold' to be picked up during the book.

Most of the people whose work is described in this chapter would not describe themselves as qualitative evaluation theorists, and maybe half of them would prefer not to be known as simply *evaluation* theorists. I could certainly have chosen other individuals whose influence on the day-to-day practice of evaluation is at least a strong as those here. Yet in my judgement these people and the persuasions they represent are those most relevant for our purposes. Campbell and Scriven have shaped evaluation theory through four decades. Campbell's work in particular will prove far more central to our concerns than may be expected by those who know him only as the high priest of experimental and quasi-experimental research design. Cronbach, while less known, may have stronger claim to holding a *theory* of evaluation than anyone, while Stake was the first major evaluation theorist to commit himself to a qualitative methodology. Weiss has had less to say about evaluation methodology, but much regarding the political context in which policy research and evaluation occur.

House takes a significant step beyond the pluralist politics of his predecessors, and argues for a reformist stance on evaluation, backed by a commitment to social justice. Evaluation has yet to see a developed theory of critical evaluation, openly committed to an emancipatory agenda. But the critique is well developed and I outline its terms.

Professionals working in social work, schools, or other local agencies, are more likely to locate their questions about evaluation in close proximity to their direct practice. Reid (social work) and Eisner (education) represent very different approaches to evaluation from the programme evaluation interests of most of the people discussed earlier in the chapter. They are both concerned with practitioner evaluation, although they proceed in dissimilar directions. The chapter concludes by picking up the interpretative, naturalistic strand in Stake's work, and depicting the radical constructivist form it takes in the work of Lincoln and Guba.

From this list of names you may conclude that evaluation was invented and developed in the USA. For programme evaluation that is certainly the case. Practitioner evaluation, democratic evaluation and participatory evaluation have emerged out of parallel and sometimes linked developments in the USA and Britain, and more recently in Australia and Canada. Critical evaluation may fit a British intellectual context at least as readily as an American one. Either way, it is likely to owe a major debt to French and German intellectual roots.

Does the work of Campbell, Scriven and so on represent models, or maybe paradigms? Our personal inclinations echo those of Stake. Of models, he says the term 'overpromises. People start relying on it as a blueprint, with a "parts inventory" and a "directions for assembly", so that, if followed carefully, a satisfactory evaluation could be assembled'. Rather, 'our so-called models are merely advocacies alluding to a few of the many responsibilities and identifying a few of the many inquiry opportunities' (Stake, 1991: 71). Of paradigm claims we might concur with Reid's observation: 'yet another instance in which Thomas Kuhn's name was taken in vain' (1990: 141). They are perhaps best described, using House's term, as 'persuasions' – and for the most part powerful ones.

Donald Campbell: probing causes

Campbell exemplifies twin commitments to understanding the positions of those with whom he may differ, and actively encouraging criticism of his own position. He is perhaps still best known for his methodological work on the design of experimental and quasi-experimental research, and for his elaboration of threats to the validity of what he describes as 'cause-probing' studies (Campbell and Stanley, 1966; Cook and Campbell, 1979).

Partly through his influence, it was widely assumed in the 1960s that experimental designs to measure the outcomes of innovative programmes were the benchmark and critical test for *all* evaluation. Campbell coined the term 'internal validity' to refer to inferences about the relationship between independent and dependent variables. He gives greater weight to internal validity than to external validity. Of what use, he would argue, is generalizing a relationship if one doubts the relationship itself. His broader political commitment has been to an emancipatory world achieved through an experimenting society.

He is a critical realist, accepting the existence of a real world beyond knowers, yet vigorously criticizing the slightest trace of naïve realism which assumes our observations or theories directly mirror reality. His emphasis on the logical impossibility of induction, and the primacy of falsification methods in justifying claims to knowledge, linked to his critical realism, all reveal his debt to Karl Popper.

He drew on his early work on cultural differences in levels of susceptibility to optical illusions, to explore ways in which cross-cultural failures of communication might be distinguished from cross-cultural perceptual differences. He concludes 'the extreme difficulty of ascertaining that the members of another culture perceive things differently' (Campbell, 1964: 325). Reflecting on this research more than thirty years later, he insists that 'to interpret as a cultural difference what is in reality a failure of communication [is] the most ubiquitous source of error in efforts to know the other' (Campbell, 1996: 165). However, he does not believe that such difficulties are insurmountable: 'Those who make knowing the other problematic are correct. Those who regard it as impossible to any degree are wrong' (1996: 169). Thus he rejects relativists ('ontological nihilists' is his term) and 'other more recent imports from the cafes of Paris' (1996: 159). He thus maintains a double-edged epistemology, emphasizing both the inevitability of doubt, but also that we can overcome this to a practically useful degree and know the other.

The ethnographer Howard Becker taught with Campbell between 1960 and 1979 and was a major influence on two essays written by Campbell in the 1970s (Campbell, 1978, 1979). He came to accept Becker's critiques of standard quantitative social science as 'valid and extremely relevant' (Campbell, 1996: 161), and criticized quantitative scientists who, 'under the influence of missionaries from logical positivism, presume that in true science, quantitative knowing replaces qualitative, common-sense knowing' (Campbell, 1979: 50). He regards qualitative knowing as both the test and the building block of quantitative knowing: 'This is not to say that such common-sense naturalistic observation is objective, dependable or unbiased. But it is all that we have. It is the only route to knowledge – noisy, fallible and biased though it be' (1979: 54).

His second contribution to qualitative evaluation is through raising the question whether qualitative methods can fulfil the same cause-probing purpose as quantitative methods. I will return to his arguments in Chapter 7, but suffice to say he uses the analogue of experimental research to suggest ways of strengthening case studies and 'constructs one of the strongest cases to date that qualitative methods can yield valid causal knowledge' (Shadish et al., 1990: 135). He has more recently observed that, 'in addition to the quantitative and quasi-experimental case study approach . . . our social science armamentarium also needs a humanistic, validity-seeking, case study method' (Campbell, 1994: x).

Campbell's work has gained new appreciation over the last decade, and remains a significant influence on qualitative research. Important criticisms have been raised regarding the apparent ambiguity of his views of causation, his neglect of 'discovery' methods of inquiry, the priority he affords to internal validity, and the utopian nature of his social vision. We will trace the development of these criticisms in the work of Cronbach, Stake, House and Weiss. Yet he provides a continuing agenda for practitioners of qualitative evaluation. This agenda includes his

- sophisticated defence of critical realism
- work on case studies and comparative ethnographies
- openness to critical comment.

Michael Scriven: a science of evaluating

Like Campbell, Scriven emphasizes evaluation as a search for effective solutions to social problems. His ideas have been the subject of contention at almost every point, and he has developed 'one of the most talked about and least used approaches' (House, 1980: 232). He has introduced new language into the field – goal free evaluation, formative and summative evaluation, meta-evaluation and probative inference. Evaluation, including qualitative evaluation, has been shaped by Scriven's work, even where it departs most obviously from it. His ideas are generatively important to the field, 'and may still not be fully appreciated' (Shadish et al., 1990: 74).

His concern is less with developing and prescribing evaluation methodology, and more with exploring the logical requirements of the task. At the core of his argument is the view that evaluation assigns merit or worth. For Scriven, the very idea of evaluators who never draw evaluative conclusions 'is not only paradoxical, but it makes the notion of an autonomous profession of evaluators redundant. They are no more than re-labelled social scientists' (Scriven, 1995: 54–55). 'The fact that evaluation, as currently conceived by most of its practitioners, can only lead to descriptive conclusions, not to evaluative ones', represents in his view 'the terminal disease' of evaluation (Scriven, 1986: 10). However, he makes careful distinctions between judgements of the merit of what is evaluated (the 'evaluand', to use the term common in American literature), *explanations* (through formative evaluation), and *recommendations* ('remediations'):

> Bad is bad and good is good, and it is the job of evaluators to decide which is which. And there are many occasions when they should say which is which whether or not they have explanations or remediations. (Scriven, 1986: 19)

'Goal-free evaluation' is Scriven's ideal means of reaching an evaluative judgement, by which he means that evaluators should proceed with a veil of ignorance regarding the goals held by programme managers and other stakeholders. Goals bias the evaluator. Rather than ask, 'there are the objectives. Have they been achieved?', Scriven would prefer, 'Here is the programme. What are its effects?' Kept in ignorance of the programme goals, the evaluator will search for *all* outcomes. The distinction between intended and side-effects is one he rejects as reflecting the intentions of the producer. The standards for judging programmes come from needs assessments, and his approach is thus consumer-driven rather than management-driven. This leads to an evaluation practice in which the lead evaluator is almost inevitably an outsider: 'Both distancing and objectivity remain correct and frequently achievable ideals for the external evaluator' (Scriven, 1997: 483). 'Distance has its price', but involvement 'risks the whole capital', and 'so-called participatory design . . . is about as sloppy as one can get' (Scriven, 1986: 488, 486).

Scriven aims to weave much of this argument into a general logic of evaluation. Without such a general theory he believes evaluation becomes lost in narrowness and lack of perspective, unable to address the internal and external battles which face it (Scriven, 1996). He aims for an evaluation theory of wide scope, addressing not only programme evaluation but also product and personnel evaluation. He regards evaluation as a 'transdiscipline', autonomous from both philosophy and social science, which should provide a process of reflexivity appropriate to all disciplines as they monitor their disciplinary boundaries.

At his worst Scriven sounds increasingly cranky, both in content and in tone. His intolerance of formative evaluation, constructivists, the 'philosophically besotted' (Scriven, 1997: 479), and what he describes as the 'lackey' view of evaluation research (Scriven, 1986: 23), feel like the 'smack of authority' delivered by a 'tribal elder' with a 'licence for irascibility' (Kushner, 1997: 364). This is unfortunate. He is an original thinker who repeatedly renders problematic what others treat in a taken-for-granted manner. House suggests, for example, that he has 'written brilliantly' about objectivity (1980, Ch. 4; Scriven, 1972), and his later work on applying an informal logic to evaluative reasoning has prompted creative work on several fronts (e.g. Fournier, 1995). Finally, 'his work on valuing is so complex, subtle and so full of information, we learn new things each time we read it' (Shadish et al., 1990: 118). But his general model of evaluation is not for the real world, and will at best be partial and selective in its consequences for qualitative evaluation.

Lee Cronbach: evaluating within programmes

The *motifs* of Campbell's and Scriven's approaches are inference from the internal validity of evaluations, and assessment of outcomes through summative comparisons of alternative programmes. Cronbach gives priority to neither of these. Against Campbell he argues the priority of *external* validity, and contrary to Scriven he advocates *formative evaluation* – evaluation *within* and not *between* programmes.

Cronbach is one of the most important and least appreciated evaluation theorists. His work is almost never cited in British evaluation literature, outside some important corners of educational evaluation (e.g. Simon, 1987), and apart from the major review by Shadish, Cook and Leviton, his work is drawn on occasionally and selectively in the American literature. Yet the work of this 'tough-minded master of conceptual distinctions' (Scriven, 1986: 15) is

> a brilliant *tour de force*, unusually rewarding if closely read, trenchant in analysis of the *status quo*, and creating truly unique alternatives sensitive to the scholarly need for general knowledge and the practitioner need for local application. (Shadish et al., 1990: 375)

At the core of Cronbach's position is the claim that '"external validity" – validity of inferences that go beyond the data – is the crux of social action, not 'internal validity"' (Cronbach et al., 1980: 231). Behind this lies a particular view of causation. For Campbell, internal validity is about the relationship between interventions and outcomes in a given random sample. Cronbach considers this concept insignificant – 'Campbell's writings make internal validity a property of trivial, past tense, and local statements' (Cronbach, 1982: 137). Cronbach prioritizes the understanding and explanation of mechanisms operating in a local context, in order that plausible inferences can be drawn regarding other settings, people and interventions that are of interest to policy-makers. It is extrapolation that matters – 'a prediction about what will be observed in a study where the subjects or operations depart in some respect from the original study' (Cronbach, 1986: 94). It is not 'before-and-after', but 'during-during-during', as he somewhere says.

To achieve this local, contextualized understanding he rejects the notion of evaluation in which 'the program is to "play statue" while the evaluator's slow film records its picture' (Cronbach et al., 1980: 56) in favour of case studies drawing primarily but not exclusively on qualitative methods. He insists many times on the need for 'flexible attack' and 'does not want a particular conception of scientific methods to trivialize the process of asking important questions' (Shadish et al., 1990: 349). 'Planning inquiry . . . is the art of recognizing tradeoffs and placing bets' (Cronbach, 1986: 103).

His pluralist view of methodology echoes his conception of the policy context in which evaluation is located. With characteristic dry wit he remarks, 'The very proposal to evaluate has political impact. To ask about the virtue of Caesar's wife is to suggest she is not above suspicion' (Cronbach et al., 1980: 163). Cronbach and his colleagues complain that evaluation theory has 'been developed almost wholly around the image of command' and the assumption that managers and policy-makers have a firm grip on the controls of decision-making. However, 'most action is determined by a pluralistic community not by a lone decision-maker' (Cronbach et al., 1980: 84). Hence, evaluation enters a context of governance which is typically one of accommodation rather than command: 'A theory of evaluation must be as much a theory of political interaction as it is a theory of how knowledge is constructed' (1980: 52–53).

Having allowed that decisions rarely hinge solely on the empirical evidence, Cronbach is ready to trade off precision ('fidelity') against relevance ('bandwidth'). He is hostile towards both goal-setting models of evaluation, and evaluation as accountability: 'We are uneasy about the close association of evaluation with accountability. In many of its uses the word becomes an incantation and one that can cast a malign spell' (Cronbach et al., 1980: 133). He regards the role of the evaluator as a multi-partisan advocator. While the evaluator may serve some partisan interest 'his unique contribution is a critical, scholarly cast of mind' (1980: 67). He sees evaluation within a context of political accommodation as both conservative and committed to change:

> To be meliorist is the evaluator's calling. Rarely or never will evaluative work bring a 180-degree turn in social thought. Evaluation assists in piecemeal adaptations: perhaps it does tend to keep the *status* very nearly *quo*. (Cronbach et al., 1980: 157)

There are problematic aspects to Cronbach's theory to which we will return in Chapter 5. His concern with large-scale policy and programme evaluation makes his ideas less readily transferable to evaluation of local projects and practices. His pluralist political stance was fashioned prior to the advent of the right wing market policies and will be unacceptable to some readers. Finally, his arguments may be too complex to provide the methods for practice that most evaluators seek. Yet his influence has already proved diverse (Lather, 1986a; Simon, 1987; Stake, 1991), and his work has extensive implications for key aspects of qualitative evaluation, including:

- generalization
- causal explanations
- multi-site case studies
- the policy relevance of evaluation.

Robert Stake: responsive evaluation

Stake was perhaps the first evaluation theorist to place qualitative inquiry and participatory methods at the forefront of the evaluative task. His position is 'complex, continuing to develop, not extremist' (Shadish et al., 1990: 468). His model of responsive evaluation has several elements:

- It orients more directly to programme activities rather than programme purposes.
- It responds to local stakeholder requirements for information.
- The different values of the people at hand are referred to in reporting the success and failure of the programme.
- It is participatory, thus increasing local control.

He makes a virtue of gradualist, incremental change, and tends to be politically conservative:

> Stake does not emphasize helping needy stakeholders, or educating stakeholders and socio-economic causes of their plight. His approach is *laissez-faire*, characteristic of a traditional 'rightist' or libertarian perspective. (Shadish et al., 1990: 296)

Stake has given more attention than many theorists to practical evaluation methodology questions, and is perhaps the leading exponent of qualitative case study methods (Stake, 1994, 1995). We say more about case study evaluation in the second half of this book. Stake harnesses his methodology to a commitment to a service model of evaluation. The test of evaluation knowledge is its usefulness, with the evaluator acting as enabler and facilitator, rather than giver of insights. He aims for a popularization and democratization of knowledge. In doing so, he refuses to go beyond descriptive approaches to values. Thus case studies should be 'oriented to understanding the case more or less as a whole, not for patching its pieces and fixing its problems' (Stake, 1991: 77).

His service model of evaluation is nowhere more apparent than in his understanding of how learning is generalized from programmes. In arguing for 'naturalistic generalizations', Stake and Trumbull say:

We believe that program evaluation studies should be planned and carried out in such a way as to provide a maximum of vicarious experience to the readers who may then intuitively combine this with their previous experience. (1982: 2)

They reject the 'tenacious expectation that *knowledge* can make a sick education well', as in the assumption that 'research leads to knowledge which leads to improved practice' (1982: 3). Such routine assumptions have, as a corollary, an emphasis on the production, utilization and dissemination of knowledge. For Stake this is a dream that distracts from practice. He and Trumbull argue alternatively that 'research can evoke personal experience which leads to improved practice' (1982: 5).

Direct cross-fertilization of evaluative thinking between the USA and Britain has been a strong feature of Stake's work and of similar evaluation models. Curriculum reform of British schools led to democratic evaluation associated with the Centre for Applied Research in Education (CARE) at the University of East Anglia (cf. Simon, 1987). McDonald, Parlett, Stenhouse, Elliott, Simon, Hamilton, Walker, Smith, Adelman and Kushner are among the names associated with CARE.

Stake's own position continues to develop, and he has reflected publicly on this development on several occasions (Stake, 1991, 1997). His extensive review of his own position traces developments in methodology, epistemology and value positions. His recent reluctant acceptance of advocacy roles seems to mark a shift to a more reformist stance (Stake, 1997), perhaps in unspoken acknowledgement of the political complacency of his earlier work. Indeed, he has recently been reported as believing that the rise of managerialism has sealed the end of responsive evaluation (Kushner, 1997).

Mainstream ethnographers have launched critiques of Stake's version of case study research and practitioner research models in education (e.g. Atkinson and Delamont, 1993; Hammersley, 1993c) on alleged grounds of methodological and theoretical naïvety. Notwithstanding, Stake's work contributes significantly to qualitative evaluation in the following ways:

- He is the first of the theorists we have examined to develop an approach to evaluation in which local practitioners are central.
- His ground breaking initiatives on participatory evaluation have had varied successors.
- His case study methodology and arguments for naturalistic generalizations lay the groundwork for continued developments.

Carol Weiss: evaluating policy

Carol Weiss's research on the political context of policy research and evaluation changed, probably for ever, the ways we understand the uses of evaluative research. Evaluative outcome research in the 1960s and early

1970s yielded at best marginal success for innovative programmes and practices. We have seen that Campbell's methodological solution to this was to develop increasingly differentiated research designs to counter threats to internal validity. The neo-conservative response questioned throwing money at social problems. Weiss later remarked on this: 'We had signed on as evaluators with the intent of contributing to the improvement of social programming, but we seemed to wind up giving aid and comfort to the barbarians' (quoted in Shadish et al., 1990: 182).

Weiss's response to early outcome research was different from both the methodologists and the conservatives. She set about rethinking the place of evaluation research in policy-making, first by explicating its political context, and second by empirical work on ways in which evaluation research is actually used.

In a paper first written in 1973 she argued that political considerations intrude in three ways in evaluation. First, the programmes and policies being evaluated are themselves the creatures of political decisions:

> They emerged from the rough and tumble of political support, opposition and bargaining. Attached to them are the reputations of legislative sponsors, the careers of administrators, the jobs of program staff, and the expectations of clients. (Weiss, 1987: 49)

The political creation of programmes gives them a lack of clarity – a 'consequent grandiosity and diffuseness' (1987: 51), so there is often little agreement on which goals are real (in the sense that effort is actually invested to attain them).

Second, evaluation entails political considerations because its reports enter the political arena. Her subsequent empirical work focused on this issue. Third, there are politics implicit in evaluation research. Research tends to accept the broad premises of the programme, and serious research 'gives an aura of legitimacy to the enterprise' (1987: 57). In consequence: 'Most evaluations – by accepting a program emphasis on services – tend to ignore the social and institutional structures within which the problems of the target groups are generated and sustained' (1987: 57). Her general conclusion was to call for more strategic research, and to lament that: 'Most of these political implications of evaluation research have an "establishment" orientation. They accept the world as it is; as it is defined in agency structure, in official diagnoses of social problems' (1987: 59–60).

The conventional rational assumption about the utilization of research was that research led to knowledge, which in turn provided a basis for action of an instrumental, social engineering kind. The historical roots of this view are deep (Finch, 1986). Weiss was not the first to question the legitimacy of this view, but her significance lies in the empirical underpinnings, explanatory cogency and plausibility that she conveys. With her colleagues she interviewed 155 senior officials in federal, state and local mental health agencies. Officials and staff used research to provide information about service needs, evidence about what works, and to keep up with the field. However, it was also used as a ritualistic overlay, to legitimize positions, and to provide personal assurance that a position held was the correct one. At a broader conceptual level it helped officials make sense of the world. For all these purposes, 'It was one source among many, and not usually powerful enough to drive the decision process' (Weiss, 1980: 390). As for direct utilization, 'Instrumental use seems in fact to be rare, particularly when the issues are complex, the consequences are uncertain, and a multitude of actors are engaged in the decision-making process, i.e., in the making of policy' (1980: 397).

Research use was also reflected in officials' views of the decision-making process. Decisions were perceived to be fragmented both vertically and horizontally within organizations, and to be the result of a series of gradual and amorphous steps. Therefore, 'a salient reason why they do not report the use of research for specific decisions is that many of them *do not believe that they make decisions*' (1980: 398). Hence the title of her paper – 'Knowledge creep and decision accretion'. This provided the basis for her argument that enlightenment rather than instrumental action represents the characteristic route for research use.

Weiss's position has been challenged especially by Patton. His argument is twofold (Patton, 1988a, 1988b). First, he reasons that Weiss is wrongly generalizing from policy research to programme evaluation. 'It makes sense that policy research would be used in more diffuse and less direct ways than program evaluation', because they are 'different kinds and levels of practice' (Patton, 1988a: 12). Second, her vision is 'quite dismal'. 'The Weiss vision, in my judgement, is not marketable' (1988a: 11). Her response is to complain that in Patton's world 'everybody behaves rationally' (Weiss, 1988: 18). She also elaborates her earlier argument regarding the politics implicit in evaluation research: 'The job of a program practitioner is to believe; the job of an evaluator is to doubt' (1988a: 22).

Theories of enlightenment are difficult to falsify or verify, but feel plausible. Weiss has become less optimistic regarding the likely benefits of basic research: 'Social science is not an easy or efficient route to social reform. It has effects but the effects are likely to be slow or erratic' (Weiss, 1987: 67). She also feels more optimistic about specific applications of research: 'Incremental improvements have been made, and cumulative increments are not such small potatoes after all' (Weiss, 1987: 67). We will have more to say about Weiss's work in Chapter 5. Her legacy for qualitative evaluation is important and broad-based. Her work has not been methodology-driven, although she published a methodology text on evaluation near the beginning of her career and has recently completely rewritten it (Weiss, 1998). Her general stance is that armed only with methodology the evaluator is ill-prepared. Her personal preference is for methodological pragmatism.

Her general approach is directly congruent with an important strand of British policy research. The research and writing of Abrams, Bulmer and

Finch typify this work, albeit all three have taken a stronger line on the necessity of qualitative methods of inquiry, and of the reformist uses of research. The interlocking strands of her work combine to open up a rich seam for qualitative evaluation:

> More than anything else she has struggled towards a realistic theory of use. These shifts started a debate in evaluation that goes on to the present day about the role in evaluation of idealism and pragmatism. (Shadish et al., 1990: 207–208)

The five evaluation theorists considered in the first half of this chapter differ from one another in important ways. Yet they share common ground regarding the terms of the debate:

- All commenced their work from a committed faith in the potential of evaluative research to uncover the real world. Campbell and Stake have both developed their positions in ways that increasingly accentuate epistemological uncertainty.
- The prominence of stakeholder interests in the work of Cronbach, Stake and Weiss has been framed within a broadly pluralist, consensus politics. Advocacy roles are eschewed by all five.
- Campbell, Cronbach, Weiss, and to a lesser extent Scriven all focus their work on wide canvas issues of programme and policy evaluation. Practitioner evaluation emerged only in Stake's approach and in the British teacher-as-researcher movement.
- All five theorists have adopted either strong or weak versions of methodological pragmatism. With the exception of Scriven all give significant place to both qualitative and quantitative inquiry methodology. Stake makes qualitative methods his usual methodology of choice.

Yet since 1980 evaluation has expanded, becoming both more assertive regarding its place in the world, yet more doubting regarding the certainty of the knowledge it produces. Pluralist consensus politics have broken down, and produced a diversified context for evaluation. House has developed social justice arguments which support a reformist position. Openly ideological positions have been developed by critical theorists and feminists, although the terms critical or feminist evaluation rarely surface in the literature.

Practitioner evaluation still lacks extensive theorizing. However, Reid's later work within social work, and Eisner's work on connoisseurship and criticism are examples of developments in this field. The interpretative thrust of Stake, Campbell and Eisner is grounded in a realist ontology. Explicitly relativist positions have been developed, notably by Guba and Lincoln, who have also challenged the dominant methodological pragmatism. I will outline the central themes of each of these persuasions in the following pages.

Ernest House: evaluating for social justice

House is not happy with most preceding approaches to evaluation on three counts. First, their value positions are subjectivist. Whether they are directed at managers, professional elites, or consumers, they distance evaluation from prescriptive recommendations. Second, their epistemology is either objectivist or intuitionist. Third, the political assumptions are uniformly pluralist. While he does not level a charge of political complacency, he complains that they are all based on essentially enlightenment philosophies: 'All assume that increased knowledge will make people happy or better satisfied in some way' (House, 1980: 64).

House's most developed response is captured in his major book, *Evaluating With Validity* (1980), and is threefold. First, he argues that the logic of evaluation is not so much rational evidence, but persuasion and argumentation. Evaluations never yield certain knowledge: 'Subjected to serious scrutiny, evaluations always appear equivocal'. The aspiration after certain knowledge 'results from confusing rationality with logic. They are not identical ... Evaluations can be no more than acts of persuasion' (1980: 72). They are acts of argumentation, not demonstration. This is as true for quantitative methodology as it is for qualitative, despite the fact that 'statistical metaphors ... give a semblance of certainty and unequivocality to evidence' (1980: 74). In summary, 'Evaluation persuades rather than convinces, argues rather than demonstrates, is credible rather than certain, is variably accepted rather than compelling' (1980: 73).

House characteristically interleaves considerations of logic and moral positions. He repeatedly claims that normative considerations have been neglected and that 'if this is a weakness in the conduct of science, in evaluation it is a fatal flaw' (1980: 251).

Second, House has developed extensive arguments for a reformist, social justice purpose for evaluation. He is not indifferent to the aesthetics of evaluation. Yet for him, 'Truth is more important than beauty. And justice more important than either' (1980: 117). Utilitarian theories of justice, based on the greatest net satisfaction, provide clear criteria for evaluating, yet tend to favour the upper classes, lead to judgements that 'do not square with one's moral sensibilities' (1980: 134), and often lead to oversimplification. Pluralist and intuitionist theory comes closest to common sense, everyday judgements of justice, and fosters a valuable emphasis on portraying the opinions of stakeholders. Yet 'the threat of relativism' (1980: 134) jeopardizes consistency of application, and it tends to place too high a value on professional judgement.

> In essence, the pluralist model confuses issues of interests with conflicts of power. It can balance only those interests that are represented – typically those of the powerful. (House, 1991a: 240)

House's conception of justice finds its most practical application in his detailed arguments for a fair evaluation agreement (1980: Ch. 8), and in his broader arguments for evaluation ethics (1993). His replacement of traditional ideas of objectivity with impartiality undergirds his explicit reformist stance. In responding to mainstream criticisms that his fair evaluation agreement is biased towards the interests of the disadvantaged, he replies:

> It seems to me that making certain the interests of the disadvantaged are represented and seriously considered is not being biased, though it is certainly more egalitarian than much current practice. (1991a: 241–242)

Third, he seeks to resolve the epistemological problems of preceding evaluation approaches through a sophisticated scientific realism, which he hopes may offer the basis of a new synthesis for resolving 'paradigm wars' within evaluation (House, 1991b). We return to this theme in Chapter 3, and simply note here that scientific realism involves understandings of 'cause' and 'objectivity' which are very different to conventional ideas. He has also sought to integrate evaluative logic and justice, in order to develop a basis for synthesizing evaluation results (House, 1995). We consider these arguments in Chapter 9.

House shares with Stake the exposure of his early work to the cross-fertilizing influence of British developments (Simon, 1987), though his later work is less thoroughly explored outside the USA. His approach to justice issues has loopholes which he generally acknowledges. His major work was completed when neo-Marxist applications of justice were still emerging, and before sustained feminist work had been undertaken. He is well aware that the underlying assumptions of such positions are different from both his own and those of his theoretical predecessors. He does tend to assume an overly consensual view of society, which limits his reformist position. He believes that, although philosophers, legislators and the public disagree, they do so 'within the frameworks of overall agreement about fundamental democratic values' (House, 1995: 44). His commitment to participatory models of evaluation is limited by his retention of an expert evaluator role.

The agenda he drafts for qualitative evaluation is extensive. His thinking on justice is subtle, whether he warns that evaluation practice is not *determined* by our views of justice, or distinguishes cultural and moral relativity in accepting the proper diversity of concepts of justice. Taken together, the work of House, Cronbach and Campbell provides a well-anchored platform for causal inferences through qualitative evaluation. Programmes are not fixed entities which 'play statue' (in Cronbach's phrase), but vary from site to site. Causes are discovered by knowledge of particulars – 'evaluation approaches that expect and track variability and irregularity of events' (House, 1991b: 8). Qualitative methodology offers his approach of choice in such circumstances. House has worked consistently with his own aspiration for 'a more complete and more translucent conceptual order and . . . a stronger sense of moral responsibility' (1980: 11).

Critical evaluation

According to House's reformist view, disagreements between the stake-holders of evaluation occur within a general consensus regarding funda-mental democratic values. He noted emerging critical models of evaluation with acknowledgement that any such persuasion regarding evaluation would stand outside his own framework for understanding the political location of evaluation.

Two decades later there is still no prominent theorist of 'critical evalu-ation' who will 'stand for' the application of critical theory to evaluation. Not that we lack animated debate on critical research (Carr and Kemmis, 1986; Harvey, 1990), and on neo-Marxist (Willis, 1977), feminist (Acker et al., 1983; Humphries, 1999), anti-racist (Whitmore, 1994), Freirian, partici-patory (Edwards, 1989; Martin, 1996), anti-disablist (Oliver, 1992), praxis-oriented (Lather, 1986b), deconstructive (Lather, 1991) and empowerment (Dullea and Mullender, 1999; Everitt and Hardiker, 1996; Miller, 1990;) ver-sions of a liberatory vision for evaluation. Each of these has implicit con-sequences for qualitative evaluation, although most of these practitioners and writers would add the suffix 'research' rather than 'evaluation' to describe their commitments.

Critical evaluation is 'critical' in that evaluation problems are concep-tualized within their social, political and cultural context. It is critical 'evaluation', to borrow a phrase from Popkewitz's excellent essay on the critical theory paradigm, because it 'gives reference to a systematic inquiry that focuses upon the contradictions of . . . practice' (1990: 46). The critical theorist reconstructs the rules of evaluation to reflect the understanding that the language categories of research and evaluation are historically related to larger social and moral issues of production and reproduction: 'Methodology is concerned with the moral order . . . presupposed in the practice of science. It is the study of what is defined as legitimate know-ledge' (1990: 51–52). It entails a theoretically-based analysis marked by scepticism towards the forces of social regulation and distribution, and sometimes also to empirical evidence: 'Whatever it is must not be taken at face value' (Harvey, 1990: 8). Critical evaluators will reject the idea of science as cumulative and progressive development. They are usually fal-lible realists in philosophy, and may be less unyielding than constructivist writers like Guba and Lincoln on the extent to which methodological accommodation may occur between holders of different paradigm pos-itions. For example, Lather refuses to demonize other persuasions and insists that 'there are no innocent positions' (1991: 85).

There is a debate among critical scientists about the extent to which they are engaged in an emancipatory and liberatory project. Some – for example those holding a feminist standpoint position – believe that the partisan role of science makes it their obligation to pursue political commitments through 'a direct and explicit involvement in efforts to transform current social relations' (Popkewitz, 1990: 49). Research is seen as praxis-oriented

(Lather, 1986b), in which a 'reciprocally educative process is more important than the product' (Lather, 1991: 72). Others, including Popkewitz, disagree, believing that 'social scientists are partisans in the forming of social agendas through the practices of science' (1990: 50).

Rather than construct an agenda for qualitative evaluation arising from a latent critical evaluation, I prefer to suggest terms in which a critique of other forms of evaluation may be developed. Most critical evaluators would, I think, *oppose* most of the following:

- Evaluation distinguished from research on the grounds that the former does not involve *theorizing*.
- Paradigm positions regarded as representing only a conflict of *ideas*.
- Evaluation based on an assumption of a democratic *consensus*.
- Evaluation as finding meaning only within the *local context* of the inquiry.
- Evaluation as primarily associated with *planned decision-making*. They may recall Marx's paradox that anyone who plans for after the Revolution is a counter-revolutionary.
- A *descriptive valuing* approach to evaluative conclusions.
- A *gradualist*, incremental assumption about desirable changes following from evaluation.
- A *management-driven* evaluation contract.
- *Naïve participatory* evaluation that does not recognize that 'an emancipatory intent is no guarantee of an emancipatory outcome' (Acker et al., 1983: 431).
- A *methodological orthodoxy* of either a quantitative or qualitative variety. Lather, for example, criticizes inquiry that fails to 'go well beyond the mere use of qualitative methods' (Lather, 1992: 91).

William Reid: evaluation for developing practice

Reid has spent his career in social work education. His early work grew from mainstream experimental outcome evaluation. His more recent work is distinctive among the theorists we have considered, in that he has harnessed continued development and evaluation of goal-oriented models to a growing engagement with qualitative, process-oriented research. His position sharpens the issues for qualitative evaluation – it extends yet questions them.

His *Brief and Extended Casework* (Reid and Shyne, 1969) reported an experimental study comparing short- and long-term social work intervention. Planned short-term service provision yielded results at least as good as and possibly better than open-ended intervention. In the context of the time, when long-term casework was regarded as the ideal, 'in this particular race (Planned Short Term Intervention) needed only a tie to win' (1969: 175).

Reid took the lead in developing and testing Task-Centred Practice – a short-term, problem-solving approach to social work where the focus is on the problems that clients acknowledge as being of concern. The model has been research-informed throughout, and has a strong empirical orientation (Reid, 1997). This connecting strand running though Reid's career provides the context for a range of evaluation-related concerns.

First, his own outcome research and review work on other studies has been one plank in the gradual renewal of confidence in such evaluative research (Reid, 1988, 1997; Reid and Hanrahan, 1982). His work notes the increasing 'dominance of structured forms of practice', in particular those influenced by 'the behaviour modification movement' (Reid and Hanrahan, 1982: 329). While he is convinced the helping professions can demonstrate they are effective, he warns that the practical significance of identified effects is often slight, and their durability ambiguous. He sometimes appears doubtful about the methodological criteria of such studies. In his chastening and memorable metaphor, 'It is like trying to decide which horse won a race viewed at a bad angle from the grandstand during a cloudburst' (Reid, 1988: 48)!

In his observations on the direction of outcome research he has commented favourably that 'The researcher as evaluator is giving way to the researcher as developer of models' (Reid and Hanrahan, 1982: 338). This reflects his second evaluation-related concern. He regards his task-centred practice research as a step-by-step process of development, testing and further development. He has sought to develop unobtrusive and practitioner-friendly methods for field testing the early trial versions of specific practice interventions (Reid, 1994b).

Reid's modest confidence in the benefits of outcome and developmental research contrasts with more bullish pronouncements regarding evidenced-based practice. Reid has responded to these with measured reviews of the empirical practice movement (Reid, 1994c; Reid and Zettergren, 1999):

> The empirical practice movement has advanced social work's long and laborious pursuit of the goal of creating a scientifically based profession. However, the gains achieved have been partial, uneven, and not always clear. (Reid, 1994c: 180)

This reflects his third contribution to evaluation – suggesting ways in which considerations of epistemology and methodology should be applied to social work. For example, he has explored the potential of 'change process research' (Reid, 1990). Practical and ethical constraints on experiments necessitate, in his view, the naturalistic study of process–outcome relations. A key notion about the process of change is that of intermediate 'micro-outcomes' depicted through intensive study of smaller elements of practice. This gives central importance to the immediate context of practice. This avenue of research has the potential to be pulled towards either a stronger naturalistic, interpretative methodology, or towards more traditional notions of rigour. Reid opposes the latter and probably the former, and prefers to see the knowledge gained as 'one kind of provisionally valid knowledge' (1990: 144). Behind this careful steering is Reid's concern to reframe debate 'away from arguments about epistemological worldviews, and devote our energies instead to clarifying and resolving the specific issues embedded in these arguments' (1994a: 465).

His concerns are for good practice, empirical work, a shared vocabulary and rationality, and a lack of enthusiasm about philosophical authority. He falls 'within the tradition of American pragmatism especially as it has been set forth in the writings of Pierce, James, Dewey and Rorty' (Reid, 1994a: 472). He also wishes to 'redefine the nature of the mainstream so that qualitative methodology is a part of it not apart from it' (1994a: 477).

There are inevitable unresolved issues raised by his work. There is a gradualist presumption in his welcome for incremental experimentation, and in his comment that 'These small successes of the present are better than the grand failures of the past' (Reid and Hanrahan, 1982: 338). Reid tends to ignore wider issues such as the politics implicit in evaluation research. He is aware that if social workers focus their energy on the achievement of effective but modest results, this can 'discourage more radical, but possibly less testable innovations' (Reid, 1988: 45).

Reid is more familiar than the majority of social work theorists with the wider literature on evaluation, though cross-fertilization is still limited in his work. This is unfortunate. Reid's commitment to developmental research is an imaginative broadening of the scope of evaluation. His work on change-process research illustrates how he has been able, 'pragmatically and effectively, to adapt a number of the ideas and procedures from this process-oriented form of research to his goal-oriented model of practice' (Sherman, 1990: 152). He has also hinted at ways in which change-process research can combine with developmental research strategies. His recent work on empirical practice as a perspective offers an interesting challenge to more entrenched paradigm claims (Reid and Zettergren, 1999). Developmental research, and his adaptation of change-process analyses of outcomes, will both enhance 'the precision with which we vex ourselves' (Geertz, 1973: 29).

Elliot Eisner: reflective evaluating

Like Reid, Eisner focuses evaluative inquiry on the immediate professional task. But that is where their common ground more or less ends. Eisner is concerned with schooling, especially with pedagogy. His aim is that teachers become 'both perceptive and the communicators of what is perceived' (Eisner, 1991a: 3) – experience and its representation. His ideas are most fully stated in *The Enlightened Eye* (1991a). Experience entails more than simply looking: 'Experience is a form of human achievement

... we *learn* to see, hear and feel' (1991a: 21). The communication of that experience vicariously is central to his approach: 'The writer starts with experience and ends with words. The reader starts with words and ends with experience' (1991a: 22).

Two ideas lie at the heart of Eisner's model – educational connoisseurship and educational criticism. Connoisseurship is the art of appreciation, involving a 'qualitative intelligence' (1991a: 64) which enables the practitioner to get beyond 'stock perceptions' and the problem that 'a way of seeing is also a way of not seeing' (1991a: 67). He uses the expression 'epistemic seeing' to refer to an appreciation that may draw on all five senses. Reflexivity – while mentioned only occasionally by Eisner – appears central to connoisseurship.

> When we are functioning as connoisseurs, it is important to focus our attention on two targets: one of these is the events themselves, the other is what those events do to our experience. (Eisner, 1991a: 189)

His second idea, educational criticism, is the art of disclosure: 'Connoisseurs simply need to appreciate what they encounter. Critics, however, must render these qualities vivid by the artful use of critical disclosure' (Eisner, 1988: 143). Connoisseurship is a private act: 'Criticism provides connoisseurship with a public face' (Eisner, 1991a: 85). While it is possible to be a connoisseur without being a critic, 'one cannot be a critic of any kind without some level of connoisseurship' (1991a: 86). He generally assumes that connoisseurship and criticism are exercised by the same person.

He has valuable things to say regarding ways in which generalization of learning takes place, and has also developed sensitive criterion tests for ethical practice. In a general sense he prescribes values, requiring the critic to judge the educational value of what is going on. It is this, in Eisner's view, that distinguishes educational criticism from ethnography. But in specific instances he is a descriptive valuer: 'I conceive the major contribution of evaluation to be a heightened awareness of the qualities of that life so that teachers and students can become more intelligent within it' (Eisner, 1988: 142).

Eisner's ideas have been described rightly as 'bold and imaginative' (House, 1980: 235), but they remain as yet incomplete and partly developed. His methodology is unequivocally qualitative. He does not preclude quantitative *elements* within this, insisting that 'in qualitative inquiry *numbers are okay*. I want to say that again: numbers are okay' (1991a: 186). Quantitative and qualitative are distinguished in a way somewhat analogous to one of his favourite aphorisms from Dewey – 'science states meanings, art expresses them'. Yet on specific methods he is distinctly vague: 'I know of no "method" for the conduct of qualitative inquiry in general or for educational criticism in particular'. And, 'Whatever is relevant for seeing more acutely and understanding more deeply is fair game' (1991a: 169, 82). He makes no mention of analysis and it has been observed that 'the dangers involved in going direct from data to narrative, seem to us to be real and serious issues for educational criticism' (Pitman and Maxwell, 1992: 750).

Despite his recurrent expositions of the defining concepts, the process remains loosely described. Is the connoisseur the teacher or another researcher? He talks in both senses, but the methodological implications are different in each case. Does he risk overstating the uniqueness of good teaching and denying the routine, even formulaic elements of some good professional practice? Does the metaphor of appreciating a good wine or a painting really 'work'? Wines and paintings do not actively interrogate the perceiver in the same sense that children may interrogate social workers, teachers or doctors (see Greene, 1992, for comparable comments on strong aesthetic emphases in constructivist evaluation). Indeed, the apparent non-participatory character of Eisner's form of evaluative inquiry is not helped by the basic metaphors.

Eisner admits that in some respects the implications of the claims are 'riddled with optimism' (1990: 101). Yet despite these criticisms Eisner's model sets a distinct and important agenda for qualitative evaluation. His carefully worked out commitment to qualitative methodology, and his distinctions between qualitative *research*, qualitative *inquiry*, and quali-tative *thinking* suggest overlapping borders with both research and every-day life activities. His approach has points of contact with other writers on reflective inquiry, such as Schon, Reason, England, Heron, Gould, Fook and Shaw, some of whom we consider in Chapter 6. Like Stake and Reid, Eisner has a practical agenda of improving local practice, and the details of his work, for example on ethics, are more plausible as a result.

Like most of the theorists we have considered, he began his work in an educational context. Unlike others, however, he has stayed close to edu-cational concerns. It may fall to others to explore the transferability of his central generic ideas to other professional contexts such as health, social work or law.

Egon Guba and Yvonna Lincoln: constructivist evaluation

Stake introduced an interpretative thrust into evaluation theory. Indeed, he has remarked 'I have increasingly replaced realist presumption with constructivist hesitation' (Stake, 1991: 81). But while Stake's epistemology remains ambiguous, Guba and Lincoln's relativist, constructivist and value-infused paradigm has changed the way in which we think about evaluation.

Their critique of conventional inquiry positions has become well known. As Lincoln summarizes it in her excellent personal account of her journey to constructivism: 'Egon and I rejected conventional inquiry on three basic grounds: its posture on reality; its stance on the knower–known relationship, and its stance on the possibility of generalization' (1990: 68).

On reality, they came to advocate multiple, socially constructed realities which, 'when known more fully, tend to produce diverging inquiry' (Lincoln and Guba, 1986a: 75). Realities cannot be studied 'in pieces' (e.g. as variables) but only holistically and in context. The traditional image of the relationship between knower and known, researcher and subject, was rejected: 'Knower and known not only *could* not remain distanced and separated in the process of evaluation, but probably *should* not' (Lincoln, 1990: 68). Hence, 'the relationship, when properly established, is one of respectful negotiation, joint control, and reciprocal learning' (Lincoln and Guba, 1986a: 75). Finally, because there are no enduring, context-free truth statements, and all human behaviour is time and context bound, 'we began to doubt seriously the possibility of generalization from one site to the next' (Lincoln, 1990: 68).

Relativism is perhaps the single most important idea in their model of 'fourth generation evaluation' (Guba and Lincoln, 1989). Guba intentionally provokes when he insists, 'The only alternative to relativism is absolutism' (Guba, 1990: 18). Relativism and constructivism hang together. For Guba and Lincoln there is no reality except that created by people as they attempt to make sense of their surroundings, and evaluation creates the reality that it presents, rather than discovering some objectively existing reality. A report is simply the 'residue' left by the process that created the 'facts'. The methodology of constructivist evaluation proceeds through hermeneutic (eliciting and refining constructions) and dialectic (comparing and contrasting, and being confronted by others' constructions). The aim is to achieve 'ever more informed and sophisticated constructions' (Guba, 1990: 27).

Lincoln and Guba's work is equally important for their analysis of other approaches in terms of paradigms, or basic sets of beliefs that guide action. Their analysis of paradigms is in terms of their critique of the nature of reality (ontology), the relationships between knower and known (epistemology) and methodology. Paradigms have been presented in various terms – for example, modernist/postmodernist and quantitative/qualitative. Guba and Lincoln distinguish positivism, postpositivism, critical theory and constructivism, although they tend (as also do most critical theorists) to regard postpositivism as a 'modified version of positivism' (1990: 20). The adoption of a paradigm 'literally permeates every act even tangentially associated with inquiry' (Lincoln, 1990: 81).

Much of their effort has been directed to developing standards of validity appropriate to naturalistic, constructivist inquiry. This has involved a set of 'trustworthiness' criteria which parallel the criteria for conventional inquiry. They subsequently developed 'intrinsic naturalistic criteria' of 'authenticity' which primarily address ethical and ideological concerns (Lincoln and Guba, 1986a).

In addition to this work they have also considered the methodology differences between conventional and naturalistic inquiry (Guba and Lincoln, 1989); the relationship between evaluation and research (Lincoln and Guba, 1986b), and the ethical issues raised by naturalistic and positivistic inquiry (Lincoln and Guba, 1989).

The work of these theorists is of major significance, and colours most of the themes discussed in the following two chapters. For the moment, we should note some of the immediate issues raised by their work. Some broadly sympathetic commentators have criticized Guba and Lincoln for not being sufficiently consistent with their principles, and for retaining conventional notions of autonomous, rational subjects (Schwandt, 1997). Much space has also been devoted to discussions of paradigms and their relation to both theory and evaluation practice. Pitman and Maxwell conclude that:

> the greatest strength of Guba and Lincoln's work is as a critique of other approaches; its greatest weakness is as a model for actively conducting an evaluation along naturalistic or constructivist lines. (1992: 742)

The criticism is not entirely fair. Guba and Lincoln's strategies for consensual validity are directly practice-oriented. A more serious criticism is of alleged inconsistency between their rhetoric and evaluation practice (Heap, 1995). I develop this criticism in the next chapter. They emphasize that values inhere in the inquirer, the inquiry paradigm, theory choices and the evaluation context, and that evaluation empowers stakeholders. However, I am uncertain whether their value position extends beyond a pluralist and potentially conservative commitment that 'all ideologies should have an equal chance of expression in the process of negotiating recommendations' (Lincoln and Guba, 1986a: 79). If, as they say, 'it is the mind that is to be transformed, not the real world' (Guba, 1990: 27), the potential for reformist or critical change may be at best indirect and contingent. Although Guba and Lincoln's paradigm has doubtless changed the way we think about evaluation, we need exemplary applications to develop and judge its viability.

Conclusion: a preliminary agenda for qualitative evaluation

I conclude this chapter with an interim stock-taking of questions suggested by a reading of the theorists introduced in this chapter.

- Is evaluative reasoning similar to or different from research reasoning?
- Is paradigm diversity helpful or unhelpful in the development of qualitative evaluation?
- What are the implications for qualitative evaluation of developments in modified versions of realism?

- What consequences for qualitative evaluation follow from a grasp of the political context in which it is commissioned and to which it reports?
- Can qualitative evaluation address problems of causal inference?
- In what ways, if at all, may we generalize from evaluation sites?
- What are the identifying problems posed by qualitative *program* evaluation and qualitative *practitioner* evaluation?
- Are qualitative *evaluation* methods different from qualitative *research* methods?
- How promising are design and development approaches for qualitative applications?
- What is the present best practice for participatory evaluation?
- What ethical problems and principles apply in qualitative evaluation at the design, data collection, analysis and report stages?
- Should qualitative evaluators adopt a descriptive or prescriptive valuing position?
- In what circumstances may a partisan or emancipatory stance be required in qualitative evaluation?
- In what ways *is* and *should* qualitative evaluation be used?
- How can a position of reflexive self-criticism be sustained in qualitative evaluation?

I do not assume coherence between these questions. The chapter offers neither a taxonomy nor a history, and these questions reflect only the themes that have preoccupied evaluation theorists. Still less do I intend to imply comprehensiveness. For example, the list includes little on methods in general or evaluation methods in particular. Indeed, questions of methods have not been central to inquiry practice for the majority of these writers. Finally, I hope I have not conveyed too strongly my predispositions. I could certainly wish there had been less methodological pragmatism in the majority of evaluation theorizing, just as I could wish for more – even *some* – intellectual cross-fertilization between evaluators in different social science disciplines and professions. The problem is admitted by Cronbach and addressed, rather idiosyncratically, only by Scriven. In the next chapter we consider broad alternatives – paradigms or pragmatism, realism or relativism and rigour or relevance.

3

Evidence from qualitative evaluation

CONTENTS

Professional practitioners act or decline to act, feel confident or uncertain they have a sound basis for their actions and decisions, draw prescriptions or confess agnosticism, and all in the light (or gloom!) of the best evidence they can reasonably assemble. But what is the status of such evidence? Can professionals safely act on the assumption that it provides a good enough approximation to reality, which will transfer to similar new situations? Or should they remain deeply sceptical of all similar information on the grounds that it is the contingent, relative product of a unique local context, and may also represent the interests and constructions of the powerful?

There is a welcome vigour in current advocacy of the need to make evidence 'work' for professional practice. The very phrase, 'evidence-based practice' captures a confident belligerence, a tone of 'prove it or else'. The language of goals, objectives, outcomes and effectiveness challenges reliance on sentimentality, opinion-based practice, intuition or lay knowledge. The phrase, along with its companion question, 'What Works?', has gradually crept into official formulations. The term was being used in academic literature on evaluation research from at least 1980 (Weiss, 1980: 387), and was common currency in official reports in the USA by the mid-1980s (US Department of Education, 1986). Although medicine is often seen as the model for aspirants to emulate (Sackett and Rosenberg, 1995), teaching, nursing, social work, youth policy, policing, prisons, pharmacy, librarians and probation work all have their performance measured against evidence-based criteria (Kirkpatrick and Lucio, 1995).

We pointed briefly in Chapter 1 to reasons why evidence-based practice should not be the first resort of professionals or evaluators eager to establish secure grounds for effective practice. However, the idea of evidence-based practice helpfully problematizes the notion of evidence in two ways. First, evidence-based practice helps support the important assumption that some central issues of evidence are not special to any given occupation but are shared across superficially very different professions. Evidence-based practice promotes this assumption by insistently asking the same core questions of all and sundry. Qualitatively grounded forms of inquiry also promote the same assumption through a more inductive, bottom-up approach to understanding practice, shorn in part of prior assumptions that we already know what a given profession is really about. Second, evidence-based practice forces attention towards direct practice rather than broader programme evaluation strategies and agendas, which have dominated the theorizing of evaluation.

This chapter explores the background issues that shape debate and practice regarding evidence. They are posed, perhaps too simply, as a series of alternatives:

- Should evaluation be based on a particular *paradigm* of evaluation practice, or on *pragmatic*, even opportunistic, initiatives?
- Can we discover an objective, *real* picture of the world, or are all evaluative accounts contingent *relativities*?
- Should evaluation be planned according to the demands of scientific *rigour* or practice *relevance*?

In Chapter 4 we move our footholds to consider how the answers to these questions need also to take into account a series of more 'use-oriented' questions.

- How do we know if we are doing evaluation right?
- Are the results of evaluation research used through direct application to problems or through a more general process of enlightenment?
- What ethical principles and decision rules should guide qualitative evaluation?
- How should our answers to these questions shape the methodology we use?

Paradigms and pragmatism

'Paradigm' is a thorny word. Indeed, it has become a 'bucket word' (Popper 1966, 1989) to hold diverse meanings. If we take it in a general sense of 'a basic set of beliefs that guides action' (Guba, 1990: 17) we are only a little further forward. It would give even a mildly tendentious philosopher a heyday with each of the five key words in this definition! How many such 'basic sets of beliefs' are there? Convinced social science paradigmists do not always agree. Perhaps there are two – qualitative and quantitative, or positivist and postpositivist, or realist and idealist? Maybe there are three – realist, hermeneutic and critical theory? But possibly there are four – positivist, postpositivist, constructivist and critical theory?

Before you despair and decide to skip this section altogether, the particular question at issue is fortunately slightly more straightforward. Is it the case that in order to be consistent, evaluators must choose one or another? Is there an inherent inconsistency in subscribing to the world-view of one approach but employing the methods of the other?

Filstead (1979), for example, advocated a strong paradigm position, as a means of promoting qualitative evaluation. He viewed the classic arguments between realism and idealism as lying at the root of the debate. Faith in reason became expressed through faith in science, and was exemplified in logical positivism. To those influenced by European idealist philosophies, the mind is the source of knowledge and the social world is created by individuals who live in it. Quantitative evaluation represents the first paradigmatic approach and qualitative evaluation the second. Jacob (1987) adopts a paradigmatic position in her frequently cited review of qualitative research traditions in American education research. However, she criticizes the treatment of qualitative research as a single approach, and draws on Kuhn's notion of 'traditions' to identify five different schools of thought. Her plea is that applied researchers should align themselves with a tradition: 'Studies outside traditions are likely to be poorly focused, conceptually unclear, and weakly implemented' (Jacob, 1987: 38).

Take for a moment the distinction between quantitative and qualitative approaches to practice evaluation. Hammersley does not subscribe to a paradigm stance. However, he helpfully summarizes ways in which others have distinguished the elements of each pole. These can be represented as in Table 3.1. Guba argues that all such paradigms respond to three basic questions (Guba, 1990: 18):

- What is the nature of reality? A question of *ontology*.
- What is the nature of the relationship between the knower (inquirer) and the known (or knowable)? A question of *epistemology*.
- How should the inquirer go about finding out knowledge? A question of *methodology*.

In the following discussion we will pursue Guba's basic questions to discern three possible paradigm positions, realist postpositivism, critical evaluation and constructivist evaluation. Each position includes major diversity over issues such as objectivity (realist postpositivism), the advocacy role of the evaluator (critical evaluation) and relativism

TABLE 3.1   *Quantitative and qualitative paradigms*

	Quantitative	Qualitative
Data is	Quantitative	Qualitative
Fieldwork in	Artificial settings	Natural settings
Empirical focus is on	Behaviour	Meaning
Natural science model is	Accepted	Rejected
Analysis proceeds by	Deduction	Induction
Theorizing seeks	Laws	Patterns
Philosophy of	Realism	Idealism

Source: Hammersley (1992: Ch. 10)

(constructivism). But the three positions have general coherence and correspond closely to major developments in the philosophy of science (Bernstein, 1976; Outhwaite, 1987; Phillips, 1987a). We should be warned that the prefix 'post' is used in different and potentially confusing ways in the literature. For example, in the term *postpositivism*, 'post' is used to convey that this is a position that keeps some of the key ontological/epistemological premises of positivism, with some more or less radical changes to doctrines of realism and subjectivity. Thus, 'post' serves to signal a greater or lesser element of *continuity* with the position it conditions. However, in the term *postmodernism*, 'post' is used to convey that the key motives and *motifs* of the modernist enterprise are challenged. What unites adherents to this position is what is challenged. 'Post' in this context serves to signal the element of *discontinuity* with the position it conditions.

Realist postpositivism

Positivist is a convenient term of abuse that has been much over-used. Yet it is rarely a term which attracts public adherents. It is, as Raymond Williams (1976) long ago remarked, 'a swearword by which no-one is swearing'. Despite claims to the contrary, positivism has been in decline for at least fifty years. Attacks on practitioners or academics as 'positivists' are generally ill-informed and damaging (Shaw, 1999). Miles and Huberman do admit to being 'soft-nosed positivists' (1994), but this merely indicates their commitment to a thoroughgoing version of realism. Positivism is no longer a serious choice within qualitative evaluation research.

For the *positivist*, 'the business of science is to discover the true nature of "reality" and how it "truly" works' (Guba, 1990: 19). It also has an objectivist epistemology, and the idea of an Archimedean point. Archimedes is said to have remarked that given a long enough lever and a place whereon he could stand, he could move the earth: 'Objectivity is the Archimedean point . . . that permits the inquirer to wrest nature's secrets without altering them in any way' (Guba, 1990: 19).

Phillips (1990a) provides a plausible account of the reasons for the demise of positivism. Three developments have been crucial in creating near unanimity among social scientists that there are no absolute justifications of scientific assertions. First, the role of observation as the final arbiter has been revalued. For example, the acceptance that some mechanisms are unobservable led to the rejection of the belief that concepts can be reduced to a set of operational, observational statements. Equally influential has been the rejection of the assumption that observation can be theoretically neutral. The recognition that all observation is 'theory-laden' is shared by all three positions described here. There is more to seeing than meets the eyeball. 'Justificationism' – the view that knowledge equals proven knowledge – is almost universally rejected. But realist postpositivists are united in arguing that theory-laden observation does not entail relativism, and that it is possible to sustain a version of a correspondence view of truth – that research can represent social phenomena that are independent of it (Hammersley, 1995: Ch. 4; Phillips, 1990b).

Second, the relationship between theory and observation was shown to be more complex than previously thought. It became clear that theories are 'underdetermined' by nature, such that we are never able to say that we have the best theory, and a variety of theories can be constructed that are equally compatible with the available evidence. This has led to the unanimous rejection of 'foundationalism' – the view that research findings of indisputable validity can be a foundation for policy. We should note, however, that this should not lead to a belief that theories are always fallible whereas the empirical base for them is not fallible. Lakatos (1970) labels this position 'dogmatic falsificationism'. He rightly rejects the caricature that 'science grows by repeated overthrow of theories with the help of hard facts' (1970: 97). This scepticism regarding the value of theory simply reinstates a new version of theory-free observation. Observations are so in the light of a given theory, and 'there are and can be no sensations unimpregnated by expectations' (1970: 99). Therefore, although there are no *absolute* justifications, this does not mean there are *no* justifications. Yet while we may be warranted in holding particular views, we cannot assert that something is true, that our warrant is unchallengeable, or that it will for ever be warranted – '*nothing* can guarantee that we have reached the truth' (Phillips, 1990a: 43). There are ironic, invisible inverted commas whenever Popper speaks of 'experiment', 'empirical base', 'observation' 'applying theories' and so on. 'If a theory is falsified, it is proven false; if it is "falsified" it may still be true' (Lakatos, 1970: 108; Shaw, 1996a: Ch. 6). Popper's falsifying arguments have been criticized. Nonetheless, the thesis that science (and hence evaluation research) should be both critical and fallible is central – both as commitment and tension – in all realist postpositivism.

Third, the view that there is a steady accumulation of findings and theories, and that science grows thus, has been effectively challenged by Kuhn, Popper, Lakatos and others.

The continuity between positivism and postpositivism should not be overemphasized. Guba (1990) is surely engaging in tongue-in-cheek mischief when he says that the only alternative to relativism is absolutism.

Phillips rightly insists, 'In no sense is [this] new philosophy of science . . . closely akin to positivism' (1990a: 39). Postpositivist evaluators and those influenced by them, actively engage in partial trade-offs, of rigour to gain relevance, precision to gain richness, theoretical elegance to gain local applicability, and measures of outcomes to promote inquiry into process, meaning and local context. They do, however, remain distant from both critical evaluators and constructivists (Phillips 1987b).

Critical evaluation

Critical theory – or more specifically *critical evaluation* – is a catch-all term to include neo-Marxist evaluation (Anderson, 1989; Lather, 1991; Popkewitz, 1990), some feminist positions (Dullea and Mullender, 1999; Swigonski, 1993), the work of Paolo Freire, and some forms of participatory inquiry (Reason and Rowan, 1981). These approaches are 'critical' in the sense that problems are conceptualized as part of the social, political and cultural patterns in which the evaluand is formed. The form of critical inquiry focuses on the contradictions of practice. Hence the basic logic is not preoccupied solely with the formal organization of argument, 'but also particular forms of reasoning that give focus to scepticism towards social institutions' (Popkewitz, 1990: 49). For example, critical evaluation of schooling is not merely about learning but has implications which continually relate the evaluation to larger issues of social production and reproduction (Carr and Kemmis, 1986). This typically involves an 'inversion' which entails 'making history fragile . . . thus poking holes in the causality that confronts us is daily life and that limits our possibilities' (Popkewitz, 1990: 49).

Hence, critical knowledge from evaluation is never neutral: 'It is always for some particular subject' (Comstock, 1982: 374). The production of knowledge is the production of values. This has major implications for the role of the evaluator:

> Social scientists are participants in the socio-historical development of human action and understanding. As such they must decide the interests they will serve. The only legitimate activity of a critical social scientist is to engage in the collective enterprise of progressive enlightenment. (Comstock, 1982: 377)

There are internal differences within critical evaluation at this point. For perhaps a majority of representatives of this position, the partisan role of science makes it an obligation to pursue political commitments through active participation in political movements. This 'entails a direct and explicit involvement in efforts to transform current social relations' (Popkewitz, 1990: 49). To quote Popkewitz's own position again, 'social scientists are partisans in the forming of social agendas through the practices of science' (1990: 50). Thus activism is implicit, whereby inquiry discloses ways in which people are to challenge the world and locate themselves in its ongoing relations.

There are lively debates within critical research and evaluation. Neo-Marxists have strongly criticized the a priori theorizing tendency of critical theorists, and have called for 'critical inquirers to practice in their empirical endeavours what they preach in their theoretical formulations' (Lather, 1986b: 258). Others have insisted that both traditional and emancipatory research need to be interrogated, 'and *both* may be found wanting' (Humphries, 1997: 4.6). Critical evaluators need to acknowledge 'the permanent partiality of the point of view of those of us seeking to construct emancipatory research' (1997: 4.8). There are differences in the extent to which critical evaluators place emphasis on the classic Marxist concept of false consciousness. Those who place heavy emphasis on false consciousness are likely to place equally heavy weight on structural conditions, whereas those who place little or no emphasis on false consciousness will give central significance to intersubjective meanings. Indeed, it may not be too much of an exaggeration to say that where people stand on this is the single most important determinant of the critical theorist's stance on epistemology and methodology. We return to some of these themes in Chapter 4.

Constructivism

The third paradigm, *constructivism*, is perhaps best known through Guba and Lincoln's book on *Fourth Generation Evaluation* (1989). The outline of their work given in Chapter 2 will stand for a sketch of the constructivist/interpretivist position. Their work has attracted inevitable discussion, both for its epistemological stance, and for its methodological strategy. Constructivism is also associated with the names of Smith and Schwandt. Schwandt seeks to recast evaluation in terms of practical acts of interpretation, often described for this reason as an interpretative or hermeneutic approach. He criticizes postpositivism on grounds of its alleged modernism:

> [We] resist three modernist tendencies: (1) . . . to conceive of knowledge only as the acquisition of power to control self, society and nature; (2) . . . to assume that method holds the key to knowledge; (3) . . . to define the individual knower as in complete control of self, nature and social arrangements. (Schwandt, 1997: 78)

The approach he advocates involves the positions

> (1) that the social world . . . can only be studied from a position of involvement 'within' it, instead of as an 'outsider'; (2) that knowledge of that world is practical-moral knowledge and does not depend upon justification or proof for its practical efficacy; (3) that we are not in an 'ownership' relation to such knowledge but we embody it as part of who and what we are. (1997: 75)

Adherents of all three paradigms accept the position that observation is theory-laden. However, constructivism enthusiastically embraces the theory-ladenness of facts, the value-ladenness of facts, and the interactive nature of inquiry whereby the knower and the known are 'fused into a coherent whole' (Guba, 1990: 26). Hence the concern of the constructivist working out of a strictly relativist position is not so much with understanding more accurately but with understanding more deeply, more truly. Inquiry is not therefore an epistemological task but a moral and practical activity. No meaning has epistemic privilege: 'The kind of understanding one has of understanding makes a great deal of difference to the understanding one has of qualitative inquiry' (Smith, 1993: 199).

While a challenging variety of constructivist positions exist, these extracts helpfully catch the recurrent *motifs* of paradigm-based constructivism. The position is gaining increasing voice in the evaluation journals, stimulated by the 1989 'Alternative Paradigms Conference' (Guba, 1990), although these sources may perhaps be less vocal in Britain than in the USA.

The basic constructivist evaluative commitment is to story-telling:

> Stories are the closest we can come to experience as we and others tell our experience. . . . Experience in this view, is the stories people live. People live stories, and in the telling of them reaffirm them, modify them, and create new ones. (Clandinin and Connelly, 1994: 415)

Much of the debate surrounding constructivism is focused on the relativist framework, and the feasibility and consistency with which that relativism is espoused (Heap, 1995; McLennan, 1995). There has also been concern regarding the even-handedness with which constructivists frame the debate. McLennan, for example, suggests extended criticism of some feminist postmodernism on the grounds that opposing views are persistently cast as 'absolutist'. He complains that this is 'a near scandalous truncation of the highly varied philosophical labours which have gone into this issue . . . [and] over-polemicizing to the point where scholarship simply does not come into the picture' (McLennan, 1995: 401). We have more to say on this issue in the second part of this chapter.

To return to our initial questions, is it the case that to be consistent, evaluators and practitioners must choose one paradigm? Is there an inherent inconsistency in subscribing to the worldview of one approach but employing the methods of the other? Lincoln answers eloquently in the affirmative:

> The adoption of a paradigm literally permeates every act even tangentially associated with inquiry, such that any consideration even remotely attached to inquiry processes demands rethinking to bring decisions into line with the worldview embodied in the paradigm itself. (1990: 81)

Smith and Heshusius similarly conclude with a qualified 'no' in answer to the question whether quantitative and qualitative inquirers can even talk to each other: 'In the end, the two sides may be close to speaking different languages – a neutral scientific or value-free language versus a value-laden language of everyday discourse' (1986: 11). Constructivists are not the only advocates of paradigm stances. Popkewitz acknowledges that accommodation occurs at the practical levels of hiring practices in universities and academic debate, but of the theoretical level, he says, 'Here, I guess, I leave the pluralism' . . .

> To include a disciplined sense of history into methodology . . . rejects 'seeing' the discrete events, whether bound to 'qualitative' or 'quantitative' techniques, in isolation from the relation of events to historical formulations. (Popkewitz, 1990: 65)

Pragmatism

However, loud replies in the negative can be heard from different quarters. The mainstream position of evaluation theorists takes a mixture of postpositivist and pragmatic positions (Cook, 1985; Patton, 1990; Reichardt and Cook, 1979; Scriven, 1997; Shadish, 1995). Chelimsky represents this mainstream position when she says,

> What should count is not the favoured method of a particular group, but rather how well we answer the question or achieve the purpose . . . it matters little which perspective or purpose has been adopted: honesty is critical and advocacy is not really an option. (1997: 109)

Some ethnographers have also argued for pragmatism. Hammersley (1995), for instance, is strongly opposed to pragmatic arguments for the validity of research. However, he is equally resistant to paradigm stances, and argues that for each of the seven elements of the divide between qualitative and quantitative methods (see Table 3.1), characteristics of each paradigm element can always be identified in examples of research conducted under the alternative paradigm. Miles and Huberman have also warned against the temptation in epistemological debates to 'operate at the poles': 'In the actual world of empirical research, we believe that all of us – realists, interpretivists, critical theorists – are closer to the centre, with multiple overlaps' (1994: 4–5). Perhaps the most well-known ethnographic voice on this issue is that of Howard Becker. Writing of epistemological issues, he says, 'I think it is fruitless to try to settle them. . . . These are simply the commonplaces, in the rhetorical sense, of scientific talk in the social sciences, the framework in which the debate goes on. So be it. . . . There's nothing tragic about it' (Becker, 1993: 219). We should take an empirical perspective on such matters, treating them as 'a topic rather than an aggravation' (1993: 222). But we should beware the paralysing effect of too much methodological discussion: 'We still have to do theoretical work, but we needn't think we are being especially virtuous when we do' (1993: 221). Rather than regard such theoretical work as the responsibility of all qualitative researchers, he is content to view it as a specialism – the profession of 'philosophical and methodological worry' (1993: 226)!

Support for some kind of pragmatism can be found also in Eisner and Stake. Eisner asks 'what can be more enslaving' than to have 'one framework, one language . . . one drummer to whom scholars and teachers . . . can listen', and suggests 'it is more a matter of seeing what works, what appears right for particular settings' (Eisner, 1991a: 211). We have already seen in Chapter 2 that Stake rejects the use of the term 'model' as raising false hopes.

Pragmatism is attractive for a variety of reasons, and makes for some unexpected bedfellows. We should distinguish between *methodological* pragmatism and *philosophical* pragmatism. Methodological pragmatism rests on an impatience with philosophy and an emphasis on real world evaluation and practice, and it is claimed that methods can be separated from the epistemology out of which they have emerged. The emphasis is thus on practical utility and the credibility of the methods used. Most of the pleas for pragmatism referred to above are of this kind. For example Patton puts forward a case for what he describes as a 'paradigm of choices': 'A paradigm of choices rejects methodological orthodoxy in favour of *methodological appropriateness* as the primary criterion for judging methodological quality' (1990: 38–39).

Gage (1989) envisages the time when there will be a triumph of pragmatic resolutions of paradigm differences, based on a realization that paradigm differences stem from researchers simply studying different topics, often from a different discipline perspective. The guidelines and regulations for professional education in perhaps all the English speaking countries typically take broadly pragmatic stances, despite lobbying from evaluation constituencies. For all those who hold this position, 'the specific methodology employed is less important than the overall approach to action and research' (Kelly, 1985: 144).

Methodological pragmatism typically leads to a rejection of both epistemological and methodological 'purism', a contentment with a 'good enough' methodology, and a pluralist approach to specific methods. Thus, in complaining about the 'philosophically besotted', Scriven says, 'it is better to build on what might conceivably be sand . . . than not to build at all . . . It is a waste of time to try to solve the problems of epistemology without getting on with the job' (1997: 478, 479). Reid argues to similar effect if more temperately for social work: 'Irreconcilable conflicts may indeed exist in the discourse of philosophers, but their perspectives are not essential to the task of resolving differences and building consensus in the practical worlds of social work' (1994b: 478). Reid wants to 'redefine the nature of the mainstream so that qualitative methodology is part of it, not apart from it . . . Neither method is inherently superior to the other, but rather each provides the researcher with different tools of inquiry' (1994b: 477).

There are overlapping concerns between methodological pragmatism and *philosophical pragmatism*. However, there are important differences. Philosophical pragmatism draws especially on the work of American philosophers, and has been invigorated by recent work by Richard Rorty (1979, 1991), whose arguments have exercised a growing influence:

> When confronted with a knowledge claim the pragmatist is less concerned with whether it is right and asks instead, 'What would it be like to believe that?' 'What would happen if I did?' 'What would I be committing myself to?' . . . This shifts the focus of inquiry from verification and the appeal to method, to practice and an appeal to deliberation and conversation. (Schwandt, 1993: 18)

Reid applies a less relativist version of some of these ideas to social work. He believes such a stance 'will take us further than grand epistemologies that trade in abstract assertions about Truth, Reality and so on', and locates himself 'within the tradition of American pragmatism, especially as it has been set forth in the writings of Pierce, James, Dewey and Rorty' (Reid, 1994b: 472). He and Zettergren (1999) develop the interesting idea of empirical practice as a *perspective* which allows an interchange with humanist and advocacy approaches.

Pragmatic arguments have also been used within some work on feminist postmodernism – one of the unexpected bedfellows referred to earlier. The element of surprise stems from the radical's fear that pragmatism tends to political complacency:

> Characteristic of these methodologies are their orientation to decision making and hence to management, their primary emphasis on producing useful information, their practical and pragmatic value base, and their eclectic methodological stance. (Greene, 1994: 532–533)

EXAMPLE 3.1   CAN PRAGMATISM BE RADICAL?

Rorty believes that pragmatist philosophy may be useful to feminist politics. He hopes that feminists will consider the possibility of dropping realism, and the notion that the subordination of women is *intrinsically* abominable. He also urges them to drop the claim that there is something called 'right' or 'justice' or 'humanity' which has always been on their side.

He is modest about the nature of the enterprise: 'Yoking feminism with pragmatism is like yoking Christianity with Platonism . . . something big and important, a vast social hope, is being yoked with something comparatively small and unimportant' (Rorty, 1991: 6).

Applying pragmatism in this way is utopian rather than radical. Radicals think there is a basic mistake deep down at the roots:

> Pragmatists cannot be radicals in this sense, but they can be utopians. They do not see philosophy as providing instruments for radical

surgery . . : Philosophy's function is rather to clear the road for the prophets and poets, to make intellectual life a bit simpler for those who have visions of new communities. (1991: 6)

It thus allows for an appeal to courage and imagination: 'On my view philosophy bites other philosophies, but not social problems as such' (1991: 12).

The application of such more careful ideas of pragmatism to evaluation is still in its infancy. But it has the potential to critically integrate aspects of postpositivist, constructivist and empowerment approaches to evaluation. My own position lies with a strong version of the *fallible* realism of postpositivism, the *constructed* character of reality, and the central role of political and personal *interests*. On paradigms, my premise is that 'the relationship between paradigms and methods is an empirical question' (Pitman and Maxwell, 1992: 732). Yet I think that Hammersley overstates the weakness of the relationship between epistemology, values and methods. People's actions, in evaluation as much as in any other activity, *are* shaped by values and worldviews, and paradigm positions do *not* inevitably tend to the intolerance suspected by Atkinson and colleagues (Atkinson, Delamont and Hammersley, 1988). Professional practitioners and evaluators have sometimes been guilty of naïve pragmatism of the variety that says, 'if it works, it's true'. I agree with Greene when she dissents from the methodological pragmatism that avers epistemological purity does not get research done. Rather, 'epistemological integrity does get meaningful research done right' (Greene, 1990: 229).

As early an advocate of paradigms as Filstead conceded that 'the middle ground of blending the assets of both approaches throughout an evaluation is optimal', and as enthusiastic a proponent as Guba allows there is now a 'more ecumenical stance' in the shared acknowledgement that both verification and discovery methods can go on in all paradigms (Filstead, 1979: 43; Guba, 1990: 23). Guba and Lincoln's case is that disagreement is at the level of basic axioms, rather than methodological postures. Writing out of a postpositivist position, Reichardt and Cook are probably safe to stop at the point that 'paradigms are not the sole determinant of choice of methods', and to conclude there is a 'real but imperfect linkage between paradigm and method' (1979: 16).

This essential tension between philosophical paradigms and practice is likely to remain contested: 'It matters to evaluators because it has important effects on how we envision and do our work' (Greene, 1996: 537). In discussing paradigmatic approaches we have touched on issues of realism and relativism, trade-offs between relevance and rigour, and the uses of evaluation. This fairly extended discussion of paradigms and pragmatism has signalled the kind of solutions I am likely to suggest for each of these issues.

Realism and relativism

We opened the chapter with the dilemma of realism and relativism as it faces professionals in their day-to-day practice. Are practitioners working with fairly direct evidence of reality, with relativist constructs, or the standpoints of the powerful? 'Realism', as with paradigm, is a word that has attracted increasingly varied and differentiated meanings. Speaking of one variety of realism, Leplin wryly remarks that, 'Like the Equal Rights Movement, scientific realism is a majority position whose advocates are so divided as to appear a minority' (1984: 1).

Realism as applied to evaluation is usually assumed to demand an absolutist view of the role of evaluative inquiry, referred to as foundationalism. This is thought to involve a strict correspondence view of truth, that evaluation can fully represent realities independent of the inquiry process. We have noted already that this naïve form of realism is a straw man, which retains the positivist adherence to the role of observation as discloser of the true nature of reality, and a confidence in the objectivity of the evaluator. However, this does not preclude the presence of strong versions of realism in some varieties of qualitative evaluation. Blumer and Harré are perhaps the best known representatives. For instance, Blumer argued that a constructivist view

> does not shift 'reality', as so many conclude, from the empirical world to the realm of imagery and conception . . . [The] empirical world can 'talk back' to our picture of it or assertions about it – talk back in the sense of challenging and resisting, or not bending to, our images or conceptions of it. This resistance gives the empirical world an obdurate character that is the mark of reality. (1969: 22)

Constructivism is not incompatible with realism. Indeed, this is simply to repeat the point we made about realist postpositivism in the context of paradigms. On this view of things we can maintain belief in the existence of phenomena independent of our claims about them, and in their knowability, 'without assuming that we can know with certainty whether our knowledge of them is valid or invalid' (Hammersley, 1992: 50).

A critical or fallible realism is the stance of most of those identified with postpositivism as well as Blumer and Harré. It is also the position of the majority of evaluation theorists such as Scriven, Campbell, House, Cook, Shadish, and, with some ambiguity, Stake:

> The essence of this position is that, although a real world, driven by real natural causes, exists, it is impossible for humans truly to perceive it with their imperfect sensory and intellective mechanism. (Cook and Campbell, 1979: 29)

A range of views co-exists within fallible realist evaluation. For example, the term 'objectivity' means different things to different realists, as does the idea of 'cause'. Some would not be very far from a strict positivist position in respect of their apparent belief that evaluation can provide an account closely approximate to reality. Others, such as the writer, take the position that, while some version of objectivity remains as a 'regulatory ideal' (Phillips, 1990a: 43), evaluative processes and results are always significantly jeopardized by interests, the social location of the evaluator and powerful stakeholders, and, in Guba's surprisingly realist phrase, 'nature's propensity to confound' (1990: 19).

Such epistemological modesty does not necessarily lead to modest aspirations for social change. For example, Campbell's strong fallibilism is harnessed to a bold vision of an experimenting society, and from within social work Reid has asked, 'Is it better to make limited but well documented progress or to work toward more important goals with less certainty of what we have attained?' (1988: 45). Yet fallible realist evaluators are less likely to pronounce confidently that they have got it right. They are likely to concur with Phillips when he admits that 'the objectivity of an inquiry does not guarantee its truth . . . *nothing* can guarantee that we have reached the truth' (Phillips, 1990a: 43).

The most influential developments in the last two decades have stemmed from the field of scientific realism. The most prominent advocates within evaluation are House in America and Pawson and Tilley in Britain (House, 1991b; Pawson and Tilley, 1997a). Scientific realism is a complex field with more than its share of internal contradictions. Leplin, for example, lists ten claims that are characteristic of realism, but no majority of which is likely to be endorsed by any one realist. Yet,

> What realists do share in common are the convictions that scientific change is, on balance, progressive, and that science makes possible knowledge of the world beyond its accessible, empirical manifestations. (Leplin, 1984: 2)

The counterpoint to this continuing commitment to a realist basis of evaluation is a radically relativist epistemology of evaluation, fashioned around assumptions that truth is a matter of consensus, facts do not have meaning except within some value framework, and causes and effects exist only in that they are imputed. Relativist evaluators unequivocally reject the whole idea of a correspondence view of truth. It requires 'independent access to both domains of mind and an independently existing reality', say Smith and Heshusius, 'which we cannot have' (1986: 10). Relativists believe that problems, findings and solutions from one context cannot be generalized to another. Evaluators are subjective partners with stakeholders in the literal creation of data, and act as orchestrators of a negotiation process. Hence, evaluation data have neither special status, but represent simply another construction to be taken into account in the move to consensus. There are consequently multiple shapers of accountability, no single one of which can be singled out for accountability.

The main criticisms of relativist evaluation are similar to those against social science relativism in general. It suffers from the well-known problem of being self-refuting, in that if it is true then it applies to itself, ... 'and therefore it is true relative to a particular culture or framework, and may be false from the perspective of other cultures or frameworks' (Hammersley, 1992: 49). Hammersley has also argued that one of the effects of relativism is that its adherents 'tend to oscillate between undiscriminating tolerance and ideological dogmatism'. The latter is a constant risk, he and Gomm suggest, because there are no grounds within a specific community to oppose enforcement of the paradigm (Hammersley and Gomm, 1997: 3.3). This can lead to stalemate, sometimes encountered in evaluation, where each side is able to claim that their views are 'true'.

A further particular problem connected with relativist evaluation is that constructions become divorced from any anchor point to structures and interests. They appear little more than personal, mental constructs, as when Guba concludes that 'realities exist in the form of multiple mental constructions ... It is the mind that is to be transformed, not the real world' (1990: 27). But reality is not simply and solely a mental product. It comprises social, collective acts, and these collective acts are material transactions with the world.

The confessedly relativist position of writers such as Guba, Lincoln, Smith and Schwandt also poses special difficulties for practising evaluators, deriving from the pressure on them to seek guidelines and support for their work which will give it credibility and trustworthiness:

> Evaluators sense particular pressure to invoke such procedures because the contexts of program evaluation continue to demand assurances of methodological quality and data integrity in evaluative work. This work can make no contributions to social policy and program decision making unless it is perceived as credible and trustworthy. (Greene, 1994: 537)

Relativism has as a consequence been troubled by practitioner struggles. Writing of qualitative evaluation Greene remarks that,

> Many qualitative practitioners struggle with the dissonance invoked by the assumed mind-dependence of all social knowledge claims in the face of the contextual (as well as personal, ego-related) demands to *'get it right'*, to *'find out what's really going on in this setting'*. (1996: 280)

The final argument that has been developed against some forms of constructivist and relativist evaluation and social problems research is that they are guilty of what has been called 'ontological gerrymandering' (Woolgar and Pawluch, 1985). The point requires a few sentences to explain the precise argument involved. Constructivist (or as Woolgar and Pawluch prefer, 'definitionist') arguments regarding social problems analyze changing definitions of behaviour and conditions, in terms of claims-making activities of the individuals concerned. A given deviant behaviour or condition – for example, child abuse, prostitution, drug abuse – becomes defined in society as gaining new or increased problem status. The most common definitionist argument is that since the basic background condition has not changed, variations in the definition of the condition must result from the social circumstances of the definers rather than from the condition itself: 'The lynch pin is the assumption that the condition itself does not vary' (Woolgar and Pawluch, 1985: 215). The problem arising from this explanatory strategy is, 'how do authors manage to portray statements about conditions and behaviours as objective while relativizing the definitions and claims made about them?' (1985: 216):

> The successful social problems explanation depends on making problematic the truth status of certain states of affairs selected for analysis and explanation, while backgrounding or minimizing the possibility that the same problems apply to assumptions upon which the analysis depends. (1985: 216)

It is this strategy of creating and managing boundaries between assumptions understood to be problematic and those understood not to be problematic, that Woolgar and Pawluch describe as 'ontological gerrymandering'. Constructivists proceding in this way fail to acknowledge that their assertions regarding the constancy of the background condition must itself be construed as a definitional claim.

Heap describes this problem in terms of monism and dualism. The meaning of monism taken by Heap is the metaphysical position that only one kind of thing exists, whereas dualism is the metaphysical position that two kinds of thing exist (mind/matter, body/soul, reality/representation, and so on). For example, the realist evaluation position described earlier in this section is clearly dualist – there is knowledge and there is 'knowledge' (representation). A strict relativist position is, on the other hand, monist. Evaluators are concerned with both the *domain* of inquiry (the evaluand) and the *inquiry* itself. For the consistent relativist 'the domain of inquiry is considered to consist of constructions, and the inquiry itself is seen to consist of constructions' (Heap, 1995: 55). There is no objective reality against which the inquirer's claim can be judged.

Heap's contention, persuasively illustrated from Guba and Lincoln's writings, is that there are deep inconsistencies between the rhetoric and practice of fourth generation evaluation. While they argue constantly that the domain of inquiry is constructed, their methodology is assumed always in dualist terms. We have seen an example of this already, in Guba's phrase regarding 'nature's propensity to confound' (Guba, 1990: 19), where he presumes a world that is not simply a mental (or social) construction. Heap gives several other illustrations of Lincoln and Guba's presumption of the existence of independent, intersubjectively accessible evaluands in the domain of inquiry.

Woolgar and Pawluch, and Heap each conclude that the inconsistency apparent here cannot be eradicated: 'Perhaps all attempts at accounting (explaining) depend upon presenting at least some state of affairs as objective' (Woolgar and Pawluch, 1985: 224). Selective relativism of the kind Heap identifies in Guba and Lincoln may not be 'mere technical difficulties in social problems arguments, but pervasive features of all attempts to explain social phenomena' (Heap, 1995: 224). Heap skips Woolgar and Pawluch's 'perhaps':

> Evaluation, and policy studies, can be taken up consistently and cogently only from a dualist social constructionist position . . . *Evaluation inquiries necessarily are dualist.* A monist position that there are no real evaluands, only constructions of them, entails the claim that there is nothing to evaluate, unless one wants to evaluate constructions of evaluands. (Heap, 1995: 58)

The arguments against relativist evaluation are generally persuasive. However, there are also serious difficulties attached to realist evaluation involving its assumptions regarding the overall progressive character of scientific knowledge.

Rigour or relevance?

Reid's choice between limited and well-documented goals or working to more important goals with less certainty, illustrates one of the central 'trade-offs' that appears to face evaluators. Some have argued for objectivity and validity as the highest imperatives of the evaluator. For the outside evaluator 'both distancing and objectivity remain correct and frequently achievable ideals' (Scriven, 1997: 483). Scriven's arguments for remaining distant, undertaking goal-free evaluation, the priority of summative evaluation over formative evaluation, and for dismissing 'so-called participatory design' as 'about as sloppy as one can get, short of participatory authoring of the final report' (1997: 486), are unlikely to find favour with qualitative evaluators. I find them either wrong-headed or otherworldly. But they remain important strands in the argument for evaluative rigour.

However, the wind has been blowing strongly in the direction of addressing issues of relevance as well as, and in some cases instead of, traditional ideas of rigour. Ironically it was the honest doubting of writers such as Campbell that opened the way for such changes. For example, writing in 1974 when 'many of our ablest and most dedicated graduate students are increasingly opting for the qualitative, humanistic mode' (1979: 49), he expounded his insistence that qualitative, common sense knowing is the building block and test of quantitative knowing.

The mainstream among evaluators has for some time abandoned the claim that experimental and quasi-experimental designs, and single system designs, can yield confident information about cause and effect. It is widely conceded that we are involved in 'social inquiry for and by earthlings' (Cronbach, 1986).

The possibility for rigorous evaluation has also been conditioned by loss of faith in the rationality of organizational decision-making, and by the extensive work done first in the mid-1970s on the nature of policy-making, and the ways in which information is used in such processes. This fed through to changed views about how evaluation is and can be used to change programmes, projects and practices. The problem of relevance arises in a sharp form in qualitative evaluation because of its idiographic approach. The findings have to be made relevant by appeal to appropriate arguments about generalization, or to inference from the design and process by which the evaluation was carried out.

Where should we stand then on issues of relevance? The question involves six different aspects. We discuss the first four aspects in the final pages of this chapter, and the fifth and sixth aspects in Chapter 4.

1 How do evaluation problems emerge and gain agreement?
2 Should evaluators be concerned to develop theory?
3 How does scientific knowledge relate to common sense and professional knowledge?
4 Can evaluation results be generalized to other similar or even somewhat different settings or practices?
5 What are the criteria for a good evaluation?
6 How are – or ought – the results of evaluation to be used?

First, relevance involves issues of how evaluation problems emerge and are agreed. Arguments for practitioner evaluation and action research are often based on claims of increased relevance, and that 'any losses in research rigour are more than compensated for by gains in the acceptability of the research' (Kelly, 1985: 148). The development of 'responsive evaluation' by Stake and others has also widened the involvement of stakeholders in practical agendas of problem setting.

Second, the rigour versus relevance issue has been pulled in different directions by the unresolved question of whether evaluators should be concerned to develop theory. By theory, we mean substantive theory. Greene has previously complained that,

> Contemporary discussions of qualitative approaches to evaluation are filled with clamorous dialogue about methodological theory and practice, but only whispers of concern about the nature and role of substantive or programme theory. (1993: 26)

'Theory' is, of course, difficult to define. Indeed, in one important sense we have already argued from the theory-laden character of observation that there is no distinction between theory and fact. Even bracketing that consideration, difficulties may still exist because theory may refer to formal propositions, a worldview, or a working hypothesis. 'You can't pick up rocks in a field without a theory', as William James apparently said.

My own answer to the question whether qualitative evaluators should engage in substantive theory development is 'in some cases'. I do not accept the position of several theorists and writers on evaluation that theory development is the task of research, not of evaluation. But the question of theory development poses special questions for evaluation. It will not do for ethnographers to simply rap the knuckles of qualitative evaluators for not being good theorizing ethnographers (Atkinson and Delamont, 1993). Greene invites us to explicate our own theoretical predispositions, describe local programme theories ('locally meaningful theoretical perspectives on data interpretation': Greene, 1993: 38), attend to emergent theoretical issues, and integrate theory into evaluation conclusions and recommendations. The unanswered problem (acknowledged by Greene), is how such theorizing should reflect contested evaluative purposes.

Those who claim to do atheoretical evaluation are actually doing one or some combination of three other things:

1 They hold their theories tacitly, without reflecting upon them or stating them explicitly.
2 They hold them explicitly but deliberately withhold them from public view.
3 They pack structural concepts that properly belong to theory into their methodology where they are hidden from their view as well as ours. (Garrison, 1988: 24)

Greene has more recently detected 'an opening up of qualitative evaluation to the potential contributions offered by theoretical ways of looking and seeing' (Greene, 1996: 282). Such developments are none too early.

Third, developments in how we think regarding the logic of evaluation have also helped to draw on practical criteria of relevance. There has been a welcome influence of ideas regarding practical reasoning, informal and working logic, and the stimulating impact of neo-Aristotelian ideas of practical reasoning. These developments all help push a distinction between mainstream research rigour and more practical, everyday reasoning and logic, which also include ethical reasoning. We should note four questions.

1 How should qualitative evaluators regard common sense knowledge – their own and others?
2 How do practitioners think regarding evaluation?
3 What is meant by arguing the practical character of a task?
4 Does practitioner evaluation rely on similar or different forms of inquiry from those of the evaluative researcher?

Common sense knowledge, especially that possessed by those on the receiving end of evaluation, has for some time been given weight (Campbell, 1978; Mayer and Timms, 1970). Smith is pushing at an open door when he proclaims interpretivists think, 'it is time to dispense with the long-standing claim that the knowledge of researchers is inevitably superior to, and thus can stand automatically in judgement of, the knowledge of others, such as parents and teachers' (1992: 100).

Anthropologists, such as Geertz, have suggested several reasons why we should treat common sense as a cultural system – 'a relatively organized body of thought, rather than just what anyone clothed and in his right mind knows' (Geertz, 1983: 75). If it *is* a cultural system and not mere matter-of-fact apprehension of reality, then 'there is an ingenerate order to it, capable of being empirically uncovered and conceptually formulated' (1983: 92). It is here, of course, that the argument 'bites' on qualitative evaluation. Pleas to treat common sense seriously must in part include pleas to treat it empirically. The common sense picture of the odd, the deviant, the tediously mundane, and the difficult, provide us with out-of-way cases. They are hence of use to us anthropologically, by setting nearby cases in an altered context.

Geertz undertakes this 'disaggregation of a half examined concept' (1983: 93). He contends that the uses we gain from common sense are by understanding its 'stylistic features, the marks of attitude that give it its peculiar stamp' (1983: 85), rather than its varied content. He identifies properties of 'naturalness', 'practicalness', 'thinness', 'immethodicalness', and 'accessibleness' as those general attributes of common sense found everywhere as a cultural form.

Common sense is much more than the explanation of the untutored citizen offered by the professional or academic expert. Recent reflections on the place of professional practice wisdom owe an indirect debt to this realization. If evaluation is to be relevant it cannot ignore the untutored (or tutored) ways in which practitioners endeavour to make evaluative sense of their practical activities (Shaw and Shaw, 1997a, 1997b). But this raises a further question. What do we mean when we describe such activities as 'practical'? In considerations of this question the renewed influence of Aristotelian views of theory and practice surfaces in various quarters, including ethnography (Hammersley, 1992), constructivism (Schwandt, 1993) and critical evaluation (Carr and Kemmis, 1986). The main effects of this have been twofold. First, it has led to a welcome reinstatement of the ethical dimension of reasoning and practice. Second, it has rescued notions of the practical from its status as second tier, derivative, and derived prescriptively from formal theory. Hence Schwab insists that by practical 'I do *not* mean . . . the easily achieved, familiar goals which can be reached by familiar means', but to 'a complex discipline . . . concerned with choice and action' (1969: 1, 2).

Reflection on common sense understandings also leads eventually to the question whether practitioner forms of evaluation rely on similar or different forms of inquiry from those carried out by the evaluative researcher. We will see in Chapter 6 that practitioner evaluation raises a range of interesting questions that differ from the arguments and solutions of some earlier programme evaluation theory.

Fourth, can evaluation results be generalized to other similar or even somewhat different settings or practices? For the moment we simply note the significance of the question posed. Generalization raises special problems in qualitative research. The greater the emphasis on the local and the contingent, the more wary one will inevitably be about extrapolating conclusions to other places and times. There are, no doubt, ways and means of addressing the task, some of which lend themselves with particular appropriateness to evaluative practice. Erikson, for instance, invites stimulating comparisons between inference in research and in the clinical setting (Erikson, 1959). Geertz has similarly suggested that the task of generalizing within rather than across cases is exactly like the clinical inference process (1973: 26). We have more to say on this question in Chapter 9.

The connection to questions of relevance versus rigour is apparent in terms of the familiar distinction between Type I and Type II errors – false positives and false negatives. Cronbach has complained somewhere that evaluation researchers have been too prone to accept Type II errors (false negatives), out of a misreading of the risk of Type I errors. We have already noted in Chapter 2 that he is ready to trade off precision ('fidelity') against relevance ('bandwidth'). There are more things in heaven and earth than are dreamt of in our hypotheses, he would doubtless say. Once we major on gaining control through enhancing the internal validity of evaluations, relevance is likely to suffer: '"External validity" – validity of inferences that go beyond the data – is the crux of social action, not "internal validity"' (Cronbach et al., 1980: 231).

Quantitative evaluation researchers are fond of accusing qualitative researchers of lack of precision, in their failure to turn their assertions of the typical into quantities. But qualitative evaluation should hold its position. The accusation fails to distinguish precision and wider accuracy. It is the latter that is important. Answers may be precise – but wrong.

We have considered three questions at the heart of understanding the evidence gained from qualitative evaluation. Should evaluation be based on a particular paradigm of evaluation practice, or on pragmatic, even opportunistic, initiatives? Can we discover an objective, real picture of the world, or are all evaluative accounts contingent relativities? Should evaluation be planned according to the demands of scientific rigour or practice relevance? We now turn our attention to more 'use-oriented' questions:

- How do we know if we are doing evaluation right?
- Are the results of evaluation research used through direct application to problems or through a more general process of enlightenment?
- What ethical principles and decision rules should guide qualitative evaluation?
- How should our answers to these questions shape the methodology we use?

4

Values, validity and the uses of evaluation

CONTENTS

The preoccupations of Chapter 3 are central to all forms of disciplined social science inquiry. The specificities of paradigms, realism and relativism, inquiry rigour, manifestations of relevance, and so on, will vary according to whether the concern is with basic research, applied research, policy research, or evaluation. Yet the basic arguments are precisely the same, whatever form of inquiry is under the microscope. The same cannot be said of most of the issues discussed in this chapter. In each case they are shaped, constrained or enriched by virtue of their evaluative purpose. Questions of the validity of inquiry, the uses to which evaluative inquiry may be put, the general approach to methods of inquiry, and even, to some extent, questions of evaluation ethics, are all given a distinctive twist by their evaluative purpose. No territorial elitism is intended by this point. I am not arguing that evaluation issues are more complex, important or even more interesting than the corresponding issues within qualitative research. But they are *different*.

Validity and values

How does an evaluator decide and apply the criteria of a good evaluation? We have tacitly presupposed different answers to this question in the previous chapter. For example, in negotiating the trade-offs of rigour and relevance we saw that Cronbach always prefers less dependable answers about a broader range of questions: 'Scientific quality is not the principal standard; an evaluation should aim to be comprehensible, correct and complete, and credible to partisans on all sides' (Cronbach et al., 1980: 11). Campbell, on the other hand, places his emphasis precisely on the scientific quality of evaluation. His work on internal validity, especially perhaps his elucidation of the threats to validity, remain the sounding board for all evaluative work, even where his original distinctions are modified or rejected. Choices and trade-offs regarding rigour and relevance thus assume questions regarding how we judge the validity of evaluative work.

Validity is at the heart of Becker's 'profession of philosophical and methodological worry' (1993: 226), so much so that any attempt to label someone's dispositions on the matter runs the risk of creating heat rather than light. Such dissension is partly a product of contested standards or criteria. But the *level* at which the judgement is made also leaves scope for confusion. Take evaluation of classroom work as an example. When we ask if this evaluation is valid we probably mean one of the following:

- The validity with which evaluators draw conclusions from their inquiry.
- The validity with which teachers draw conclusions from such studies.
- The validity with which teachers draw conclusions from their own experience.

However, it is reasonably safe to say that any given evaluation writer will adopt one of the five following orientations to questions of validity:

1 Reliance on internal rigour and validity, including claims as to whether evaluation is dependable, confirmable and can be generalized.
2 Reliance on broader criteria of plausibility, credibility, external validity and relevance.
3 Interpretative criteria, which commence from the position that evaluation inquiry is not a technical task but a moral and practical activity.
4 Validity judged according to fulfilment of a model of evaluation as service or reform.
5 Openly ideological evaluation where the evaluation is judged according to its catalytic impact on the lives of the powerless, and by the fulfilment of an advocacy role by the evaluator.

In saying someone will hold *one* of these positions, we should be clear that this applies to the argument or rhetoric adopted, and not necessarily the practical stance implemented in a given evaluation. Evaluators may shift from one position to another, or hold elements of more than one position at the same time. This is especially likely where two or more evaluation researchers are working as a team. However, general distinctions can be made. The internal validity orientation is especially associated with experimental and quasi-experimental designs. The sketch of Campbell's position in Chapter 2 is sufficient for our purposes, and I do not intend to elaborate it further. However, the 'sounding board' quality of his work, mentioned above, will be evident more than once in the following paragraphs.

Plausibility and credibility

Mainstream ethnographic evaluators, postpositivist evaluators, and those committed to more pragmatic philosophical positions on evaluation are often characterized by the *second* position. Hammersley has provided one of the fullest defences of this general view of validity.

EXAMPLE 4.1   HAMMERSLEY ON VALIDITY

Hammersley's position has been developed partly over against more recent arguments for validity based on relativist epistemologies, and advocacy stances within research. His arguments have been brought together in his *What's Wrong With Ethnography?* (1992) and *The Politics of Social Research* (1995).

Hammersley's general view regarding the purpose of research is that, 'The function of research is to provide information that is both true and relevant to some legitimate public concern' (1992: 68). Truth and relevance are not always in harmony. False claims can be fruitful (useful) and we cannot always anticipate the future usefulness of true but apparently trivial claims. But Hammersley believes the basic criteria still hold good.

He believes we should resolve disputes regarding the validity of research in terms of their plausibility ('consistency with existing knowledge whose validity is taken to be beyond reasonable doubt'; 1995: 75) and credibility ('the likelihood that the process which produced the claim is free of serious error'; 1995: 75). The idea of 'reasonable doubt' is important in that it acts as a check on the possibility of an infinite regression of claim and counterclaim.

The central questions are, is the research/evaluation claim reasonable given present knowledge? If not, is it credible? He acknowledges, in a significant caveat, that, 'While [consistency with existing belief] does not rule out the acceptance of new beliefs . . . it makes this less likely than on the foundationalist model' (1992: 72). He also points out that there has to be a good faith assumption that people are ready to be convinced. The existence of different stakeholder audiences will involve different criteria of plausible evidence.

Is the claim central to the overall argument being put forward? If so, then the evidence will need to be more convincing. The type of claim will effect the criteria used. Hammersley distinguishes definitions, descriptions, explanations and theories. Description is local and time bounded. Theory is neither of these:

> The assessment of validity involves identifying the main claims made by a study, noting the types of claim these represent, and then comparing the evidence provided for each claim with what is judged to be necessary, given the claim's plausibility and credibility. (1992: 72)

It is clear from this that while the criterion of validity is viewed as constant across audiences, its implementation in particular cases may vary considerably. His views about the process through which disputes about research should be resolved are shaped by his understanding of rational discourse. He proposes a conception of discourse which has the following ground rules (1995: Ch. 4):

- The overriding concern should be the truth of claims, and not their political or practical consequences.
- Arguments should be judged solely on the grounds of their plausibility and credibility, and not on the grounds of the personal characteristics of those advancing the argument.
- Researchers should be willing to change their views, and should behave as if other researchers are also so willing, at least until there is strong counter-evidence.
- Where agreement does not result the researcher should accept there is some reasonable doubt regarding the argument they are advancing.
- There should be no restriction on participation in such discourse on grounds of political or religious attitude.

Hammersley has framed these ground rules deliberately to exclude relativism and strong activist conceptions of the purpose of research. He also wishes to retain the status of scientific truth claims against lay claims.

Aspects of this argument are sometimes found as part of rather different evaluative positions. This is because evaluative researchers who accept either relativist or openly ideological forms of evaluation often draw on validity criteria that parallel conventional *rationales* (Lather, 1986a; Lincoln and Guba, 1986a; Reason and Rowan, 1981). Reason and Rowan, for example, cite evidence of ability to describe and discriminate what is there as one criterion of the validity of experiential knowledge, and set this in direct parallel to the traditional criterion of measurement validity. The earlier work of Lincoln and Guba offers a carefully developed version of this naturalistic analogue to conventional versions of rigour (Table 4.1). The criteria in the right-hand column should be read as 'analogs or metaphoric counterparts' to positivist criteria (Lincoln and Guba, 1986a: 76). By *credibility* they include prolonged engagement, persistent observation, triangulation of different kinds, and member checks. *Transferability* achieves plausibility through the evidence of 'thick description' (Geertz, 1973) – narrative about the context. External audit of the process of evaluation will enable the evaluator to deduce *dependability*, and external audit of the product will facilitate the deduction of *confirmability*.

Evaluation as a moral and practical activity

While Lincoln and Guba regard their trustworthiness analogues as a significant advance on conventional validity criteria, they have since moved towards more characteristically relativistic criteria of validity, anchored in the category of *authenticity*, which largely addresses aspects of ethical and ideological concerns. This third approach to establishing the criteria of good evaluation more or less forgoes criteria which can meaningfully be described as validity. It rests on a rejection of realism, in which no meaning has epistemic privilege and the 'validity' of evaluation is not concerned with understanding more accurately but with understanding more deeply and truly. Tests of good evaluation are in terms of fairness, an increased awareness of complexity, and an increased understanding of and respect for the values of others.

Smith is an uncompromising advocate of this stance. He regards the regulative ideal for this attempt to understand as human solidarity rather

TABLE 4.1 *Naturalistic analogue to conventional validity criteria*

Values	Conventional criteria	Problem countered thereby	Achieved by	Trustworthiness analogues
Truth	Internal validity	Confounding	Control, randomization	Credibility
Applicability	External validity; generalization	Atypicality	Probability sampling	Transferability
Consistency	Reliability; replicability	Instability	Replication	Dependability
Neutrality	Objectivity	Bias	Insulation of researcher	Confirmability

than objectivity. The procedural choices one makes in ascertaining the quality of a study are choices of a moral nature:

> For example one might undertake member checks because it is the morally and ethically correct thing to do under the circumstances, not because they will lead to a more objective study. (Smith, 1992: 103)

Hence 'our judgements of goodness are practical accomplishments, undertaken within the context of dialogue and persuasion, that we work out as we go along' (1992: 103). As Reason and Rowan express it, 'valid knowledge is a matter of relationship . . . more personal and interpersonal, rather than methodological' (Reason and Rowan, 1981: 241, 244). The consensual approach to validity judgements means that within this approach 'valid is a label applied to an interpretation or description with which one agrees' (Smith and Heshusius, 1986: 9), and therefore an honorific term.

This position is not equivalent to an emancipatory position or even a reformist one. Thus, when Smith illustrates what he means by human solidarity he explains that reading good research has 'allowed me to understand the people and the situations they studied differently and, I hope, with greater depth and sensitivity' (Smith, 1992: 105). We reviewed in Chapter 3 the main problems with relativist positions of the kind Smith adopts. In the present context we appear to have encountered another problem of the relationship between rhetoric and practice in constructivist evaluation. Vicarious understanding and sensitivity seem rather small potatoes for all the heavy ethical and ideological rhetoric behind them. The elephant of rhetoric has brought forth a mouse of practice – a desirable mouse for all that, but a mouse nonetheless.

Woolgar and Pawluch's criticism of constructivism has been on grounds of inconsistency, in that such analyses usually assume some knowledge of real social conditions. This is often in the form that relativizing claims are made while the underlying condition is assumed to remain unchanged. Following this accusation of 'ontological gerrymandering' there has been some clarification of various positions within constructivism. As a result of this, Best (1989) plausibly suggests there exist, in fact, three kinds of constructionists.

First, *strict constructionists*, who accept the criticism made by Woolgar and Pawluch (1985; and by Heap, 1995; and see this volume, Chapter 3), and consistently refuse to make any assumptions. Second, *debunking constructionists*. These are at heart objectivists, in that they assume the social construction takes place, but that it is mistaken. In other words, constructivist claims are a distortion of knowledge. In between these positions lies, third, probably most constructionist research and evaluation, called by Best *contextual constructionism*. These constructivists accept that some assumptions are being made about social conditions, and also that such assumptions *can* be made: 'Contextual constructionists argue that any claim can be evaluated . . . [they] assume that they can know – with reasonable confidence – about social conditions' (Best, 1989: 247). This position clearly echoes the fallible, critical realism of some postpositivists, which we discussed in Chapter 3.

Reformist evaluation

Evaluation as service is perhaps one way of distinguishing evaluation from research, in terms of its *purpose* rather than its *methodology*. This fourth general approach to evaluation and its corresponding stance on validity is summarized by Simon as 'a practical, particularistic, political, persuasive service' (1987: 8). After describing the development of demo-cratic evaluation, she confesses that, 'Personally speaking, the attraction of the democratic model for me lies in its educative logic rather than in its politics of opposition' (1987: 53). In Britain the policy research stance of Finch (1986) reflects this rejection of the view that the evaluator is a technician, and in the USA, Greene has insisted that, 'No longer can we shroud our citizen-selves behind our scientific subjectivities. We must become scientific citizens' (1996: 287).

Holders of this position often reason that evaluation should be educa-tive and democratizing. Varying emphases on the role of advocacy can be found within this approach, from the pluralism of Cronbach and Stake to the reformist positions of House, Simon and Finch. House has long been the advocate of a social justice criterion for evaluation, based on a concept of justice as fairness and impartiality. More recent work has aimed to develop ideas of justice as a criterion for judging evaluation (e.g. Altheide and Johnson, 1997; Kirkhart, 1995). While there are thorny questions to resolve regarding different philosophies of social justice, it is an area that will reward attention. We consider questions of justice in relation to inquiry design decisions in Chapter 7.

Openly ideological standards

Commitments to justice are also part of the fifth stance on evaluation and validity – that associated with openly ideological evaluation. Its adherents share with constructivists a determination to shift the grounds of the debate regarding validity away from the nature of the world, and how we may know it, to questions of values and morals, where the moral stand-points of the evaluator are central.

What place is there for advocacy through evaluation – this 'controversy of the first water' as Chelimsky (1997: 109) describes it? Is she right when she concludes that 'advocacy is not really an option' (1997: 109)? Are Ham-mersley and Gomm fair and correct when they uncompromisingly claim that advocacy undermines public confidence in the impartiality of social evaluation and research and,

> to the extent that such developments amount to redefining the goal of inquiry as the promotion of some practical or political cause, we see them as motivated bias, and believe they must be resisted by researchers. (Hammersley and Gomm, 1997: 5.4)

If evaluation is to achieve Chelimsky's aspiration of standards of quality and practice that are 'inclusive of all legitimate purposes of evaluation and not merely serve to sanctify one perspective at the expense of another' (1997: 108), then the evaluation establishment has to face difficult issues rather than define the boundaries in order to exclude them.

Lather has suggested an especially creative exploration of issues of validity in openly ideological evaluation and research. She confesses that, 'What I have found over and over again in the methodological literature of openly value-based research is a fuzziness on the need for data credibility checks' (Lather, 1986a: 77). She concludes that the minimum standards that evaluation needs to build into its designs to address validity are:

- Triangulation of *methods*, *data sources* and *theories*.
- Reflexive subjectivity (some documentation of how the researcher's assumptions have been affected by the logic of the data).
- Face validity (established by recycling categories, emerging analysis and conclusions back through at least a subsample of respondents).
- Catalytic validity (some documentation that the research process has led to insight and, ideally, activism on the part of the respondents).

Lather warns that 'if we fail to develop these procedures, we will fail to protect our work from our own passions, and our theory building will suffer' (1986a: 77). Lather tackles one remaining tricky problem – false consciousness. Neo-Marxists typically see the evaluator as the interpreter of the world and the exposer of false consciousness. Lather criticizes the tendencies to elitism and alienation engendered by this view of the role of the researcher:

> This non-dialectical perception of the role of the researcher confounds the intent to demystify the world for the dispossessed ... While there is at last some needed revision of the tendency to dismiss resistance to Marxist interpretations as 'false consciousness' ... empirical and theoretical insights continue to be aimed at other intellectuals. (1986a: 75)

In her own research on student resistance to a liberatory curriculum, Lather declined to dismiss it as false consciousness. Rather, 'I want to explore what these resistances have to teach us about our own impositional tendencies' (1991: 76). She recognizes the tension that such praxis-oriented researchers have to live with:

> The development of emancipatory social theory requires an empirical stance which is open-ended, dialogically reciprocal, grounded in respect for human capacity, and yet profoundly sceptical of appearances and 'common sense'. (Lather, 1986b: 269)

Questions about validity

A clutch of difficult issues about validity remains. We simply note them here. First, the crucial question of whether evaluators should be partisan

TABLE 4.2 *Should evaluation and policy research be partisan?*

Solution	Associated with
Non-partisanship	Scriven, Hammersley
Multi-partisan	Cronbach, Stake
Reformist	House, Finch
Radical partisan	Lather, Oliver

is not going to disappear. I have implied in the previous paragraphs that there are four broad answers to this question – non-partisanship, multi-partisanship, reformist positions, and openly ideological, radical partisan approaches (see Table 4.2).

Second, we have argued in the previous chapter that qualitative evaluation has given too little attention to the question of whether the products of evaluation *generalize* to other settings. Cronbach's criticism of Campbell's arguments for internal validity has been widely acknowledged, although it is still far too little known and reflected on. We noted Cronbach's argument that external validity – the validity of inferences that go beyond the data – is the crux of social action, not internal validity. The consequences of his position are methodologically radical. He is convinced that Campbell's formulation of external validity is ultimately trivial, and that the issue for generalization is how we may generalize to people, interventions and settings *that were not sampled and are different*.

Relativist epistemologies, together with a substantial proportion of orthodox ethnographic approaches to evaluation, reject ideas regarding generalization based on implicit probability inferences. A smaller proportion also believes that the local relevance of evaluation is all we have. We argue in Chapter 9 that qualitative evaluators do not need, and cannot afford, to take this last position.

Third, should evaluators regularly recycle evaluation back to those who gave information? This is usually referred to as member validation. There are three basic possibilities, although they are not entirely mutually exclusive. First, we can opt for a realist understanding of member validation (and also triangulation) as a method of validating data. Researcher and respondent views enable us to locate and position what is really happening. Second, it has been argued that this corroborative view of member validation is unduly naïve, and that member responses should be 'viewed instead as further important data, an occasion for extending and elaborating the researcher's analysis' (Bloor, 1997b: 48). Third, we may choose to retain a process of member feedback and response not on epistemological grounds but on ethical and moral commitments to participatory, democratizing evaluation. This is similar to the argument we encountered in Smith's version of validity. The question becomes pressing when planning for the analysis of evaluation, and we consider it in more detail in Chapter 9.

Fourth, what value positions should be adopted by evaluators regarding the conclusions of their inquiry? The general divide on this issue is between those who take a descriptive position and those who adopt a prescriptive stance. A *descriptive* position typically concludes an evaluation by saying, 'These are the value positions adopted by stakeholders in this evaluation, together with the possible consequences that appear to follow if this or that position is adopted.' Constructivist evaluators tend to be descriptive evaluators, as do evaluators such as Stake who place importance on the decisions of stakeholders. Lincoln and Guba, for example, say that 'all ideologies should have an equal chance of expression in the process of negotiating recommendations' (1986a: 79). A *prescriptive* valuing position seeks to persuade key people of the merits or otherwise of the evaluand, and recommendations are made regarding future action. There is no hard and fast way in which valuing positions map on to the stances on partisanship in Table 4.2. Scriven, for example, is a prescriptive valuer, as is House. Most radical partisanship evaluators also hold prescriptive positions.

There are problems with either pole of this debate, and attempts have been made to develop mediating positions. Eraut provides an example of such a position in his discussion of handling value issues in evaluation. He is rightly unhappy with Scriven's insistence that evaluators must bring their evaluation argument together into a summary judgement: 'Conflicting values cannot be condensed without imposing some superordinate ethical framework' (Eraut, 1984: 31). Neither is he comfortable with a neutral, descriptive evaluating position. Data selection and interpretation are intimately connected, so 'putatively descriptive accounts embody hidden principles of selection. The evaluator saves his [sic] own conscience at the expense of not helping his clients' (1984: 31).

Eraut's tentative solution is what he calls 'divergent evaluation':

> One of the tasks of the evaluator is to explore the connections between empirical evidence and the various values which might provide criteria for judging it . . . By showing linkages between the empirical evidence and certain values he is aiding those who espouse those values. (1984: 32)

Thus far this is similar to a version of the descriptive position which has been proposed elsewhere in the literature (Shadish et al., 1990: 101). However, Eraut adds an important new element by adding that the same service is offered to rival values which may not be represented within the evaluation. This enables people to see values as problematic and,

> Allows the evaluator to introduce values not heeded by any of his respondents without giving them any special priority. Thus divergent evaluation aims to increase sensitivity to other viewpoints, to represent all the value positions of involved parties, and to introduce additional values where appropriate. (Eraut, 1984: 32)

Eraut's position fits closely the multi-partisan position in Table 4.2.

Engineering or enlightenment?

Some vision of purpose is, at root, what guides evaluation practice. Close to the centre of that vision is a view of evaluation as having a usefulness for policies, services and practice. Until the 1970s that use was assumed to be relatively straightforward, and to consist of applying the results of evaluation in a direct instrumental or social engineering mode to the problem addressed by the evaluation. In the USA this was supported by the early work of Campbell and Scriven, and in Britain represented in the Fabian model of the researcher–policy-maker relationship.

The shift in assumptions regarding the balance of rigour and relevance outlined in the last chapter contributed to a new focus on the uses of evaluation. One key figure in these changes was Carol Weiss. In the outline of her position in Chapter 2 we noted her argument that political considerations intrude on evaluation in three ways:

1   The programme and policies being evaluated are themselves the creatures of political decisions.
2   Evaluation includes political considerations because its reports enter the political arena.
3   Politics – usually establishment ones – are implicit in evaluation research.

Weiss's empirical work led to more realistic theories of evaluation use, in contrast to the more utopian aspirations of Campbell's vision of an experimenting society. She introduced the ideas of 'decision accretion' and 'knowledge creep' to describe the way in which policy decisions are not made at a single point in time, but by the build up of small choices, the closing of small options, and the gradual narrowing of available alternatives (Weiss, 1980). Weiss argued that policy-makers' decisions reflect an enlightenment model of use, whereby there is a diffuse and indirect infiltration of research ideas into their understanding of the world. Ideas of use as enlightenment have become the established orthodoxy.

The view taken on the uses of evaluation will in turn effect how the task of dissemination of information is envisaged. The work of Weiss and others implies that we should not regard this as a matter of technical communication, but that it will raise issues of how we view social change. Professions and their researchers have tended to treat dissemination and research utilization skills in an unproblematic fashion (Fisher, 1997). We explore the implications of the work of Weiss, Cronbach and others for information use in policy research and evaluation in Chapter 5.

There is a link back to the discussion of paradigms in the previous chapter. It will be clear that the position that is taken on matters of evaluation use will be shaped by one's evaluation worldview. Postpositivist realists are more likely to adopt a social engineering view of evaluation use, constructivists may regard use as a form of story-telling, while critical evaluators will see use in terms of political engagement and action (Greene, 1990).

We should not overdo the stress on enlightenment, and neither should we assume that ideas on use developed in the fields of programme evaluation and policy research will transfer easily to practitioner evaluation.

Enlightenment models are more likely to be linked to:

- Longer-term change through evaluation research.
- Evaluation that aims to change the way people conceptualize their experience.
- Programme evaluation.
- Theorizing about the targets of evaluation.
- Evaluation based within higher education.

Instrumental views of evaluation are more likely to be associated with:

- Shorter-term, immediate applications.
- Practitioner evaluation.
- Limited social science theorizing.
- Evaluation that is local organization-based and may be carried out by 'insiders'.

The problem of use can be given too much emphasis. Chelimsky rightly points out that 'use is a good thing . . . but too much zeal about it will make us bland and innocuous when we really should be questioning prevailing policies, and challenging the status quo' (1997: 105, 108).

Evaluation ethics

Naïvety about ethics is itself unethical. If Lincoln and Guba are correct, there are definite grounds for concern:

> Respondents' values *are* systematically disregarded as mere opinions with no foundation in scientific knowledge. Purposes of research *are* systematically withheld from subjects on the grounds that were they to know them, the 'technical adequacy' of the study would be compromised ... Protected personal information *is* accessed when the researcher believes it useful to his or her larger search for truth. (1989: 225)

The concerns raised here are about the day-to-day process of ethical decision-making rather than broader ethical principle. Yet even at the more general level there are different views about what broad ethical principles should govern evaluation. Eisner (1991a), for example, occupies familiar territory when he suggests that the three main principles are informed consent, confidentiality, and the right to opt out of research at any time.

House takes a rather different view. He suggests that the three ethical principles are mutual respect, non-coercion and non-manipulation, and upholding democratic values (House, 1993). He elaborates these through, for example, the setting up of a fair evaluation agreement (see Chapter 7), but he admits that which actual values his third principle entails is contestable.

Warwick believes that ethical principles can be subsumed under the single principle of maintaining human freedom. He considers a study perhaps most discussed for its ethical implications, Laud Humphreys' *Tearoom Trade*. Humphreys adopted a covert 'watchqueen' role for the participant study of (then illegal) male homosexual activity. He observed some 200 sexual acts. Some men knew of his research, and others did not. He subsequently illegally obtained the addresses of men in the study and interviewed them, unrecognized, regarding a 'health survey' (Humphreys, 1975).

Under the general rubric of human freedom, Warwick outlines the potential costs and benefits to human freedom of conducting research. Potential *benefits* include opportunity for self-expression through the findings, the satisfaction of sharing important things with someone else, the intellectual satisfaction of participating in research, and the possible personal benefits from talking about a problem. Potential *costs* include deception, the invasion of privacy, and the misuse of information. He wonders whether we need to question liberal assumptions regarding the value of information. He asks, 'Does research reinforce the tendency of individuals to be wary and to live for the record?' (Warwick, 1982: 52). He suggests that research consumes resources of money, personnel, goodwill and tolerance, all of which are finite. While there is an obligation to study controversial topics, that does not include the right to deceive, exploit or manipulate.

Warwick's discussion applies equally to evaluation ethics. However, Guba and Lincoln adopt a different approach to ethics, tying their analysis firmly to their paradigm position.

EXAMPLE 4.2 ETHICS: HAS POSITIVIST SCIENCE FAILED?

Lincoln and Guba believe that the failures of ethical decision-making suggest three lessons. First, 'much depends on the "moral boiling point" of the individual inquirer; different inquirers will make different decisions even when confronted with similar circumstances' (1989: 226). Second, nothing inherent in conventional modes of social science research either mandates or rewards ethical behaviour. Finally, 'inquirers have managed to find many apparently sound reasons for avoiding "wisdom ethics" – the ideal ethical practices – in conducting their research' (1989: 226).

The main thrust of their argument is directed to the second problem – what they describe as the ethical 'tilt' of the conventional paradigm.

The essence of their case is that the conventional paradigm holds an absolutist view of truth, assuming that unassailable knowledge can be obtained:

> With such a metaphysical warrant for the search for truth in hand, the social scientist is free to argue convincingly that his or her research requires and justifies deception ... Presumptions about the nature of reality reinforce – and indeed require – treating human subjects as though they were objects. (1989: 226–227).

Lincoln and Guba believe that the naturalistic paradigm – while not free from its own ethical dilemmas – is more ethical than the conventional. Because it has no underlying premise about the way things really are, deception is 'absolutely counterproductive' (1989: 230). Also, the relationship between researcher and respondent is one between equal partners with equal voices. The respondent therefore keeps control of the process.

The argument helps to reinstate ethical issues as central to research and evaluation. However, several questions are raised by their analysis:

- Are Lincoln and Guba justified in adopting the position that some paradigms are more ethical than others?
- It is a matter of judgement whether the ethical problems of naturalism are preferable to those of conventional research ethics. For example, Lincoln and Guba say that 'confidentiality and anonymity obviously cannot be guaranteed' in naturalistic inquiry (1989: 233).
- Lincoln and Guba run together positivism and realist postpositivism in their critique. However, the two hold very different positions regarding the possibility and nature of objectivity. Their critique may lose part of its force once we recognize this distinction.
- Is it apparent that naturalistic inquiry guarantees freedom from deception? It has a certain rhetorical plausibility, but several commentators have asked whether ethnography may be *more* prone to deception than traditional methods of inquiry (Stacey, 1988). While egalitarian relationships *do* counter deception, one problem, discussed in the previous chapter, is that much ethnographic, interpretative evaluation makes a dualist distinction between stable researcher constructs and unstable, contingent respondent constructs. Heap has suggested that this is morally suspect, in that 'respondents will be treated as metaphysical fools, dumb dualists, while the otherwise honest and forthright evaluator knows the truth: it's all constructions, nothing is real' (1995: 59).

Our accounts and comments on evaluation ethics have been deliberately general. The more specific problems and dilemmas are considered in later chapters, in accord with our general perspective that evaluative purpose should be the central consideration. Specific questions of ethics are considered in connection with evaluation design, fieldwork and analysis, in Chapters 7 to 9.

Methodology and methods

There is an ambiguity surrounding attitudes to methodology and methods within evaluation theory, which is a mix of bane and blessing. Much of the writing since the 1970s has served to underscore that evaluation is not and should not be solely methodology-driven. It has become orthodoxy – although not one shared universally – that 'armed only with methodology, the evaluator is ill-prepared' (Shadish et al., 1990: 183). Methodological purism has come to be mistrusted (Hammersley, 1993b).

There are several reasons for these doubts about methods:

- First, they stem in part from the emphasis, especially within qualitative and constructivist evaluation, on the use of the self as instrument, and in the mistrust of methods as a modernist search for the key to knowledge. Interpretivists are suspicious of researchers who are 'too enamoured of procedures or methodology' (Smith, 1992: 104). Eisner is in tune with this position in his somewhat disdainful remark that 'in qualitative matters cookbooks ensure nothing' (1991a: 169). Lincoln and Guba say that, 'The relativism of naturalism suggests that it is impossible (and always will be) to specify any ultimately true methodology for coming to know' (1989: 231).
- Second, methodological doubt may be one consequence of acceptance of the theory-laden character of observation. Garrison infers that only theory can turn phenomena into meaning. Methods 'only provide the syntax, never the semantics' (1988: 25).
- Third, a diminished concern with methodological cogency may follow from the shift to an enlightenment view of evaluation, where instrumental procedures take second place to wider political issues and trade-offs in evaluation.
- Finally, we cannot ignore the probability that methodological indifference is due partially to a simple lack of methodological imagination, often manifested in naïve methodological pragmatism.

For these reasons the methodological implications of the issues we have discussed are more general. For example, broad methodological leads follow from the different paradigm positions. This link is fairly transparent in both critical evaluation (Comstock, 1982) and constructivism (Smith and Heshusius, 1986). It also follows from the postpositivist shift in mainstream evaluation. This has led to an emphasis on multiple methods ('critical multiplism' to use Cook's ugly phrase; Cook, 1985). There is a danger here in the current emphasis on a 'horses-for-courses' approach to evaluation design decisions. It is suggested, to caricature slightly, that quasi-experiments will still be appropriate when measurement of causes, effects and impacts is needed, whereas discovery methods and case studies will be fine when evaluators are asked to provide broad-scale pictures and story-telling. This is too comfortable and results in a premature closure on debate about methods and methodology, which is influenced no doubt by the weariness with what in America have been called the 'paradigm wars'. Indeed, the central claim of this position is far from straightforward. For example, Campbell's own work on case studies 'constructs one of the strongest cases to date that qualitative methods can yield valid causal knowledge' (Shadish et al., 1990: 135). Causal questions in connection with the design and analysis of qualitative evaluation are an important example of how evaluative purpose gives a distinctive shape to qualitative evaluation, in ways which are less likely to surface in mainstream qualitative research. This is reflected in the space given to these issues in Chapters 7 and 9.

Cronbach's work also has methodological consequences. It pushes him towards evaluation *within* programmes rather than evaluation *between* programmes. He 'is dragged by his conception of social program realities toward methodologically looser conceptions of evaluation designs', and 'does not want a particular conception of scientific method to trivialize the process of asking important questions' (Shadish, et al., 1990: 349). He views evaluation design as a series of 'artful trade-offs' (Cronbach et al., 1980: 225), which are not solely technical but part of political accommodation. '*Leverage* is the bottom line. Leverage refers to the probability that the information – *if* believed – will change the course of events' (1980: 265; italics in original). For him this is not a move back to an instrumental view of how evaluation will be used, because 'the questions with the greatest leverage are the ones that contribute to insight' (1980: 266). Similar commitments to loose designs are accepted by constructivists.

We have observed the ways that views about the uses of evaluation, its general logic, paradigm positions, and views about validity and generalization will give a special purchase on methodology. We saw in Chapter 3 the way also that allowing *theory* a central location in evaluation steers us away from the view of evaluators as technical experts. Evaluators and practitioners will need to be increasingly self-conscious of where they stand on such issues. Only then are they likely to reach resolutions to the twin methodological questions for evaluation, namely, what methods are most likely to meet the purposes of a given evaluation, and what special purchase and 'take' will evaluative purpose give to those methods.

Underlying this second question is a wider problem of the relationship between evaluation/research practice and professional practice. It has frequently been argued (Bloom, 1999; Gould, 1999), that the two kinds of practice are closely akin to one another. This has usually been in the form, 'teaching/legal practice/social work/medical diagnosis/management is like evaluation/research' rather than the converse. In other words it appears a way of shifting community perceptions of the *professional* task rather than the *research/evaluation* task. It has a long pedigree. The problem with such assertions is that they have been used to support a cluster of apparently incompatible claims – for management-by-effectiveness approaches, scientific practice, reflective practice, and so on. Thomas (1978) gave warnings against a naïve assumption of common purpose or method between researchers and practitioners over twenty years ago in a social work context. Yet the idea is interesting, and evaluators and practitioners should continue to explore the correspondences and disjunctures of research and practice.

The position adopted on evaluation methods in this book is that there are no distinctive evaluation methods. I dissent from Lincoln and Guba's (1986b) apparent view that the techniques used to arrive at data in research, evaluation and policy analysis only occasionally overlap. It does not follow from this that evaluators have little to say about methods. We explore in Chapters 7 to 9 the distinctive character that evaluative purposes give to design, data collection and analysis.

Conclusion

The wide canvas questions we have considered in the last two chapters are in no way neatly resolved. Indeed, Becker is probably right when he implies they will continue to be custom and practice within social science inquiry. If that is so, then a self-assigned prescriptive stance may be in order. My own preferred approach includes commitments to:

- Empirical work on how members of cognate professions (and superficially very different professions; Schon, 1983) make evaluative sense of practice.
- Fresh examination of the risks and benefits attached to paradigmatic commitments and to different forms of pragmatism.
- Caution regarding both relativist and strongly realist assumptions about evaluation knowledge.
- Disaggregation of global judgements about whether evaluation should emphasize rigour or relevance.
- Elucidation of validity criteria accepted in qualitative evaluation projects.
- Prior agreement on procedures whereby eventual validity judgements will be reached.
- Identifying the range of expectations which qualitative evaluators are likely to face regarding eventual use of the inquiry.

- Development of case studies of ethical principles and decision-making.
- Review the adequacy of qualitative evaluation methods.

The sources used in this book suggest the more promising ways forward. Selective reworking of some of the major evaluation theorists will repay effort. For myself, I find Cronbach, Weiss, House, Greene, and aspects of Lincoln and Guba's and Stake's work to be especially fertile ground. Dialogue, ideally face to face, between evaluators working in different professional fields will especially foster good evaluation within professional groups. This will require collaboration across discipline and national boundaries. The remark of George Bernard Shaw, familiar to British ears, that 'the Americans and the British are two people separated by a common language', offers insight regarding the similarity and yet differences in the way evaluation has developed from one country to another.

5

Evaluating programmes and policies

CONTENTS

Evaluation may address policies, programmes, projects or elements of service within a programme or project. Each of these may be any stage of development from the preliminary 'drawing board' stage, through feasibility status and exemplification, to full realization and funding. Evaluation is not limited to the measurement of results of established public policies and programmes. Neither is there a single evaluative purpose of the kind that seeks to ascertain whether an observed change is the result of a given intervention. My starting point for this book was the assertion that the purposes of evaluation also include gaining understanding of public issues and of present and previous attempts to address them, the promotion of both reflective and empowering practice, and the development of cultures of evaluation.

We should not conclude from this, however, that evaluative issues are much the same whether we are concerned with policies, programmes or individual practitioners. Cronbach and his colleagues were only slightly exaggerating when they remarked that, 'If any single intellectual sin is responsible for the present chaos, it is the readiness to make general assertions that supposedly apply to all evaluations' (Cronbach et al., 1980: 51).

Take, for instance, the question of the uses of evaluation. We have seen in the previous chapter how the work of various people such as Weiss and Cronbach has led to the well nigh universal acceptance of the limitations of a model of use based on an assumption of direct, instrumental application of findings to a given, pre-specified problem. Yet a moment's reflection will suggest that, if we are considering the evaluation of an individual practitioner's work, a longer-term enlightenment model of use will make little sense, and may place at jeopardy the rights to service of existing patients, clients and pupils. Enlightenment models of use have been developed mainly at the levels of policies and broad programmes rather than local projects and practice.

In this chapter and the following one we will consider some of the more specific questions that occur in qualitative evaluation work which addresses programmes, policies and practices. Programme evaluation, along with the methodology of randomized controlled trials, is often still treated as the 'gold standard ... Rolls Royce of evaluation approaches' (Chelimsky, 1997: 101). In the first half of this chapter we will reflect on some of the special issues that occur when we embark on qualitative strategies of *programme* evaluation. The term 'programme' is used fairly flexibly in this context. Nominally independent and uncoordinated agencies, schools or projects providing broadly analogous services, or addressing a comparable cluster of problems, will be regarded as constituting a programme. In the second half of the chapter we will look more generally at debates and issues posed by qualitative evaluation of *policies*. In Chapter 6 we will describe and consider some of the more recent and innovative approaches to qualitative evaluation within direct *practice*.

Programme evaluation

Joseph Wholey offers the following definition at the start of his major handbook on the methodology and methods of programme evaluation:

> Programme evaluation includes the measurement of programme performance – resource expenditure, programme activities, and programme outcomes – and the testing of causal assumptions linking these three elements. (Wholey, 1994: 15)

Unfortunately this definition poses more problems than it solves. Perhaps its only advantage is that it maps the minefield. There are four obvious problems. First, it is tied too explicitly to the identification of outcomes. Programme activities *are* mentioned, yet the implication is that the identification of causal linkages will reveal the real significance of these activities in relation to programme outcomes. Second, Wholey goes on to underscore the contribution of programme evaluation to improving programme performance: 'One important potential contribution of programme evaluation is its use by policy makers, managers and staff to change programme resources, activities, or objectives to improve programme performance' (1994: 15). Yet this is only one of numerous reasons for carrying out evaluation. Indeed, Cronbach believes that 'an evaluation of a particular project has its greatest implications for projects that will be put in place some time in the future' (Cronbach et al., 1980: 267). Policy values are too limited if we restrict their relevance to a programme now in place. Third, the central emphasis on measurement in this definition and the omission of any clear reference to the wider political context of programmes, suggests a view of the purpose and process of evaluation which is far too unproblematic. Finally, there is an unhelpful managerialist note to Wholey's understanding of programme evaluation.

We gain a clearer differentiation of programme evaluation questions if we relate the discussion to the different *genres* of programme evaluation. For example, Greene closely anticipates distinctions in Chapter 3 of this book and suggests there are four. She names these as postpositivism, pragmatism, interpretivism, and critical or normative evaluation (Greene, 1994). The typical evaluation questions addressed by postpositivist evaluation are: Are the desired outcomes attained and attributable to the programme? Is this programme the most efficient alternative?[1] Pragmatic evaluations focus on questions such as: Which parts of the programme worked well and which need improvement? How effective is the programme with respect to the organization's goals, and to the beneficiaries' needs? Interpretivist evaluation typically starts by asking how the stakeholders experience the programme. Critical, normative evaluation addresses questions such as: In what ways are the premises, goals or activities of the programme serving to maintain power and resource inequities in society? How might the evaluation process challenge these structured inequities?

EXAMPLE 5.1   EVALUATING PRE-NATAL PROGRAMMES

It will help to provide a naturally occurring illustrative contrast from the literature. Wholey describes the preliminary assessment of the evaluability of the Tennessee Pre-Natal Programme. Whitmore also describes the evaluation of an education programme for single expectant mothers in a low income area of Halifax, Nova Scotia (Whitmore, 1990, 1994; Wholey, 1994).

The Tennessee Department of Public Health ran a five-year project 'Toward Improving the Outcome of Pregnancy' (TIOP) from 1977 to 1982. An evaluation of the programme was funded for the final year. Wholey led an assessment aimed to plan the evaluation activities that would be most useful. He involved budget staff, senior management and executive staff, a deputy commissioner of health, senior project staff, and others in work and policy groups. Following this exercise various design options were put forward which included:

- Success in meeting state-wide standards.
- Intra-programme comparisons among TIOP projects and counties.
- Before-and-after comparisons and interrupted time-series analyses using birth data.
- Before-and-after and time-series data comparing TIOP counties with others not served by TIOP.
- Before-and-after and time-series analyses comparing TIOP projects offering different services at different costs.

Agreement was reached in the light of this to focus on success in reducing numbers of low birth weight infants, as a surrogate indicator of risk of infant morbidity and mortality, and of learning disability. Programme representatives thought this was both a realistic goal and one for which they could be held accountable. Infant mortality targets were also retained on the advice of the Deputy Health Commissioner, who believed questions would later be asked on this indicator.

The programme in which Whitmore was involved had run for three years when the evaluation was invited. Whitmore offered to facilitate a participatory inquiry. As many as possible of the women who had previously used the service were contacted and invited to apply to join the evaluation team. Four women were appointed, with the brief to formulate the design, collect and analyze data, and present the results. Whitmore describes participatory research and evaluation as combining:

> investigation, education and action in an effort to improve the social and economic conditions under which people live. Its main goals involve broad social change, justice and equality, achieved by seeking to empower less powerful constituents. (1990: 216)

Data collection was based on unstructured interviews and questionnaires. There were understandable difficulties. The women found it difficult to separate the data from their own opinions. There were group tensions, which led to one member leaving. Contact with the media proved 'extremely destructive to our collective process and ultimately to group cohesiveness' (1990: 221). There were also communication and trust difficulties. One woman said:

> Our world is different from yours. The fear is that people always want to humiliate you, put you down [for being on welfare] . . . We have a different lifestyle from you. We just don't trust people the way you do. (Whitmore, 1994: 92)

Yet the net results were positive. They had successful contacts with the Advisory Group, addressed a conference and took a university class. In addition, Whitmore and the group concluded that there had been gains at individual, group and wider social environment levels (see Table 5.1).

TABLE 5.1   *Outcomes of pre-natal programme evaluation*

Level of practice	Component of empowerment
Individual	self-confidence
	knowledge/skills
	enthusiasm and enjoyment
Group	overcoming isolation
	developing trust
Environment	educational opportunities
	speaking to outside groups
	challenging the social service system
	employment opportunities

These brief descriptions of each project accentuate how programme evaluations which start from different frameworks will vary in the key values they promote, the audiences they address, the methods preferred and the typical evaluation questions asked.

Issues for qualitative programme evaluators

Although there is no single good practice model for qualitative programme evaluation, there are a number of questions whose answers set the broad parameters of a qualitative stance on evaluation. Qualitative programme evaluators:

* Will consider the *process* of programme activities and delivery prior to considering programme outcomes.
* Will be mistrustful of programme delivery and evaluation which depends heavily on assumptions of *rational decision-making*.
* Should not ignore the significance of *theorizing* about programmes.
* Will be less enthusiastic about the value of *accountability* models of evaluation.
* Include a range of positions on the place of programme evaluation in contributing to *social change*.

The tentative resolutions of these dilemmas, outlined in the following paragraphs, illustrate that qualitative evaluation should not be viewed as a pragmatic, horses-for-courses option that tucks in behind more established quantitative evaluative research, in the way too often favoured by the evaluation establishment. Rather, they present an agenda for critical negotiations.

Processes, outcomes and rationality

The doyen of randomized field experiments and quasi-experiments is Donald Campbell. We saw in Chapter 2 how his earlier work – elaborated through his successive expositions of threats to the internal validity of such studies – provided the benchmark for future cause-probing work in field settings. He argued that they led to more certain causal inferences. He debunked claims about the limited applicability of random assignment, and was happy about the ethical consequences of treating scarce resources like a lottery. He argued that the major obstacle was political will.

Yet there are other, far more ambivalent, passages in Campbell's writings. He acknowledges that:

- There is a precarious rigidity in measurement systems.
- Process is often neglected and thus, even when we learn programme effects, this knowledge has at best equivocal implications for programme improvement.
- Changes in the intervention programme are almost inevitable during the evaluation.
- Even under well-controlled situations experimentation is tedious and equivocal.
- The political usefulness of experiments is limited by the slowness with which they are completed.

Similar conclusions were reached following British field experiments in the 1960s and early 1970s (Brody, 1976; Clarke and Cornish, 1972).

Whereas Campbell aimed to improve evaluation designs, Cronbach adopted a more radical position. At its core, as we noted in Chapter 2, is the claim that '"external validity" – validity of inferences that go beyond the data – is the crux of social action, not "internal validity"' (Cronbach et al., 1980: 231). Arising out of this analysis, Cronbach prioritizes the understanding and explanation of mechanisms operating in a local context, in order that plausible inferences can be drawn regarding other settings, people and interventions that are of interest to policy-makers. It is extrapolation that matters – 'a prediction about what will be observed in a study where the subjects or operations depart in some respect from the original study' (Cronbach, 1986: 94). He is careful never to reject the logical argument for comparative experiments with controlled assignment when the evaluator needs to address a summative and causal question, but he nonetheless marginalizes such research because he believes internal validity is 'not of salient importance in evaluation' (Cronbach et al., 1980: 314).

The last decade has seen a partial revival of faith in outcome-focused effectiveness evaluation. This has been stimulated by the political commitment of several western governments to management-by-effectiveness approaches, public sector accountability, and the adoption of performance indicators for schools, hospitals, social work agencies and the whole gamut of public sector services. Suffice to say that I am not convinced the problems raised by Campbell and Cronbach have been adequately resolved by the new generation of evidence-based evaluators. In some cases they have not even been acknowledged.

Rationalist ideas of efficiency do not sit comfortably with ideas of democratic participation. Cronbach goes as far as to say that, 'Rationalism is dangerously close to totalitarianism' (Cronbach et al., 1980: 95). In response to arguments that quasi-experimental designs are convincing and plausible, he and his colleagues say tartly that:

> The demand that an argument be 'convincing' is nothing more than a rationalist attempt to define a category of conclusions that in no way rest on belief and values; in evaluation it is an attempt to place decisions outside politics by establishing an inescapable conclusion. (1980: 292)

There is a further problem too little appreciated. The question, 'Does it work?', is a sceptical question and 'functions as an exclusionary gatekeeper' (Bogdan and Taylor, 1994: 296). Even assuming the design problems could be solved the question still would not be helpful to practitioners: 'Conscientious practitioners do not approach their work as sceptics; they believe in what they do' (1994: 297). Bogdan and Taylor have worked to develop what they call 'optimistic research'. 'We have evolved an approach to research that has helped us bridge the gap between the activists, on the one hand, and empirically grounded sceptical researchers, on the other' (1994: 295). The main focus of their research has been on questions of how people with severe disabilities can be integrated into the community. Rather than ask whether services are effective, they ask, 'What does integration mean?', and 'How can integration be accomplished?'

Theorizing about programmes

Taking sociology as an example, theory may mean either a sociological framework (e.g. 'feminist theory') or substantive theoretical knowledge of a sociological kind (e.g. risk, or stigma). Greene (1993, 1994) is perhaps the most vocal advocate of the place of substantive theory in qualitative programme evaluation. The *nature* and *form* of theory for interpretivist evaluation approaches will be context-specific, with multiple meanings emergent from portrayals of the programme. The *rationale* for theory generation should avoid being content with simply understanding, but must promote scientific responsibility. On questions of how such theory should be incorporated into evaluation Greene asserts:

> the challenge rendered is to incorporate theory-related issues into qualitative evaluation, to inform these issues via local, contextualized perspectives and understandings, and thereby to contribute an interpretive programme theory to science and infuse an interpretive voice in the broader policy domain. (1993: 35)

She suggests four ways in which this may be done.

The first involves explicating the evaluator's theoretical dispositions – their beliefs, hunches, prior experiences and knowledge on such issues – which should then be linked to a programme theory framework. This is similar to McCracken's invaluable recommendation regarding conducting a cultural review (McCracken, 1988; Shaw, 1997). Second, through the description of local programme theories – 'theory as intended'. This will help provide locally meaningful theoretical perspectives on data interpretation and enable understanding of how future recommendations may be responded to. Third, attend to emergent theoretical issues. In this respect the qualitative stance of openness 'is often diffuse and ill-focused, like antennae waving around in search of some signal' (Greene, 1993: 38). Finally, integrate programme theory into evaluation conclusions and recommendations. In this, Greene wishes evaluators to steer between the classic inductivist ethnographic stance, and a priori theorizing. In all, she urges 'a more proactive, theory-sensitive role for evaluators' and 'a stronger, more assertive, and more persuasive role for interpretivist social science' (1993: 40). 'By accepting such a challenge, qualitative evaluators' stories can gain broadened responsiveness and enhanced authority' (1993: 41).

In an endnote to this paper Greene acknowledges that the response of critical evaluators will be 'broadened responsiveness' to whom, and 'enhanced authority' for what purpose? She has sought to develop a response to these questions in later work in which she argues:

> Absent an engaged, accountable position like scientific citizenship, I fear that qualitative evaluation will be relegated to the sidelines of important debates about pressing public issues ... No longer can we shroud our citizen-selves behind our scientific subjectivities. We must become scientific citizens. (Greene, 1996: 286–287)

Critical theorists may wish to go further, as illustrated from the work of Carr and Kemmis in Example 5.2.

EXAMPLE 5.2   CRITICAL PROGRAMME THEORIZING

One of the most extended arguments for a critical redefinition of the relationship between theory and practice in evaluation is that by Carr and Kemmis (1986). Practical problems, they reason, are always solved by doing and never by knowing, and the test of educational research is whether it resolves educational problems and improves practice. Both theory and practice are 'practical' undertakings. Theory as substantive theory about something, always derives from theory in the sense of a framework. Likewise, practice derives from theory in the sense of a framework. Thus educational problems are always in this sense problems of theory/practice relationships.

Therefore, when theory/practice relationships are seen as the failure of practitioners to apply the theories developed by those who are engaged in theoretical pursuits, this distorts reality. To regard theory and practice problems as a breakdown in communication that afflicts practitioners is to fail to see that practical problems of this kind occur in the course of any theoretical undertaking. To assume that difficulties of this kind can somehow be identified and tackled in theory and then 'applied' in practice tends to conceal how they are in fact generated out of practice. Also, converting theoretical knowledge into rules of action overlooks that it is practitioners who solve practical problems. It is the theory guiding *their* practice that provides the guiding principles and not some theory external to them. Carr and Kemmis summarize the defects of positivist and interpretative approaches by saying:

> The scientific approach, by ignoring the fact that educational problems are always pre-interpreted, effectively eliminates their *educational* character. The interpretive approach, by insulating the self-understandings of practitioners from direct, concrete and practical criticism, effectively eliminates their *problematic* character. (1986: 117–118)

In response to this critique they develop a critical approach to theory and practice based on the work of Habermas, and practised as a participatory science of those who 'create, maintain, enjoy and endure' educational arrangements (1986: 158).

There are problems with critical positions arising from a priori theorizing, and from a tendency to proclaim the possibility of critical evaluation while not exemplifying it. But unless evaluation combines theory and a common normative purpose, it will remain without direction or vision. One question raised by normative purpose is whether commitments to social justice should be part of evaluation. We will return to that question in Chapter 7.

Evaluation and accountability

Chelimsky (1997) suggests three conceptual frameworks for evaluators, namely, evaluation for accountability, evaluation for development, and evaluation for knowledge. Cronbach, because he believes that evaluation is to be 'judged by its contribution to public thinking and to the quality of service provided subsequent to the evaluation' (Cronbach et al., 1980: 64), regards accountability as a limited view of programme evaluation: 'Evaluation is not best used, we think, to bring pressure on public servants' (1980: 17). 'All too often, assignment of blame to individuals becomes the prime use of the accounts, while system improvement is forgotten' (1980: 135). The evaluation then falls heavily on the wrong person: 'Accountability is most demanded of those public servants condemned to farm rocky ground, under capricious weather conditions' (1980: 137). His conclusion is that a demand for accountability is a sign of pathology in the social system: 'Such a demand, each time it has occurred during the past century, has been a sign of discontent: those in charge of services are believed to be inefficient, insufficiently honest, or not self-critical' (1980: 139).

However, because most evaluators are commissioned by those with managerial or political authority, 'the dominant image of evaluation is still "retributive"' (Eraut, 1984: 36). Qualitative programme evaluators will wish to treat issues of accountability in a more problematic fashion. Lyman and Scott's analysis is helpful at this point. They distinguish two kinds of account, namely, 'excuses' and 'justifications' (Lyman and Scott, 1970). An excuse is offered when someone accepts that an action is bad, wrong or inappropriate, but denies responsibility. Justifications take the form of accepting responsibility, but denying the pejorative quality of the action. This basic distinction can be more fully elaborated in the following way (see Figure 5.1).

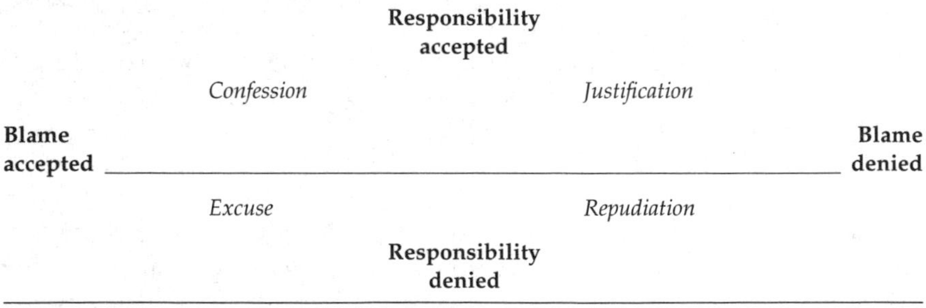

**Responsibility
accepted**

Confession　　　　　　　　　　　*Justification*

Blame　　　　　　　　　　　　　　　　　　　　　　　　　　**Blame
accepted** _____ **denied**

Excuse　　　　　　　　　　　　*Repudiation*

**Responsibility
denied**

Source: Bull and Shaw (1992: 641)

FIGURE 5.1　*Conceptualizing accounts*

Social work practitioners, for example, appear to be strongly preoccupied with accountability. Research has elicited recurring instances of ways in which practice regarded by social workers as having not gone well is likely to trigger deep uncertainties in the mind of the reflective practitioner

(Shaw and Shaw, 1997a). This research suggests there was a widespread sense that outcomes, both positive and negative, were beyond prediction, and will never cease to jump out and surprise the practitioner. Second, social workers display a hesitation about claiming credit for 'good' work or blame and responsibility for 'bad' work. The two realities – predicting and accountability – are linked. In the words of one practitioner:

> I think, bearing in mind the fact that you can't predict what judges are going to do, you can't predict what magistrates are going to do, in a sense you can't take the blame for a failure. If you can't take the blame if it doesn't work, how can you take the credit if it does? (quoted in Shaw and Shaw, 1997a: 77)

Conceptualizations and empirical evidence of this kind suggests a rich perspective for qualitative programme evaluation research (Bull and Shaw, 1992).

Evaluation and social change

We have already anticipated this point. The exchanges within qualitative evaluation between evaluators committed to an interpretivist or naturalist approach, and those with commitments to various versions of critical theory, mean that considerations about social change are permanently near the surface, yet remain a continuing source of disagreement. For example, interpretivist evaluators often espouse a social action agenda. Yet,

> In consonance with interpretivism, the specific contours and facets of that action are not prescribed but rather emerge from the setting. In this way constructivism differs from the more prescriptive empowerment, equity and social justice agendas of critical, feminist and other normative inquiry approaches. (Greene, 1994: 540)

Greene has been critical of interpretative positions in this regard. She is only partially persuaded by the blurring of boundaries between ways of knowing offered by social science and by literature and other humanities:

> Unlike the writer, the artist and the historian, the applied social inquirer is responsible for how his or her stories are read, understood and acted upon, and for who benefits and who doesn't as a result of the inquiry. Responsible social inquiry must attend to its consequences as part of its intent. (Greene, 1992: 42)

Interpretivism justifies values, but it does not justify any particular ones. It remains at root pluralist. Greene concludes that unless this essential relativism can be modified, 'interpretivist inquiry will always be judged by standards that ineluctably reflect the intents and purposes of the judge' (1992: 43).

Policy evaluation and information use

Evaluation is much more than programme evaluation. It is *very* much more than programme *outcome* evaluation. We have already seen how the work of Weiss, and others who addressed similar problems, changed the face of evaluation in the 1970s. She addressed three related issues. First, she delineated the political context in which evaluation is located. Although she has been primarily concerned with evaluation and policy research at the federal level, her empirical work with policy and programme staff resonates throughout evaluation theory and practice. Second, she exposed the limitations of conventional instrumental views of the political use of information, through her conceptualization of use as enlightenment. To similar effect Finch criticizes knowledge-driven and problem-solving models of research use for their basis in a rationalistic model:

> The rationalist model of policy making sees it as a series of discrete events, where each issue to be decided is clearly defined, and decisions are taken by a specific set of actors who choose between well-defined alternatives, after weighing the evidence about the likely outcome of each. (1986: 149–150)

The enlightenment model 'offers far more space to qualitative research, through its emphasis on understanding and conceptualization, rather than upon providing objective facts' (1986: 154).

Third, Weiss imbued models of use with a realistic view of the public interest: 'More than anything she has struggled towards a realistic theory of use. These shifts started a debate in evaluation that goes on to the present day about the role in evaluation of idealism and pragmatism' (Shadish et al., 1990: 207–208).

Questions of the use of research information are central to any analysis of policy evaluation. In words that echo the poetry of Ronald Laing, Chelimsky captures the complexities of information use in a series of aphorisms:

- You don't know, but you don't know you don't know: so you take chances.
- You don't know, but you *know* you don't know: so you're a little more prudent.
- You know, but you don't really know that you know: so you hesitate.
- You know and you know that you know. (1995: 99)

If decision-making in policy and political communities is unpredictable and contingent, it is also envisaged in various ways within the evaluation community. For example, evaluation empowered by emancipatory, critical ethnography has a very different view of social change, information use, and the relationship of politics to evaluation, from the assumptions implicit in discovery-oriented, constructivist, enlightenment models of evaluation of the kind associated with Stake and others.

There is, however, broad general support for ideas of information use which include a central role for enlightenment. Cronbach and his colleagues provide support for this analysis through their work on the context of governance, and their ideas regarding the policy shaping community. We noted in Chapter 2 that Cronbach and colleagues argue how evaluation enters a context of governance that is typically one of *accommodation* rather than *command*. They complain that evaluation theory had been developed 'almost wholly around the image of command', with an associated view of managers and policy officials having a firm grip on the decision-making controls. On the contrary, they believe that 'most action is determined by a pluralistic community, not by a lone decision maker' (Cronbach et al., 1980: 84).

In a modified version of Cronbach's argument, we suggest that the audience for evaluation consists of public servants and the public. Public servants include elected members, policy officials, responsible programme officials, and operating personnel, such as teachers, social workers, nursing staff and housing managers. The relevant public for a programme includes the immediate constituencies of the programme clientele, and those Cronbach describes as illuminators (e.g., reporters, academics, some novelists and dramatists, media commentators). We might also include the major lobbying groups which in some cases may be close to public servant roles (arm's length political 'think tanks', or non-governmental organizations, for example), and in other cases more associated with illuminators (as in the example of lobbying groups for the homeless). It is important to recognize that the policy-shaping community will expand and contract according to both the issue and the phase of any programme.

Nevertheless we should not overemphasize the significance of phases of programme development and maturity. It can suggest an unduly rational view of programmes and projects. Furthermore, it does not reflect the political reality of the present. Many programmes never move to established programme stage, and from day one are working within a fixed term budget. Much of the poverty programme research in Britain and the USA was of this kind. Government support for innovative programmes and projects is often premised on the assumption that the ethos, standards and innovatory practices of a given 'prototype' will permeate existing services, and that funding responsibility will shift from central revenue to state or local government revenue at the end of the 'pilot' period. This often depends in part on meeting the hurdle of a development evaluation.

There has been a tendency to treat Weiss's analysis in simplistic ways, and to assume that all information use is through gradual enlightenment. Chelimsky makes some valuable points arising from her long experience in perhaps the most influential evaluation post, as Assistant Comptroller General for Program Evaluation and Methodology in the United States

General Accounting Office (GAO). For instance, she suggests that evaluation use can operate by means of a *deterrence* function: 'In other words, the mere presence of the function, and the likelihood of a persuasive evaluation, can prevent or stop a host of undesirable government practices' (Chelimsky, 1997: 105). We can turn this same coin over and suggest that a more positive but general stimulus to a reflective and accountable practice can also be the spin-off from the presence of evaluation.

Chelimsky adds, 'More importantly . . . it is often the case that both accountability and knowledge evaluations are undertaken *without any hope of use*' (1997: 105). Expected non-use is characteristic of some of the best evaluations, including 'those that question widespread popular beliefs in a time of ideology, or threaten powerful, entrenched interests at any time' (1997: 105). Thus, 'there are some very good reasons why evaluations may be expert, and also unused' (1997: 105). Chelimsky's comments are both sane and plausible:

> To justify all evaluations by any single kind of use is a constraining rather than an enabling idea because it pushes evaluators towards excessive preoccupation with the acceptability of their findings to users, and risks turning evaluations into banal reiterations of the status quo. (1997: 106)

This analysis should not be used to wipe the slate clear, forget the work of Weiss, and start again with a simple ad hoc view of information use. We should not be persuaded, for example, by the rationalist grounds on which Patton (1988a) defends an instrumentalist theory of use. To reconfigure the conclusions we drew in the previous chapter, enlightenment and instrumentalist explanations of use are likely to be associated with one or more related characteristics of evaluation (see Table 5.2).

TABLE 5.2 *Evaluation models and information use*

Model of use	Evaluation focus	Evaluation base	Discipline links	Time span for action
Enlightenment	Policy evaluation Programme development Advocacy evaluation	Higher education	Stronger discipline links Commitment to theorizing	Longer term
Instrumental	Project evaluation Programme feasibility studies Practitioner evaluation	Agency sponsored 'Insider' evaluation Self-evaluation	Limited social science theorizing	Immediate 'applications'

The connections in Table 5.2 should not be over-interpreted. The table suggests the probable tendencies with which a given notion of use is most compatible. It should *not* be read, for example, to conclude that theorizing is out of place in practitioner evaluation, or that advocacy evaluation always takes place in higher education, and has a long-term action-agenda!

Chelimsky's analysis of some of the ironies and paradoxes of information use suggests a corresponding view regarding the negative and positive influences of the political process. We are familiar with the arguments for ways in which the political process may act in negative ways. They include:

- Pressures to limit the scope of an evaluation.
- Demand that evaluators meet unrealistic time frames.
- Indirect pressure to distort the study results through requests that alternative interpretations of the data are considered.
- The selective dissemination of evaluation results.
- The suppression or critical delay of publication of the report.

These could all provide anecdotes at some imaginary evaluators' party.

Yet Hedrick, who notes all these negative influences and others beside, suggests, from his experience working in the GAO, ways in which politics can provide paradoxical support for evaluation. His basic case is that evaluation often functions as a solution to political disagreement. While this may itself be a negative consequence, it can have positive effects. For example, political disagreements can serve as stimuli for the initiation of evaluative studies:

> While it would be reassuring to believe that evaluation studies are done primarily to find out whether a particular programme is working, or what a specific policy change has wrought, it is likely that many studies are initiated to confirm existing beliefs or a policy position. (Hedrick, 1988: 9)

In addition, the political use of evaluation as a delaying tactic can have the positive result that 'the scope of questions to be addressed can be expanded and researchers can adopt a long-term perspective of adding to the knowledge base about a social program or problem' (1988: 9). In other words, political fire-fighting to limit the direct instrumental utilization of evaluation may unwittingly feed longer-term enlightenment uses of evaluation.

Furthermore, 'political disagreements, by their very adversarial nature, can be a major factor in supporting the existence of organizational entities that conduct evaluation studies' (1988: 9). In specific instances such disagreements can serve to increase the visibility of the results of evaluation studies. Chelimsky cites an interesting instance of this in the case of a controversy following an early GAO synthesis of studies on chemical warfare for the Department of Defence (Chelimsky, 1995).

Policy evaluation and social policy

Has all this analysis of models of use made any difference to the contribution that policy research, and qualitative policy research in particular, makes to public and social policy? One commentator thinks not, and suggests that part of the responsibility for this state of affairs lies with the academic community: 'There is no broad-based and sustained tradition within contemporary social science of focusing qualitative work specifically on policy issues' (Rist, 1994: 556). This conclusion is unduly negative, and insufficiently informed by research and experience outside the USA. Yet work done in Britain suggests there is little ground for complacency.

British policy researchers working within a qualitative tradition have produced comparable analyses of the relationship between knowledge and policy. Bulmer, for example, distinguishes empirical, engineering and enlightenment models. *Empiricism* entails 'a conception of social research involving the production of accurate data – meticulous, precise, generalizable – in which the data themselves constitute an end of the research' (Bulmer, 1982: 31). The task of social research is to produce facts for use. He associates this with the tradition leading back through Townsend and Donnison to Titmuss and then to Rowntree and Booth.

The *engineering* model operates with both a clear distinction between basic and applied research, and an explicit customer/contractor relationship for applied research and evaluation. The problem is defined, the missing knowledge is identified, invitations to tender are prepared, and the research is commissioned. The problem is defined outside any particular social science discipline, and the resultant research is a product for the policy community and not for the academic discipline. Much evaluation research and theory has developed around this model in both Britain and the USA. In Britain it has its origins in the highly influential Rothschild Report (Rothschild, 1971). Bulmer complains that the engineering model underestimates the blurring of boundaries between pure and applied research, and turns the researcher into a technician. He argues for an *enlightenment* model in terms almost identical to Weiss. One important possible consequence of an enlightenment model is that it seems to provide the justification for arguing that greater priority be given to basic research that may ultimately be proved useful – 'strategic' research to use the language of British government research councils.

Finch (1986) argues three reasons why qualitative research and evaluation has had little impact on educational and social policy in Britain. First, the utility of statistics and politically neutral 'facts' from the perspectives of governments gives specious attractiveness to statistical and survey-based reports. Second, the Fabian model of the researcher/policy-maker relationship has been dominant. Sidney and Beatrice Webb articulated and consolidated a model which became tied in to Labour Party policy. It influenced Labour especially when in opposition and to some extent when in power. Figures such as Halsey and Donnison were part of a small elite of high status academics with congenial political positions, wishing to act as professional adviser and expert to those in power. They represented a social engineering model aimed at social justice through the Fabian belief in the 'inevitability of gradualness' and research which was both partisan and rigorous. This tradition inherited the assumption of politically unproblematic facts which would speak for themselves.

Third, social administration and sociology developed as separate disciplines in Britain. When qualitative methodology permeated sociology it was usually without a policy focus. There resulted an anti-quantitative thrust in sociology, and the empirical tradition within social administration was one target of this attitude. By the end of the 1970s British sociology had a well-nigh universal distaste for social reform.

This position has changed since then, partly through the emergence of action-oriented forms of research of the kind we describe in the next chapter. Writing in the mid-1980s, Finch wondered if 'the climate is now right for a degree of intellectual reintegration of social problems with sociological problems, and that qualitative research can make an important contribution to this' (Finch, 1985: 112).

There is now a gradual acceptance of the limitations of quantitative research and evaluation. In addition to the relatively modest argument that there are complementary aspects to qualitative and quantitative research, qualitative policy evaluation is superior in three ways. First, it studies social processes and actions in context. For example,

> Reliance on quantitative research as the basis for understanding how deviance occurs in schools . . . will inevitably be inadequate because it cannot satisfactorily take account of the way in which different contexts produce different outcomes. (Finch, 1986: 165–6)

Second, it studies processes over time. Finch comments on her three-year ethnography of working class playgroups for pre-school children. She considered the question, Why do playgroups fail? The point of interest is that her work addresses a kind of question rarely considered empirically in evaluation (why do programmes fail?). In addition, this was a question which only emerged during the research when three of the five groups she first elected to study closed. Without the longitudinal dimension of qualitative research, this central evaluative question would never have been considered.

Third, it enables theoretically grounded research. Finch argues that a blend of theory and data is the hallmark of good qualitative work and that 'this particular blend produces precisely the kind of work which is likely to make an impact upon policy because it offers theoretical insights grounded in evidence' (1986: 174).

Finch does not duck the criticisms that qualitative research has weaknesses. She says we must recognize that policy-makers schooled in the dominant tradition will always raise criticisms on the grounds that qualitative research is too small scale, not representative and hence cannot be generalized, and fails to demonstrate causal adequacy through its emphasis on meaning. She suggests three broad solutions. First, qualitative and quantitative methods should be combined. Second, when findings are presented the researcher should give enough information about methodology to enable the policy maker to assess it, and to demonstrate that control over methodology has been maintained throughout. She also advocates imaginative presentation of findings. Third, qualitative researchers should develop comparative studies to overcome the weakness of the single, free-standing case study. We pick this idea up again in Chapter 7.

Changing political contexts make the positions discussed and recommended in this chapter provisional. Cronbach and colleagues remarked with the irony of hindsight that 'Our theses will have to be revised to fit the United States of the year 2000' (Cronbach et al., 1980: 14). Hammersley is sympathetic to the argument that suggests high expectations regarding influencing policy are misguided, and that research is not a primary source of consideration in the policy process. He occasionally leaves the impression that this is only as it should be (Hammersley, 1994; 1995). Finch's tentative alignment with a reformist position does not persuade Hammersley: 'It is becoming increasingly difficult to defend this enlightenment optimism' (Hammersley, 1994: 146). However, there are developments in the field of practitioner evaluation, which are premised on a more optimistic reading of the potential value of evaluation. We now turn to these developments.

Note

1 Greene is one of the most incisive writers on evaluation at the present time. However, she does tend to adopt, here and elsewhere (Greene and McClintock, 1991), a definition of postpositivism which seems unduly influenced by Guba's misleading emphasis on the continuity between positivism and postpositivism (Guba, 1990).

6

Practitioner evaluation

CONTENTS

Evaluation is more than policy and programme evaluation. Its purpose, scope and methodology become partial and myopic whenever practitioners of evaluation succumb to this misreading of its potential. Stake was perhaps the first evaluation theorist to recognize this through his growing emphases on the quality of evaluation activities rather than outcomes; the importance of tacit and implicit understandings; local and grassroots audiences for evaluation; 'social anthropological viewing' (1991: 76); responsive evaluation; and the limits of accountability models of evaluation. He provided the stimulus for project and practitioner evaluation in addition to policy and programme evaluation.

He lays part of the responsibility for the failings of mainstream evaluation at the door of those who place the production, dissemination and utilization of knowledge centre-stage: 'Researchers have had scant inter-est in studying the intertwining, personalistic, and crisis-like problems of daily practice' (Stake and Trumbull, 1982: 4). They prefer to 'fiddle with models' and focus on change efforts in classroom and agency, and in con-sequence their research 'has not presented practitioners with the vicarious experiencings which could alter conviction and practice in the schools' (1982: 11).

Qualitative practitioner evaluation has been the site of innovative developments in the last few years, and will continue to be so. The title of this chapter is, of course, question begging. By 'practitioner' we are not referring to the evaluator but to professionals who deliver a service of some kind in organizations, hospitals, schools, social work agencies and so on. But does it mean evaluation *of* practice and practitioners by quali-tative researchers? Evaluation *by* practitioners? Evaluation which is *for* practitioners rather than academic researchers, programme directors, or policy-makers? And what about evaluation carried out on a participatory basis *for* and *with* parents, children, patients and other citizen users of public services? This chapter explores these distinctions. We will consider four areas of evaluation practice which can be subsumed under the broad title of practitioner evaluation:

1 Research and evaluation carried out by practitioners.
2 Participatory research.
3 Evaluation as a dimension of direct practice, through, for example, reflective inquiry.
4 Evaluation *for* practitioners carried out usually by academic researchers.

Questions for practitioner inquiry

It will be clear, recalling the discussion of paradigms in Chapter 3, that the adopting of qualitative evaluation methodology will not solve overnight the problems posed by more traditional quantitative methodologies. Indeed, without proper safeguards, some of the problems may be still *more* troublesome. For example, McNamara complains vociferously that class-room participant observers often 'fail significantly to understand and appreciate the realities of classroom life as seen from the point of view of the practitioner. They retain the parochial and limited view of the out-sider' (1980: 114). They 'use their fieldwork experiences to promote their own research goals' and 'do no service to the teachers who have welcomed them into their classrooms' (1980: 115). While McNamara displays scant regard for the subtleties of his argument, and is directing his fire at main-stream qualitative research rather than practitioner evaluation, it does evaluators no harm to hear their shibboleths under attack from such broadsides.

We will return to the ethical issues posed by such criticisms in Chapters 7 to 9. But we should note that they raise two general problems. First, how should we understand the relationship between practitioner understanding or inquiry, and evaluative research? Second, is tacit, implicit understanding, of the kind referred to by Stake, in tension with more explicit, planned, qualitative inquiry when carried out by practitioners?

Practitioner inquiry and evaluation

We considered the general form of the first problem in Chapter 1, when we asked whether research and evaluation are more or less the same or different enterprises. There are contrary arguments a-plenty in the literature in support of seeing practitioner evaluation and practice as either very *different* from or *similar* to evaluative research in general. Cochran-Smith and Lytle believe that the main styles of educational research – whether oriented to outcomes or to understanding 'classroom ecology' – have missed the teachers' voices, 'the questions teachers ask, . . . the interpretive frames teachers use to understand and improve their own classroom practices' (Cochran-Smith and Lytle, 1990: 2). They claim that teacher research ('systematic and intentional inquiry carried out by teachers'; 1990: 3) is not an imitation of university research but is 'its own *genre*' (1990: 4).

Their measured defence of this position is not always reflected in other defenders of practitioner evaluation as a distinct mode. Distinctions between evaluative research and practitioner evaluation are too often cited in a self-serving manner, to defend the 'relevance' of practitioner work. For example, Fortune (1994) argues that the differences between ethnography and social work practice include:

- 'Practice is action-focused, while qualitative methods, including ethnography, intend only to describe' (1994: 64).
- The practitioner needs additional skills in deductive and inductive logic 'as well as a fine sense of timing about when to stop data gathering' (1994: 65).
- Ethnographers seek to generalize, whereas in social work practice 'there is no inherent need to communicate that reality to other persons or to generalize beyond the experience of that individual' (1994: 65).
- Micro-ethnographic studies enhance social work practice and may 'generate immediately useful information' (1994: 65), while macro-ethnographies are time consuming and difficult and 'only indirectly relevant to social work' (1994: 68).
- Because social workers' time and interests are spent in practice and action, micro-ethnographic studies fit well with the resources and energies available.

These ways of distinguishing practice and evaluation are almost one hundred per cent unhelpful. The claims for distinctive practitioner skills, the assumptions regarding ethnography, the unproblematic ways in which generalization and usefulness of information are introduced, and the writer's naïve aspirations regarding the feasibility of practitioners conducting micro-ethnographies, are almost breath-taking. Fortune's argument does little to unsettle Smith and Klein's view that distinctions based on epistemology or methodology are 'tenuous if not untenable' (Smith and Klein, 1986: 55). In fairness it should be acknowledged that this failing is not the sole province of practitioners. When made by academic researchers, a strong distinction between practitioner inquiry and evaluative research sometimes reads like an élitist defence of the conceptual sophistication and superiority of ethnographic methodology (cf. Atkinson and Delamont, 1993).

There are, however, important differences of *purpose* between evaluative research and practitioner inquiry. Matters of prior evaluation agreements, likely audiences and the utilization of results, all raise special issues for practitioner evaluation. For example, it is not obvious that the important work of Weiss and others on enlightenment models of policy and programme evaluation will transfer readily to practitioner inquiry, where *immediate* use is likely to figure more prominently than longer-term use. There are also important differentiations *within* evaluative research, roughly captured in distinctions between evaluative *research*, evaluative *inquiry*, and evaluative *thinking* (see Eisner, 1991a). These differences can helpfully be explored and tested by reflecting on the inferential processes engaged in by different professionals and researchers. The psychotherapist, Erikson, has contributed valuably to this as part of an early symposium on evidence and inference in the human sciences (Lerner, 1959). He complains that 'clinical workers often fail to make explicit, even to themselves, what inventories of evidential signs they regularly but unwittingly, scan' (Erikson, 1959: 82).

Tacit knowledge and qualitative inquiry

The *second* question is whether tacit, implicit understanding is in tension with more explicit, planned, qualitative practitioner thinking. Stake may seem to suggest as much when he and Trumbull argue that 'for practitioners . . . formal knowledge is not necessarily a stepping stone to improved practice . . . We maintain that practice is guided far more by personal knowings' (Stake and Trumbull, 1982: 5). Although they do not dismiss formal knowledge, 'the leverage point for change too often neglected is the disciplined collection of experiential knowledge' (1982: 8–9). On this view, good practitioner evaluation will reveal tacit knowledge – 'the largely unarticulated, contextual understanding that is often manifested in nods, silences, humour and naughty nuances' (Altheide and Johnson, 1994: 492). There are actions, judgements and recognitions which we accomplish spontaneously. We do not have to think about them prior to performance. We are often unaware of having learned to do them. While we may remember once being aware of the understanding necessary for action, we typically are now unable to describe the knowings that our actions reveal. It has become 'thinking as usual' knowledge (the phrase is Schutz's): 'Tacit knowledge exists in that time when action is taken that is not understood, when understanding is offered without articulation, and when conclusions are apprehended without an argument' (Altheide and Johnson, 1994: 492).

The evaluation problem posed by this largely non-discursive knowledge is 'how to talk about what is seldom spoken about' (1994: 493). Evaluators share with researchers ambivalence regarding such knowledge, tending to oscillate between seeing it as potentially liberating or constraining (cf. Scott, 1990). This is illustrated in some feminist approaches to evaluative research. Hawkesworth, for example, criticizes the appeal to intuition in some feminist standpoint research on the grounds that:

> Intuition provides a foundation for claims about the world that is at once authoritarian, admitting of no further discussion, and relativist, since no individual can refute another's 'immediate' apprehension of reality. (Hawkesworth, 1989: 545)

Most evaluation theorists probably share Hawkesworth's rejection of this kind of appeal to intuition, preferring instead to interplay some kind of 'rational reality' with 'experiential reality' (Stake, 1991: 83). This is sometimes described as the exercise of 'practice wisdom' on the part of practitioners. For example, Schwab's influential paper on understanding curriculum argues for a language of the practical rather than the theoretical. By practical 'I do *not* mean . . . the easily achieved, familiar goals which can be reached by familiar means' (Schwab, 1969: 1), but rather 'a complex discipline . . . concerned with choice and action' (1969: 1–2). Schwandt, drawing on Aristotelian thinking proffers a more radical solution. He distinguishes theoretical knowledge ('knowing that'), craft or skill knowledge ('knowing how'), and practical-moral knowledge ('knowing from'). Ethical reasoning takes place through practical wisdom. Schwandt wishes to recast evaluation as a whole within this kind of practical hermeneutics: 'Practical-moral knowledge aims to actually move people, not simply give them good ideas' (1997: 81).

This preamble has a fairly obvious message. Tread carefully, eschew snap solutions, and keep evaluative purposes on the front burner.

Practitioner research

Practitioners as researchers is no new idea. The clinical research model has honourable precedents in the work, for instance, of doctors who trialled their vaccination methods on themselves, and in the clinical research of psychotherapy. It is not new in younger professions. Charles Loch spent much energy in the late nineteenth century arguing that social work is like science: 'It is science – the science of life – in operation – knowledge doing its perfect work' (quoted Timms, 1968: 59). What is new is the range of arguments and exemplars offered for practitioner research, its independent emergence in British and American education in the 1970s, in American social work in the 1970s, and in a different form in 1980s British social work, and in the gradual development of qualitative methodologies. We will consider the varying forms and arguments for the teacher-as-researcher, qualitative clinical research, and practitioner social work research.

Teacher-as-researcher

A plausible case can be made for tracing the origins of the teacher-as-researcher movement in America to the strong post-war action research interest through writers such as Lewin. It was initially linked to quantitative research and objective setting. The parallel but probably autonomous emergence of teachers as researchers in Britain revolved mainly around the major curriculum reforms of the 1960s and 1970s. In Britain a greater emphasis was placed on the process of teaching rather than objective setting and effectiveness research. Hammersley suggests that the shift to broadly progressive ideas about pupil–teacher relationships also prompted the movement within curriculum studies 'from bureaucratic to professional conceptions of teaching, and from the researcher as developer and evaluator to facilitator' (1993a: 427). In other words, 'discovery' and 'inquiry' concepts came first into education and thence into research and evaluation. We noted in Chapter 2 how the work of Stake coalesced with the emerging British work at the Centre for Applied Research in Education (CARE) at the University of East Anglia.

There were distinguishable strands in this work from an early date. An influential early argument was that put forward by Parlett and Hamilton (1972) for illuminative evaluation. Classical evaluation was criticized as artificial, in that 'rarely can "tidy" results be generalized from "untidy" reality' (1972: 5), and a case was advanced for evaluation of educational innovations in which 'attempted measurement of . . . products is abandoned for intensive study of the programme as a whole' (1972: i). They distinguished the formal 'instructional system' from the informal 'learning milieu' in which the instructional systems get reinterpreted every time for a particular setting. Hence the setting – the learning milieu – becomes the main focus of research interest. Central to this was the idea of the hidden curriculum through which students assimilate the 'conventions, beliefs and models of reality that are constantly and inevitably transmitted through the teaching process' (1972: 15).

With regard to its planning and methodology, 'Illuminative evaluation is not a standard methodological package but a general research strategy'

(1972: 15), based on a process of progressive focusing through multiple methods but with primacy given to a range of observation methods. Parlett and Hamilton encapsulate their argument in an apt analogy.

> To know whether a play works one has to look not only at the manuscript but also at the performance; that is, at the interpretation of the play by the director and the actors. (1972: 30–31)

Illuminative evaluation seeks 'to study an innovation through the medium of its performance' (1972: 31).

The transfer of weight to qualitative methods has been more marked in some representatives of this approach than others. In a frequently cited paper written in the 1970s, Stenhouse – important in early British developments – preferred the 'social anthropological' approach which 'above all ... attempts not merely generalization but also the characterization of the uniqueness of particular situations' (1993: 225). Some writers have gone further and advocated the application of ethnomethodology to classroom research by teachers (Payne and Cuff, 1982).

Others have espoused a methodological eclecticism. Kelly, for example, argues that the specific methodology employed is less important than the overall approach to action and research, and has been ready to employ 'hard data' to support her case to audiences sceptical of ethnographic data: 'They need statistics and percentages to convince them that we are not part of a lunatic fringe, that we know what we are talking about' (Kelly, 1985: 145). Some take eclecticism further and appear sceptical of any methodological reflection. Bassey opens his chapter on 'Does Action Research Require Sophisticated Research Methods?' with 'I am tempted to write the shortest chapter in this book by responding to my title with one word: NO' (1986: 18). Emphases within this tradition have also varied on matters such as relationships to stakeholders, the place of theorizing, epistemology, and the political role of evaluation (Simon, 1987: Ch. 3).

Clinical research

Qualitative clinical research has not thrived in medicine. Speculatively one may suggest that this may be due to the strong quantitative traditions of epidemiological research and the strength of mainstream ethnographic research within the sociology of medicine. There is, however, a growing literature on qualitative methods in nursing and the para-medical professions. Some of this shares the eclecticism of some educational evaluation, although a strong case has been made for qualitative clinical research by Miller and Crabtree. They describe much clinical research as 'many conversations behind walls, but increasing suffering in the clinical world', and urge qualitative clinical researchers to 'move from behind their walls, engage the clinical experience and its questions, and practice humility and fidelity within a community of discourse at the walls' (Miller and Crabtree, 1994: 340, 349).

Most published clinical research consists of clinical trials and epidemiology which fails to speak to 'the real world of clinical practice, involving intentions, meanings, intersubjectivity, values, personal knowledge and ethics' (1994: 341). Miller and Crabtree outline a threefold strategy:

- Create an open research space which celebrates qualitative and critical approaches.

  > We propose that clinical researchers investigate questions emerging from the clinical experience, pay attention to and reveal any underlying values and assumptions, and direct the result toward clinical participants. (1994: 342)

- Provide tools necessary for discovering and confirming clinical stories and knowledge.
- Identify and describe means for sharing the stories and knowledge.

'Local context and the human story . . . are the primary goals of qualitative research and not "generalizability"', and the rules of evidence 'can be translated for clinical audiences in the form of telling methodologically, rhetorically and clinically convincing stories' (1994: 348).

Qualitative practitioner social work research

Practitioner research in social work is different between Britain and America. In the USA there is a vigorous 'scientific practitioner' movement based in general on outcome-oriented and quantitative methodology. The most commonly discussed form of evaluation within the scientific practitioner movement is single system designs. The social work journals are the scene of continuing debate about the contribution of the empirical practice movement. The arguments for qualitative practitioner research stem in part from observers within the empirical practice tradition. We have observed Reid's contribution to this development in Chapter 2 (Reid, 1990; Sherman and Reid, 1994). Epstein has argued that both mainstream evaluation and social work practice have come to take 'psychic determinism' positions, 'that locate the source of human trouble inside the individual person, in some non-empirical site such as the soul, the spirit, the psyche, the mind, personality structures and similar venues' (Epstein, 1996: 115). While one appeals to scientific psychology and the other to what she calls expressive psychology, both are 'concentrating on reading and changing the minds of poor people and those who are otherwise distressed and deviant' (1996: 115). 'The problem in both cases is that the context is missing' (1996: 116). The implicit answer to her appeal appears to include a more sociological and qualitative practitioner research strategy. One approach to constructing such a strategy has been to analyze the differences in the data processing strategies of social work and qualitative research to assess the ways in which they might be implemented.

Lang, for example, explores the data gathering and data processing strategies of social work and qualitative methodology, and recommends the adoption of the latter within social work, not only for knowledge building purposes, but also for 'action-deriving purposes' (Lang, 1994: 277). She instances the data processing of qualitative researchers and practitioners, and suggests that 'The practitioner "names" the data through reference to theory; the researcher "names" the data through a conceptualizing process that derives from the features of the data' (1994: 271). She believes that several problems follow for social work because, 'The press to know what to do, what action to take, may close the avenue of knowledge development from practice for many practitioners' (1994: 271). She invites an inductive, theory-building approach to practice: 'Existing theory must have a more provisional status, a less central locus in our practice teaching, in order to open the possibility of theory-building' (1994: 276). Social workers should pull action out of the features of the data rather than turn to existing theory as a first resort. Ruckdeschel has begun to develop comparable methods for qualitative case study. He is one of several evaluators influenced by the work of Geertz (1973). He follows Denzin's idea of 'behavioural specimens' as nearly complete descriptions of interactions between individuals within particular time frames (Denzin, 1989), and also accepts that the case study's task is 'to give the poor a voice' (Ruckdeschel et al., 1994: 255). He believes that in American social work the official scepticism of qualitative methods, noted for education by Kelly, is now largely in the past (Ruckdeschel, 1999). While there are some difficulties in applying such models, they have real promise for the development of a qualitative practitioner evaluation.

Developments in British social work have followed a more pragmatic line. The leading commentators on practitioner research espouse an eclectic methodology without giving primacy to any one approach (Cheetham, 1998; Fuller and Petch, 1995). Evidence-based practice approaches are exercising a growing influence through the work of writers such as Sheldon, Macdonald, Kazi and McGuire (cf. Shaw, 1996a: Ch. 9, and Shaw and Shaw, 1997b, for discussions of these developments).

The main British developments in qualitative practice research have been in the growth of participatory research and reflective inquiry approaches, which we discuss, in the following pages. A more extended development of a similar case to that advanced by Lang is put forward in Shaw (Shaw, 1996a, 1997, 1998), who argues for and illustrates the gains from 'colonizing' and 'translating' qualitative methodology for evaluating as a direct dimension of practice.

Critical practitioner research

The methodological pragmatism and perceived political complacency of much practitioner inquiry has strengthened the hand of those who believe a more radical, critical conception of practitioner research is called for. Within social work this has manifested itself primarily in participatory research. In education there is much less tradition of participatory research, but a strong tradition of critical case study research and critical ethnography. Carr and Kemmis's *Becoming Critical* (1986) is probably the most influential example of critical case study and action research.

Their premise is that the teacher-as-researcher movement has emerged as the product of various social, political and professional pressures, and in consequence has been opportunistic and pragmatic. They regret and reject strong distinctions between theory and practice, on the grounds that it leads to the dominance of technical language: 'The "moral" dimension of education is inadvertently suppressed and education becomes a purely technical matter' (Carr and Kemmis, 1986: 38). Teaching strategy should proceed guided by a consciousness that education is historically located, a social activity, and intrinsically political, and as such intrinsically problematic. Such teachers will engage in 'critical self-reflection' (1986: 40) and construct opportunities to carry this private discourse into discussion and debate with others, to help establish critical communities of enquirers. This provides scope for teacher research. At times such research 'will only be a restless enquiring attitude about teaching and curriculum' (1986: 40), but in cases where a teacher adopts a 'project perspective':

> *actions* taken will be regarded as 'tentative' or 'experimental', . . . the *language* in which actions are described and understood will be critically examined, *social consequences* will be scrutinized and reflected upon, and the *situation* in which action takes place will be examined to see how it creates and constrains the potential of the chosen strategy. (1986: 40)

In short, they say, 'teachers become critical'. This will reawaken the disposition of moral judgement, and promote a 'critical educational science' which 'is not research *on* and *about* education, it is research *in* and *for* education' (1986: 156). Such a science must provide for the participation of all those who 'create, maintain, enjoy and endure' educational arrangements (1986: 158), and transform not only practitioners but education itself.

Ethnographic criticisms

The development of practitioner research has received a more or less warm welcome in social work and nursing. Some public funding has been available in both Britain and America for practitioner research in these areas and in teaching. However, the welcome has been less warm from mainstream ethnographers. Some are content to explore the methodological problems that may be underestimated by the teacher-as-researcher movement (Burgess, 1980; Burgess et al., 1994). Others, especially in Britain, have been far more ascerbic, implying that the whole movement is something of a circus, based on methodological cop-out and theoretical naïvety (Atkinson and Delamont, 1993; Hammersley, 1992, 1993a). For example, Atkinson and Delamont accuse case study researchers of being 'content to invoke anthropology in a ritualized fashion. It has a totemic or fetishistic significance' (1993: 207). 'Methodological sophistication is not a marked characteristic of the *genre*' and its practitioners are 'anti-intellectual' and guilty of a 'lack of scholarship' (1993: 210). They accuse case study research of primitivism – 'an emphasis on research as an essentially vernacular or demotic undertaking' (1993: 211) – and talk of 'the paradox of a group of "experts" in evaluation, part of whose stock in trade consists in a denial of expertise' (1993: 213).

Hammersley avoids the churlish, élitist disdain and oversimplification that mark Atkinson and Delamont's work, and raises more careful questions regarding the underlying assumptions of the approach. First, he is not happy that teaching should be regarded as 'isomorphic with inquiry' (Hammersley, 1993a: 441) and also thinks there is a risk of overestimating the benefits to be gained from research: 'The products of systematic inquiry will not necessarily be better than the presuppositions built into traditional ways of doing things. It is a modernist fallacy to assume otherwise' (1993a: 438). He is concerned this may represent a form of teacher imperialism. Despite its egalitarian language it may serve as a professionalizing strategy. Second, he believes the critique of conventional research advanced by people within the democratic evaluation field is based on too narrow a concept of research relevance and an overly optimistic faith in the ability of research to influence policy and practice. He suggests two grounds for arguing 'there are good reasons to believe that research cannot routinely solve teachers' problems' (1993a: 430). 'There is no scientific method that guarantees results' (1993a: 430) and teacher circumstances are diverse and unlikely to be amenable to action in any routine sense. Rather, 'sound practice cannot amount to the straightforward *application* of theoretical knowledge, but is an activity that necessarily involves judgement and draws on experience as much as on . . . scientific knowledge' (1993a: 430). Third, he doubts whether it is helpful to regard practitioner inquiry as research. He accepts the place of different forms of practical inquiry such as problem-solving investigations and reflection. But, 'while there are forms of inquiry that are closely related to practical activities, and while these may usefully draw on ethnographic ideas, it is important to distinguish them from ethnography' (Hammersley, 1992: 152).

While there may still be traces of academic élitism in these arguments, the issues raised merit a considered response from within practitioner research. Wherever it has developed, it has been marked too frequently by naïve pragmatism, such that it runs the risk of being absorbed into providing technical support for the status quo. Yet to characterize the whole movement in this way is to engage in caricature.

Participatory evaluation

The critical case study methods of Carr and Kemmis include, as we have seen, the participation of all stakeholders. Co-operative and participatory forms of evaluation have developed in various ways although it is still uncertain how far this extends beyond rhetoric. There are as yet too few accounts of participatory research. Heron offers a summary of the arguments typically put forward for such inquiry. Inquiry into the human condition is not possible from outside, but entails 'your own intelligent, personal action in co-operation with others with whom you choose to share the given condition' (Heron, 1996: 201). Persons become such only in relation to others. Unless we are in mutual relation with them we cannot research them properly as persons: 'Unless you co-opt your human subjects as equal co-researchers, they are not fully present as persons and become persons suborned' (1996: 202). And,

> Doing research involves an inescapable educational commitment: to facilitate in research subjects the development of their self-determination in acquiring knowledge of the human condition. (1996: 208)

Participatory researchers give greater or lesser emphasis to five commitments (Cancian and Armstead, 1992):

1 Participation by the people being studied.
2 Respect for popular knowledge in agreeing, conducting and reporting research.
3 A liberatory focus on issues of empowerment.
4 An educative dimension through consciousness raising.
5 Political action and social transformation.

However, this understates the diversity within participatory evaluation. In Chapter 4 we distinguished pluralist, reformist and emancipatory positions on the political stance of evaluation. Each of these can be found within participatory evaluation, and all have been adopted to justify participatory commitments. While participatory researchers hold in common some degree of commitment to an instrumental, activist view of research, some would argue that good evaluating is transformative because it is true, while others would claim it is true because it is transformative. I will reflect first on those forms of participatory evaluation that retain a stronger commitment to understanding and knowledge, before considering approaches where personal and political change are seen as the main and perhaps sole criterion of validity.

Participatory inquiry

There are various strands of participatory inquiry that go under names like Co-operative Inquiry, Action Science, Action Inquiry and Participatory Action Research, and are associated with the writings of Heron, Reason, Whyte, Schon, Argyris and Tarbert. We will refer to Schon's work in the section on reflective inquiry. For the moment I will refer briefly to

Reason's work and that of Heron. At the risk of oversimplifying, the main recurring themes in participatory inquiry are:

- Subjectivity: 'Valid human inquiry essentially requires full participation in the creation of personal and social knowings' (Reason, 1994b: 332).
- The models of 'normal science' are, to varying degrees, replaced with an emphasis on the value of lay knowledge, and by the use of less conventional methods.
- Knowledge arises *out of* action and is *for* action. The aim is to develop a genuine science of action rather than an applied science: 'Practical knowledge, knowing how, is the consummation, the fulfilment, of the knowledge quest' (Heron, 1996: 34).
- Knowledge is tested in live-action contexts.
- Unlike more explicit advocacy evaluation approaches, egalitarianism is tempered by a reliance on leadership.

Peter Reason has made one of the most sustained cases for participatory inquiry. He rejects positivist and modernist worldviews on the grounds that they separate the knower from the known. Proceeding on the basis that 'a participative methodology needs to rest on a participatory worldview', he is 'much persuaded' that 'the purpose of human inquiry is not so much the search for truth but to *heal* the alienation . . . that characterizes human experience' (Reason, 1994a: 1, 10). He shares with Heron the belief that 'we can only truly do research *with* persons if we engage with them *as* persons, as co-subjects and thus as co-researchers' (1994a: 10).

Heron defines co-operative inquiry as involving 'two or more people researching a topic through their own experience of it, using a series of cycles in which they move between this experience and reflecting together on it' (Heron, 1996: 1). His elaboration of kinds and levels of participation is based on what he describes as 'participative reality' which gives his participative paradigm two 'wings' – epistemic and political. By political he intends decisions regarding research thinking and decision-making. By epistemic he means the experiences and action that are the focus of the inquiry. On this basis he distinguishes political and epistemic participation. The key issues are whether and to what extent *researchers* are part of the epistemic *experience*, and *subjects* are part of political research *decisions*. He presents the participatory nature of conventional (usually quantitative) inquiry as shown in Table 6.1. The contrast with the full version of co-operative inquiry is shown in Table 6.2.

Heron believes mainstream 'qualitative research *about* people is a half-way house between exclusive, controlling research *on* people and fully participatory research *with* people' (1996: 27). Qualitative researchers have a partial sharing of epistemic experience through methods such as participant observation, and subjects have a partial sharing in political decisions through a fuller informed consent. But he criticizes the emphasis on access in qualitative research as 'empowerment under the aegis of

TABLE 6.1 *Conventional (typically quantitative) inquiry*

	Researcher	Subject
Participation in decisions	Full	Nil
Participation in experience	Nil	Full

TABLE 6.2 *Full co-operative inquiry*

	Researcher	Subject
Participation in decisions	Full	Full
Participation in experience	Full	Full

subtle benign oppression' and 'luring gatekeepers and informants into being studied by a design in which they are not invited to collaborate, and to which, at best, they are only invited to give informed consent' (1996: 28).

Heron admits that co-operative inquiry may not achieve the full participatory ideal. While the epistemic and political separation are broken down, co-operative inquiry fails to break down 'the difference, at the outset of the inquiry, in methodological know-how and facilitative guidance, between the initiating researcher and the other co-researchers' (1996: 23). He describes this as 'one of the major challenges of co-operative inquiry, and its highly vulnerable Achilles' heel' (1996: 23). Furthermore, full epistemic participation by researchers may not be feasible, especially when they are external researchers.

Participation in advocacy evaluation

'We ourselves are reluctant to separate epistemology from ideology, findings from yearnings' (Stake, 1997: 471). Thus Stake poses the central agendum of evaluation approaches where personal and political change are seen as the main and perhaps sole measure of validity. Diversity is once more the hallmark of this evaluation field. For example, advocacy evaluation in the health and social care fields has almost always included aspirations to include those on the receiving end of health and social care services. Educational versions of advocacy evaluation have more often developed forms of participation which involve other professionals rather than children and students.

Early appeals for participatory evaluation drew their strength from a *redistributive welfare* position. For example, Holman, the British community worker and social policy researcher, pleads for 'research from the underside' because 'the values I hold are such that I long for the end of poverty and the promotion of equality. My interest in research is just this, how can research help the poor?' (Holman, 1987: 669). He criticizes much otherwise good poverty research as being *about* rather than *by* or *with* the poor, and proposes a bottom-up model in which the investigated become the investigators.

There have also been efforts to bring *Third World development research* closer to development practice (Booth, 1994; Chambers, 1983; Edwards, 1989, 1994; Hall, 1979). Edwards draws on his experience of working in Non-Governmental Organizations when he lists the problems of

> the 'professionalization' of development studies and the devaluation of popular knowledge; the values and attitudes of researchers and practitioners that prevent them working as equals; the control of knowledge by elites; and a failure to unite understanding, action, relevance and participation. (1989: 133)

He laments the creation and perpetuation of a series of divorces, the most complete of which 'lies between research output and the subjects of this research – poor people themselves'. While he is insistent that method has not been the only problem, he nonetheless insists that 'participatory research is the vehicle for understanding and changing the world simultaneously' (1989: 128). In the telling words of a Mexican proverb which he quotes, 'we make the path by walking it'.

Participatory evaluation of this kind offers no panacea. There has been some heat generated at western colonizing of this explicitly liberationist strategy, and there has been some tempering of enthusiasm caused by the difficulties of securing authentic participation in projects which almost always originate with 'experts'. There has been continued discussion on two issues. First, what do we mean by claiming that an evaluation is relevant? Is relevant evaluation the same as participatory evaluation? In a subsequent paper Edwards appears to moderate his position. He allows that we need not require all inquiry to be participatory. This may apply especially to evaluation of higher management levels of development programmes. However, 'to be relevant, research must *in some way* be linked to the real experience and concerns of people at grassroots level' (Edwards, 1994: 284).

Second, what is the relationship between grassroots evaluation and 'higher level' evaluation? One of the dangers of post-Marxist shifts to adoption of explanations based on culture, diversity, agency and actor constructions is that the relationship between the micro-level of individual practice and the structural level is ignored. How can development workers be committed to evaluation at the grassroots level and yet keep the macro issues firmly on the table?

Participatory strategies have also followed from some versions of *feminist research*. For instance, feminist standpoint theory values epistemological egalitarianism, draws on an activist view of evaluation as undertaken for explicitly political purposes, is committed to empowerment, and entails a model of evaluation that works towards the participation of members of oppressed groups in every phase of research activity.

There has been extensive concern in feminist research and practice regarding the risks that emancipatory evaluation may carry impositional risks (e.g. Acker et al., 1983; Ellsworth, 1989; Stacey, 1988). We have seen in Chapter 5 how Whitmore's account of an evaluation of a pre-natal programme for single, pregnant mothers illustrates how positive outcomes may on balance be achieved. The evaluation was carried out over several months by four women who had themselves been through the programme, with Whitmore as consultant to the project. There were tensions in the group and communication failures. One member left and another protested to Whitmore that:

> Our world is different from yours. The fear is that people always want to humiliate you, put you down [for being on welfare] . . . We have a different lifestyle from you. We just don't trust people the way you do. (Whitmore, 1994: 92)

But the strength of their final achievements is evidence that participatory evaluation with oppressed groups is not only political rhetoric.

Whitmore concluded that she could never entirely share the worlds of the women with whom she worked: 'My small words were often their big words. What I assumed was "normal talk", they saw as "professor words"' (1994: 95). Martin (1994, 1996) arrived at similar conclusions from her own feminist participative research, concluding that such research 'places unrealistic expectations on the extent to which the researched can become involved in the research process', and that 'even when problems are a major concern to people [the researched] they have work and private lives which usually take priority, whereas research IS work for the researcher' (Martin, 1994: 142).

A sensitive and arresting example of participatory research is provided by Miller's account of three years' collaborative research with teachers who had until that time been her postgraduate students (Miller, 1990, 1992; Miller and Martens, 1990). They aim to 'extend the concept of teacher as researcher into reciprocal and interactive forms' with an emancipatory agenda (Miller, 1990: ix). The accounts portray the sustained commitments of the group as they 'continue to struggle with ways in which the intentions and forms of emancipatory pedagogy and research both attract and confound us' (Miller and Martens, 1990: 45).

Focus groups can also provide a means for emancipatory evaluation. Plaut's account of the use of focus groups for community mobilization among poor, white, politically conservative, rural communities, and Jarrett's work with black women at risk of long-term poverty both exemplify empowerment benefits of focus groups (Jarrett, 1993; Plaut et al., 1993).

Stake remains reserved about advocacy evaluation: 'I feel our stance should be to resist advocacy, to minimize advocacy, even though it is ever present, to help to recognize worthy and unworthy advocacies but to resist joining them' (1997: 474).

Evaluators committed to critical evaluation may have less doubt regarding good and bad advocacies. Yet all participatory evaluators face the possibility that their research may be used to support causes of which they disapprove. Edwards does not duck this problem, accepting the inherent ambiguity of participant evaluation: 'By its very nature the process of empowerment is uncertain ... the ultimate destination is unknown' (1994: 288).

Evaluating-in-practice

Such evidence as is available suggests there is little or no association between knowledge of relevant research and an ability to think critically about one's practice (Gibbs et al., 1995). Practitioners who come into contact with evaluative research face something of a conundrum regarding the relationship between such research and their practice. One 'solution' we have noticed previously is to loosen the Gordian knot of practice/research by claiming that practice is a kind of research, or that research is a species of practice or service. We noticed that solution in some versions of practitioner research. Goldstein claims a natural affinity of this kind when he says 'the language of ethnography is the language of practice', and that 'both the qualitative researcher and the practitioner depend on similar talents' (1994: 46, 48).

I do not find this argument persuasive. Though frequently appealed to, dilemmas of practice and evaluation are not resolved by solutions of the 'one-bound-and-he-was-free' variety. A more subtle argument is developed by those who advocate reflective inquiry and evaluation. The underlying argument in such cases is that there exists an evaluative dimension to professional practice which is indigenous to practice rather than being 'on loan' from research or evaluation methodology. We saw in Chapter 2 how Eisner has developed such a model of reflective inquiry for education based on connoisseurship and criticism, in which inquiry is regarded as more akin to art than to traditional understandings of science. Schon has developed a broader inquiry model that is intended to address the character of reflective work in all professions (Schon, 1983, 1992, 1995; see England, 1986, for a comparable approach for social work).

Eisner and Schon share a rejection of older positivist conceptions of knowledge and its relation to theory and action. For example, Eisner (1988) criticizes scientific and technological approaches to schooling on four grounds. First, 'the uniqueness of the particular is considered "noise" in the search for general tendencies and main effects' (1988: 139). Second, the technological orientation to practice 'tends to encourage a primary focus on the achievement of some future state and in the process tends to undermine the significance of the present' (1988: 140). Objectives are always out of reach. Third, there is an agenda to objectify knowledge so that the qualities to which one chooses to attend must be empirically manifest. Finally, standardized tests in schools come to act as if they were themselves educational goals, and uniformity becomes an aspiration. Decisions about forms of evaluation have consequences for the character of teaching, curriculum and educational goals. Schon extends this criticism of technical rationality to the tacit model of the research/practice relationship:

> Research and practice are presumed to be linked by an exchange in which researchers offer theories and techniques applicable to practice problems, and practitioners, in return, give researchers new problems to work on and practical tests of the utility of research results. (Schon, 1992: 53)

Empirical evidence

Recent empirical work has shed some light on how practitioners seek to make sense of and resolve evaluative issues in their day to day work. Elks and Kirkhart urge that 'an alternative research model is needed, one that is exploratory rather than confirmatory, building a model of evaluation from the practitioner's own accounts rather than superimposing an ideal model and testing for conformity' (1993: 555). They interviewed seventeen social workers asking them how they evaluated what they were doing, and how they knew whether they were doing a good or bad job. Practitioners acknowledged difficulty in knowing if they were effective. They also perceived an incompatibility between the roles of evaluator and practitioner. The researchers suggest that practitioners hold an implicit model of practice evaluation which they describe as a 'pragmatic–professional model'. This included a reliance on intuition and experience, an internalized notion of an ideal practitioner, a dependence on feedback from colleagues, friends and family, and a model of an ideal client which always included growth and change.

Humphrey and Pease conducted a corresponding study in which they interviewed British probation officers regarding their perceptions of probation effectiveness. Probation officers tended to 'de-couple' the process of supervision from the out-turns of probation. Thus one person said, clients 'frequently get into more trouble but I don't think that in any way is a reflection on whether or not I have been effective'. Indeed, there was widespread belief that an element of luck operated in being effective. One might do 'brilliant' work but if the circumstances are against you they will still re-offend. Thus, 'if luck is seen to determine outcome, probation supervision becomes merely a matter of keeping an offender in the community for luck to strike' (Humphrey and Pease, 1992: 40).

Subsequent work by Shaw and Shaw suggests that social workers appear to have two contrasting models of evaluation in their heads – a formal 'evaluation proper' and self-evaluation. Formal evaluation is experienced as largely alien to the realities of social work and in almost complete contrast to social workers' evaluative 'maps' of their actual day-to-day evaluating (Shaw and Shaw, 1997b). Evaluation strategies were constructed from a 'game plan', the success of which was viewed – as in Humphrey and Pease's research – as partly contingent on the untoward operation of 'sheer luck'. Social workers judged their practice according to whether their work produced emotional rewards; the case was 'moving'; intervention won steady, incremental change; practice was accomplished without inflicting harm through the operations of the welfare system, and confirming evidence was available from fellow professionals. These practitioners were preoccupied with causes and reasons for outcomes of their work, held strongly worked views about the complexity and ambiguity of social work evidence, and were aware of the constant interplay of knowing and feeling in practice (Shaw and Shaw, 1997a). The significance of emotions echoes Erikson's remark of the clinician that 'The evidence is not "all in" if he does not succeed in using his own emotional responses during a clinical encounter as an evidential source and as a guide to action' (Erikson, 1959: 93).

Reflective inquiry

Donald Schon would doubtless comment on these practitioners' reflections in the light of his understanding of reflective inquiry. He sees our knowing as ordinarily tacit and *in* our action, and our workaday life thus reveals 'a pattern of tacit knowing-in-action' (Schon, 1992: 56):

> In his [sic] day-to-day practice he makes innumerable judgements of quality for which he cannot state adequate criteria, and he displays skills for which he cannot state the rules and procedures. (Schon, 1983: 50)

We referred to tacit knowledge of this kind in the opening part of this chapter. Yet tacit knowledge breaks down when we encounter surprises due to the fact that our spontaneous responses to the phenomena of everyday life do not always work. This often produces what Schon labels 'reflection-in-action', whereby problems are resolved through 'inventing on line' and on-the-spot experimenting: 'Stimulated by surprise, they turn thought back on action and on the knowing that is implicit in the action' (Schon, 1983: 50).

Schon's presentation of reflection-in-action captures the following qualities of reflective evaluating:

- It is a disciplined activity in which the sources of understanding and action are not automatically picked off the surface: 'Skilful action often reveals 'a knowing more than we can say' (1983: 51).
- Reflective evaluating involves a reflexivity – a testing by reflection. Erikson's injunction is apt. We should be constantly trying to 'force our favourite assumptions to become probable inferences' (Erikson, 1959: 94). Practitioners are not simply users but generators of knowledge.

- There is an inherent comparability between 'professional' and lay persons' capacities for displaying the elements of reflective inquiry.

Schon puts flesh on this image when he describes the relationship he envisages between a professional and the client. The relationship:

> takes the form of a literally reflective conversation . . . He attributes to his client, as well as to himself, a capacity to mean, know and plan. He recognizes that his meanings may have different meanings for his client than he intends . . . He recognizes an obligation to make his own understandings accessible to his client . . . [He] tries to discover the limits of his expertise through reflective conversation with the client. (1983: 295–296)

Schon's work is open to several criticisms. He makes no acknowledgement of power issues in either the relationship or the service. Neither does he appear to envisage any directly participative dimension. His examples focus extensively on the practitioner in discussion with colleagues and supervisors, rather than involving students, children or other service users (Schon, 1995). He may also underestimate the extent of routine decision-making that comprises everyday practice in hospital, school, or social work agency (Bloor, 1978). Yet his analysis is original and provocative. He is the only theorist in the field of practitioner and reflective evaluation who has developed a model which is not specific to any one profession. This in itself presents an agenda for comparative ethnographic evaluation of services which has yet to be addressed. Schon's concerns are relevant to, but do not actively exemplify, qualitative evaluation. There is, however, an emerging literature on qualitative reflective inquiry (Fook, 1996; Gould, 1999; Gould and Taylor, 1996).

Qualitative evaluation for practitioners

The focus of this chapter has been on 'insider' practitioner evaluation. I would not be misunderstood here. It has sometimes been argued by evaluators that insider evaluation is more valid than evaluation carried out by outsiders, on the grounds that practitioners have access to their own intentions, motives and feelings; that they know the setting first hand; and that they are in a better position to gain access, and so on. My stress on insider evaluation does not reflect this view. I agree with Hammersley that no position guarantees valid knowledge and no position prevents it either (Hammersley, 1993a).

We should note in conclusion, however, that practitioner evaluation may also draw on evaluative research which has a more or less direct relevance to practice. I do not refer to ethnographies such as Atkinson's (1995) research on medical talk and medical work, Pithouse's (1998) study of a child care team in a British Social Services Department, or

Hargreaves's interactionist studies of classroom behaviour. While such studies have evaluative relevance, their direct practice implications remain implicit.

Nonetheless, there has been insufficient attention given to the *evaluative uses of ethnography*. Recalling the admittedly strident complaints of McNamara (1980) regarding the irrelevance of ethnography, work on the practitioner uses of ethnography is needed. Bloor and McKeganey, and Silverman have provided precedents in this regard that are too rare among ethnographers (Bloor, 1997a; Bloor and McKeganey, 1987, 1989; Silverman, 1993, 1997a). Bloor is not optimistic about the potential for policy impacts from research. Unlike the almost total focus of work by Weiss and others on uses of research for the policy process, Bloor argues that 'the real opportunities for sociological influence lie closer to the coal-face than they do to head office, that the real opportunities for sociological influence lie in relations with practitioners, not with the managers of practice' (1997a: 234).

In reviews of a street ethnography of HIV-related risk behaviour among Glasgow male prostitutes, and comparative ethnographies of eight thera-peutic communities, he suggests there are two ways in which ethnogra-phy might speak to the practitioner. First, it may 'model' a service delivery that can be transferred to service providers. For example, 'ethnographic fieldwork, in its protracted and regular contacts with research subjects, has much in common with services outreach work' (Bloor, 1997a: 227). This point has some similarities with the argument of reflective evaluators that ethnography may be colonized and translated in ways that may be util-ized in direct practice. From the therapeutic community studies, Bloor suggests the very act of comparative judgement can model helpful service practice: 'Rich description of particular kinds of therapeutic practice can assist practitioners in making evaluative judgements about their own practices' (1997a: 229). Second, ethnographers may, where appropriate, draw practitioners' attention to practices they think worth dissemination and further consideration. Bloor and McKeganey (1989) list seven prac-tices which seemed to them to promote therapy in their original settings, and which they discussed with the practitioners in the therapeutic com-munities.

Incidentally, they point out the corresponding implications for ethno-graphers, in that 'any attempts to further exploit the evaluative potential of ethnography for a practitioner audience must be paralleled by a growth in ethnographic studies which focus on practitioners' work, not prac-titioners' conduct' (Bloor and McKeganey, 1989: 210). Until that time, when 'citizens themselves commend the work of practitioners, then it is not the place of sociologists to murmur of false consciousness and demand resistance to pastoral care' (Bloor, 1997a: 235).

In the last two chapters we have explored the special considerations that arise in the conduct of qualitative evaluation of programmes, policies and individual practice. The differences between them are far from superficial or marginal. Yet these differences provide no grounds for fragmenting evaluation and policy research into multiple discrete forms of inquiry, each with its own axioms and methodology. In the chapters that follow we seek to illuminate how evaluative purposes undergird differentiated but coherent approaches to decisions of design, fieldwork and qualitative evaluation analysis.

7

Decisions for evaluation design

CONTENTS

> The ethnographer 'inscribes' social discourse; he writes it down. In so doing he turns it from a passing event, which exists only in its own moment of occurrence, into an account, which exists in its inscriptions and can be reconsulted. (Geertz, 1973: 20)

Geertz's view of the characteristics of ethnographic descriptions, as interpreting the flow of social discourse and trying to 'rescue the "said" of such discourse from its perishing occasions and fix it in perusable terms' (1973: 20), reflects key aspects of the understanding of the methodology of qualitative evaluation which we describe in the following three chapters.

The chapter divisions are, superficially at least, conventional. Evaluation design is followed by data collection in Chapter 8 and analysis of evaluation in Chapter 9. Yet in the practice of qualitative evaluation this clear-cut distinction of three phases of knowledge seeking may not normally be possible. Certainly, they may not exist as autonomous operations.

Substantial space is devoted in this chapter to evaluation ethics, participatory evaluation, and qualitative work on the outcomes of policies, programmes and practice. However, these are not exclusively 'design' matters any more than they are matters of the fieldwork process or of analysis, and they all reoccur in the following chapters.

Two preliminary questions raise their heads. What purchase will qualitative evaluation provide on design decisions? Are there specific qualitative evaluation methods? The position taken throughout this book has been to argue that there is no intrinsic methodological distinction between qualitative research and qualitative evaluation. Notwithstanding the arguments to the contrary by writers such as Lincoln and Guba (1986b), I see no contradiction whatever in the phrase 'evaluation research'. The line taken in this book is that there is a cluster of recognizable evaluation purposes which overlap partly but not completely with the purposes of research. Hence, evaluation and research design decisions draw from the same wide choice of methods. Where evaluation differs is in the steer which the evaluation of new or established policies, programmes or practices gives to the choice and uses made of chosen methods: 'Design is the logical sequence that connects the empirical data to a study's initial research questions and, ultimately, to its conclusions' (Yin, 1994: 19). In this sense, 'a research design deals with a *logical* problem and not a *logistical* problem' (1994: 20). The logics and values of evaluation shape decisions regarding design. Logistically, qualitative evaluation differs little from qualitative research. Thus evaluation design 'focuses on asking the right questions and selecting appropriate methods so that credible claims about the phenomenon under study can be made' (Fournier and Smith, 1993: 315–316).

However, I depart sharply from the mainstream position regarding evaluation design decisions – one which we have described as a 'horses-for-courses' position. The standard line is that qualitative designs – often identified with case study approaches – are best fitted to answer questions about *processes*. Questions regarding *outcomes* are better served, so it is argued, by traditional comparative designs which address the measurement of outcomes. There is sometimes more than a hint of disparagement of qualitative evaluation in this distinction, illustrated, for example, in Scriven's comment that formative evaluation focused on programme processes and improvement, is in reality an interim version of summative evaluation, which provides information on 'mid-stream merit' (1997: 499). Shadish and colleagues are less tendentious than Scriven but the net effect is similar (Shadish et al., 1990). They conclude that qualitative designs make sense when:

- The evaluator wants breadth.
- Few questions are known ahead of the evaluation.
- The evaluation will be used by readers who cannot experience the programme themselves.

- Evaluators can forgo higher quality answers to more specific questions.
- A succinct summary of results will not be a priority.
- Generalizations across sites are not a priority.
- Discovery is a higher priority than confirmation.
- The evaluation client will regard qualitative evaluation as credible.

Their conclusion is that qualitative case studies may be helpful in the early stages of the implementation of a new programme. In other words, they rehash the long-discredited notion that qualitative research performs an exploratory pretesting function. We are left with an impression of qualitative evaluation as an imprecise, ill-focused, descriptive, inductive exercise, strong on vicarious experience, but chronically at risk of failed credibility in the eyes of the people who count – the client.

I reject this mix and match approach to qualitative and quantitative alternatives. Qualitative evaluation problematizes and picks away at conventional stereotypes of the respective scope and division of labour between the two. For example, we saw in Chapter 1 that Williams provides a more even-handed, thought-provoking inventory of differentiating questions in answer to the inquiry, 'When is naturalistic evaluation appropriate?'

Take the following examples from his list:

- Are official definitions of the evaluand sufficient or are emic perspectives required?
- Is evaluation of the processes by which the evaluand is addressing its outcomes necessary?
- 'If the outcome includes complex actions in natural . . . settings . . . a naturalism component would allow . . . more dependable and credible judgements' (Williams, 1986: 88).
- Is there time to study the evaluand through its natural cycle?
- 'Can the evaluand be studied unobtrusively, as it operates, in an ethical way?' (1986: 89).

These questions imply a very different list of criteria from those given by most mainstream evaluation theorists. During this chapter we prioritize issues regarding evaluation ethics, and in doing so argue that social justice concerns should be central to qualitative evaluation. We reject the assumption that qualitative evaluation is hamstrung by questions of outcomes, and argue that case studies and other qualitative designs can provide an understanding of causes and outcomes which in many cases is better fitted to the purposes of evaluation than more conventional designs. We pick up the discussions of participatory and reflective evaluation, which were central to Chapter 6, and conclude the chapter with a consideration of how they shape and enrich evaluation design. Before considering matters of ethics and social justice, we briefly consider the preliminary problem of whether an evaluation is feasible in a given instance.

Assessing evaluability

Wholey identifies several problems which, if not resolved, will render any evaluation nugatory. He suggests that:

- Lack of agreement on goals, objectives, side-effects and performance criteria will lead to an evaluation which focuses on non-representative or non-relevant questions.
- Unrealistic goals and objectives, given the level of programme resources and activities will lead to a programme which inevitably 'fails'.
- When relevant information regarding the programme cannot be made available the evaluation will be inconclusive.
- If policy-makers or managers are unwilling or unable to act on the basis of evaluation in order to change the programme, then the result will be 'information in search of a user' (Wholey, 1994: 16).

Assessment of evaluability shows whether a programme can be meaningfully evaluated and also if such evaluation is likely to lead to action to maintain or change the policy, programme or practice evaluated, or some future evaluand.

Wholey's analysis of the problems and their consequences is generally helpful. He underscores the factors which prevent an unproblematic application of a goals and outcomes model of evaluation, and makes clear that there are some evaluation-related activities which will enable a better understanding and improvement of the evaluation process. There are some remaining problems in his formulation. For instance, he gives too high a profile to goals and objectives, and his analysis reflects his view that programme managers are the primary recipients of evaluation. But the more serious difficulty lies in the solution he proposes. His solution is that programme designs should be clarified, programme realities explored, and programmes redesigned where necessary so that:

- Goals, objectives, side-effects and priority information needs are well defined.
- Resources, activities and goals are changed to become plausible.
- Relevant and feasible measures of programme performance are in place.
- There is agreement among intended users on how the information will be used.

While some of the problems in Wholey's initial list *can* be mitigated, evaluation cannot be contingent on solving them through the rational formula suggested here. They will always be present to a greater or lesser extent. For instance, his distinction between intended and side-effects betrays a mechanical or maybe chemical metaphor of programmes. He also relegates the politics of evaluation to an unproblematic and invisible status. For example, he does not reflect on ways in which the agreement to focus on programme goals excludes the problems which Weiss and others have raised regarding the tacit legitimation of establishment goals by evaluators (House, 1993; Weiss, 1987). His belief that prior agreement can be reached on how the information from evaluation will be used lets slip an implicit assumption that evaluation use is primarily instrumental. We have seen in Chapters 4 and 5 that this is at best a one-sided notion of information use, and in most cases is unduly rationalist. Finally, his view of prior evaluability assessment has no place at all for any participatory practice. While he does talk about involving the intended users of evaluation, and not imposing expert assumptions, the people he has in mind are budget staff, senior management and senior project staff, as we saw in his account of the evaluation of the Tennessee Pre-Natal Programme, in Chapter 5.

Evaluability assessment may or may not be appropriate. It presupposes the possibility of a consensual strategy for evaluation, and as such perhaps best fits a model of qualitative evaluation which is based on a responsive stance towards key stakeholders and interest constituencies.

EXAMPLE 7.1 EVALUABILITY ASSESSMENT

Pulice (1994) illustrates a stakeholder-focused evaluability assessment in his discussion of qualitative evaluation methods in the public sector with seriously mentally ill adults. He recommends identifying relevant constituency groups at all levels and completing preliminary interviews with key informants on the reason for the evaluation request, the likely time frames, and their views regarding intended uses of the evaluation. He also advises a literature search of legislation, agency documents, and committee reports 'to determine the nature and content of documentation relative to the evaluation question' (1994: 307).

He then suggests that the evaluator/s develop a preliminary taxonomy of the identified constituency groups in terms of their likely role as advocates, planners, facilitators, monitors or managers. Finally, he recommends conducting semi-structured interviews that focus on the broad evaluation questions. It would be possible to use focus groups for this stage.

Evaluability assessments will reflect the underlying perspectives of the evaluators. For example, critical evaluators may wish to explore – with a view to mitigating – the potential for imposing their own worldviews on those participating in the evaluation. Where such imposition seems unavoidable, it may be decided that evaluation is not feasible. Evaluators who commence from a constructivist and relativist standpoint will wish to explore the feasibility of an authentic evaluation which takes local context into account, and empowers stakeholders. Rodwell and Woody believe that: 'Constructivist methods to determine evaluability are very appropriate when the goal is to have all possible stakeholding groups involved in the process, while having problems emerge from observation, from experiences, and from the data' (1994: 319).

They describe a proposal for an evaluation of a clinic setting, which went astray: 'We ignored the context of our deeds' (1994: 324). When, following the evaluability assessment, the proposal was made it was turned down, on the grounds that it did not follow the research policy of the agency; that it threatened the homeostasis of the organization through having too broad a focus, and too short a time frame to accomplish it; and that such detailed study was not needed but that the agency wanted comparison studies with similar services and using quantitative methods. The authors believe their failure stemmed in part from not taking criteria of authenticity into account. Such assessments can 'create a referent in a not so rational program evaluation environment' (1994: 326).

Design ethics and social justice

The ethical problems of evaluation have usually been discussed as roughly synonymous with the ethical problems of (quasi-)experimentation. The experience and reflection of qualitative researchers and evaluators has fortunately rescued us from that myopic perspective on evaluation ethics. House (1993) has distinguished four areas in which ethical problems face the evaluator:

1 Withholding the nature of the evaluation research from the participants.
2 Exposing participants to acts that would harm them.
3 Invading the privacy of participants.
4 Withholding benefits from participants.

Take, for example, the first of these problems. Covert evaluation is 'a particularly dangerous example of covert social research, because the findings are not being used merely to illuminate our knowledge of the social world, but potentially to change it' (Finch, 1986: 203). Bottom-up forms of evaluation are less at risk of this problem due to the closeness of those involved, and the participant aspects of such evaluation. However, there remains what Stacey (1988) has called the delusion of alliance, and the problem that participants may reveal more than they intend. In traditional evaluation it is probably relatively clear to the participant when the evaluator is 'working' and when she is having 'time out'. The participants are likely to assume that when they are in informal settings the evaluator is having time out. But this is not likely to be the case in qualitative evaluation, and the participants face the risk of unwitting disclosure.

The principle of informed consent has often been appealed to, in order to protect participants against this abuse. The problem arises, of course, because it 'implies that the researcher knows *before* the event . . . what the event will be and its possible effects' (Eisner, 1991a: 214). This is often not the case, especially in qualitative evaluation.

EXAMPLE 7.2   INFORMED CONSENT

Staff of a residential home for older people are told:

> We are seeking your permission to observe in your home for the elderly for eight weeks. At the end of the eight weeks we will be happy, if you wish for it, to provide feedback on what we have seen and what we think it means.

This approach has the virtues of stressing the voluntary nature of the agreement. It explains the duration and general form of the study, and promises feedback to those who request it. But there are several unanswered question:

- Will the study be published?
- And to what readers?
- Will staff have the right to read and comment on the report before it is published?
- Will their comments be included in the report if they believe there has been serious misunderstanding and/or misrepresentation?
- Will residents be interviewed?
- If so, how will *their* informed consent be negotiated?
- What will the researchers' role be during the observation period?
- Will the evaluation entail additional work for staff?
- How will confidentiality be protected?

Some participants will be less sophisticated than others in raising issues:

> Do researchers have an ethical responsibility to serve in a dual role: first, as researchers with a project aimed at satisfying their research purposes, and second, as advocates for the practitioners, raising questions that the researchers know should be raised in order for practitioners to make a competent assessment of the risks? (Eisner, 1991a: 217)

Problems of *confidentiality* are also sharper in qualitative evaluation. Quantitative evaluators can often deal with confidentiality issues through the sampling process, and through technical safeguards when the data are analyzed. We may decide to guarantee the privacy of disclosures. But, do all evaluation participants have equal rights to privacy? Tabloid newspaper revelations of the lives of those in the public eye are often treated differently from similar revelations of the less powerful. Does a commitment to privacy cover all circumstances? We may feel fairly clear what we would do if we saw a teacher sexually fondling a young child. But what about blatant incompetence by a professional practitioner? Or incidents which we judge to be clear examples of racism? The response is less clearcut. The school or agency may already know. Also, whistle-blowing during the evaluation may forfeit the opportunity for whistle-blowing in the final report. Less usually, what should the evaluator do if she encounters outstanding but unrecognized accomplishments by someone who may have a reputation as a poor or 'difficult' practitioner by managers? The general point is much the same as that raised regarding consent – 'do researchers have an ethical responsibility to foster fair treatment of those they observe?' (Eisner, 1991a: 219).

Evaluation standards have been developed in America (Stufflebeam, 1991), but the problem of applying ethical principles to the conduct of evaluation still remains. House believes that the balancing of principles in concrete situations is 'the ultimate ethical act' (1993: 168). For example, it is possible that adherence to ethical principles may prove detrimental to programme effectiveness (Lewis, 1988). A hospital manager may decide to lessen workloads to limit burdens on staff, and so reduce the number of patients that can be seen. Reflecting on his own experience of ethical mistakes, Eisner concludes,

> We might like to secure consent that is informed, but we know we can't always inform because we don't always know. We would like to protect personal privacy and guarantee confidentiality, but we know we cannot always fulfil such guarantees. We would like to be candid but sometimes candour is inappropriate. We do not like to think of ourselves as using others as a means to our own professional ends, but if we embark upon a research study that we conceptualize, direct, and write, we virtually assure that we will use others for our purpose. (Eisner, 1991a: 225–226)

Evaluating for social justice

The issues of social justice for evaluation have been addressed patchily, although there is a growing literature. Evaluators 'do not live in a state of methodological grace' (House, 1991a: 245), and justice considerations impinge on decisions regarding evaluation design. I will briefly consider just two approaches, briefly outlining the key ideas, suggesting an example, and noting the issues that each approach poses.

Justice as fairness   One of the clearest examples of this position is that held by Ernest House. He believes that none of the dominant theories of justice is entirely satisfactory as a basis for evaluation. He advocates a moral basis of evaluation resting in principles of moral equality, moral autonomy, impartiality and reciprocity, without being sure how they are to be balanced against each other in every situation. None should have particular priority and decisions should be made in pluralist fashion, with considerations of efficiency playing a part but with justice as prior. In other words, he offers a strong dose of John Rawls, and also of more intuitionist approaches, with a slight dash of utilitarian efficiency.

He develops the example of negotiating a fair and demanding evaluation agreement (House, 1980: Ch. 8), in which all participants should meet the demanding conditions that they:

- Not be coerced.
- Be able to argue their position.
- Accept the terms under which the agreement is reached.
- Negotiate. This is not simply 'a coincidence among individual choices' (1980: 165).
- Not pay excessive attention to one's own interests.
- Adopt an agreement that affects all equally.
- Select a policy for evaluation that is in the interests of the group to which it applies.
- Have equal and full information on relevant facts.
- Avoid undue risk to participants arising from incompetent and arbitrary evaluations.

House defends this reformist position. In response to critics who say he is biased to the disadvantaged he responds, 'It seems to me that making certain the interests of the disadvantaged are represented and seriously considered is not being biased, though it is certainly more egalitarian than most current practice' (1991a: 241–242).

Constructivist justice   The constructivist shift in sociology poses special questions about justice. Some explicit work on justice from a reflexive stance has been undertaken by Johnson and Altheide (Altheide and Johnson, 1997; Johnson, 1995). They reject contemporary theories of justice and Johnson argues that a reflexive theory of justice should include the following emphases. Justice is:

- A struggle: 'our struggle to live with virtue in our social and communal lives' (Johnson, 1995: 199).
- Fundamentally emotional. Our judgements stem from our experience.
- Developmental, changing over time, and changing standards as we change in time and place.
- Gendered. Our struggles include 'an abiding concern with how to live peacefully and productively with the members of the other genders' (1995: 201).
- Personal: 'The pursuit of justice lies not in our words and our theories but in our concrete actions to help other people' (1995: 201).
- A matter of social interaction: 'We typically join together with others . . . Justice is communal and processual' (1995: 202).

- Our effort to 'figure out what is going on in the world' (1995: 202).
- Selfish: 'Selfishness is the foundation for altruism' (1995: 203).

This approach pushes us to an empirical concern with 'how justice is constituted, communicated and experienced in everyday life' (Altheide and Johnson, 1997: 184). The main focus of criticism of constructivist and interpretivist positions is on their relativism and hence their potential political complacency. Greene concludes:

> Questions about the political and moral aims of interpretivism are the most deeply disquieting. The essential relativism of interpretivism argues for no particular role in the world. There is no commitment . . . to reinforce the status quo or to challenge it, to condone racist or sexist practices by one's silences or to actively seek to redress observed inequities, to remain neutral on issues of political beliefs or to openly advocate for a chosen ideology. (1992: 43–44)

Designing qualitative evaluation for outcomes

> Qualitative studies are not designed to provide definitive answers to causal questions . . . [but] it can still be an appropriately qualified pursuit. (Lofland and Lofland, 1995: 136, 138)

Miles and Huberman are even less reserved: 'The conventional view is that qualitative studies are only good for exploratory forays, for developing hypotheses – and that strong explanations, including causal attributions, can be derived only through quantitative studies'. They describe this view as 'mistaken' (Miles and Huberman, 1994: 147), and insist that qualitative evaluation research:

- Identifies causal mechanisms.
- Deals with complex local networks.
- Sorts out the temporal dimension of events.
- Is well equipped to cycle back and forth between different levels of variables and processes.
- Analytic induction provides a way of testing and deepening single case explanations.

Qualitative evaluation can address outcome problems and questions of causal attribution in three ways. First, there are design solutions analogous to designs which entail a degree of control. These owe their main inspiration to the work of Donald Campbell. Design solutions from the same broad family have been adopted by those, such as Cronbach and Yin, who advocate the use of multiple case studies. Second, the shift of emphasis from internal validity to questions of external validity and generalization, has led to a greater sensitivity to the micro-processes of practice and programmes. Third, the impact of scientific realism has led to a radical rethinking of notions of causality. We will consider each of these.

Campbell and case studies

Campbell's early position was that 'one-shot' case study designs are uninterpretable with regard to causal attribution. However, through exchanges with Becker and Erikson, he came to the position that the analogy of degrees of freedom provides a major source of discipline for interpreting intensive, cross-cultural case studies. The logic entails testing theories against the predictions or expectations it stimulates, through a general process he describes as pattern matching, based on the premise that 'experimental design can be separated from quantification' (Campbell, 1978: 197).

Campbell (1964) suggests a paradigm which entails a whole-hearted commitment to both ethnography and comparative studies (see Figure 7.1). In this model two anthropologists from different cultures would each study a third and fourth culture. The net effects are 'read' as follows:

- The attributes common to ethnographies 1 and 3, but not shared with 2 and 4, can be attributed to ethnographer A.
- The attributes common to ethnographies 2 and 4, but not evident elsewhere, can be attributed to ethnographer B.
- The attributes common to ethnographies 1 and 2, but not present in 3 and 4, can be attributed to culture C as 'objectively' known.
- The attributes common to ethnographies 3 and 4, but not found in 1 and 2, can be attributed to culture D as 'objectively' known.

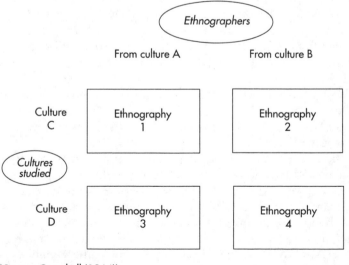

(*Source*: Campbell (1964))

FIGURE 7.1 *Multiple-ethnography design to extricate the ethnographer-contributed content from the culture studied*

Attributes common to *all four* ethnographies are inherently ambiguous, interpretable either as shared biases on the part of the ethnographers or as shared characteristics of both cultures. Interpreting features *unique* to any given ethnography are indeterminate, due to specifics of the ethnographer, the culture, or interactions between the two.

The full implementation of this model would be resource intensive and frequently not feasible. But, it would be a significant gain to operate just the top half of the figure. Another variant would be for two ethnographers to study each other's culture, with implicit bases of reference provided by the ethnographers' descriptions of their own cultures. It would be desirable on this model to have ethnographers from cultures as different from one another as possible.

Micro-processes

We saw in Chapter 2 that William Reid has been attracted by the potential of 'change-process' research. He does not reject the role of controlled experiments but concludes that 'practical and ethical constraints on experiments necessitate a reliance on the naturalistic study of these relations' (Reid, 1990: 130). This entails a focus on the processes of change during the period of contact between the professional helper and the client system. Rather than relying on aggregated, averaged summary measures of outcomes, this approach returns to the content-analysis tradition in social research, through a greater focus on micro-outcomes.

Reid applies his ideas to social work, although the logic would presumably apply to other forms of change-oriented professional service. A systemic view of intervention is at its root, in which professional and service user are viewed in a circular, mutually influencing interaction. In this model 'conventional distinctions between intervention and outcome lose their simplicity' (1990: 135). 'It then becomes possible to depict change-process research as a study of strings of intermixed i's and o's' – interventions and outcomes (1990: 136). While Reid seeks to defend experiments, he suggests a more naturalistic stance when he says that 'averages of process variables that are devoid of their contexts at best provide weak measures' (1990: 137).

This approach holds promise especially in case studies where the unit of analysis is an individual, and where the evaluand includes a one-to-one delivery of a service. The evaluation of micro-processes is not, of course, restricted to outcome-oriented evaluation. We noted Silverman's critique of some established forms of evaluation research in Chapter 3. He has applied conversation analysis to the evaluation of the sequential organization of talk in HIV counselling. He argues that conversation analysis is appropriate to an understanding of complex data of this kind, but also that it can demonstrably establish a fruitful dialogue with practitioners in a range of work settings (Silverman, 1997a: 37).

Cause and causal models

The third qualitative line of approach to the methodological problems posed by outcome evaluation is rather different. It stems from the stimulus provided by changed thinking regarding the nature of cause, and the corresponding models of causal hypotheses which flow from that thinking. We outlined the background to these changes in Chapter 3 in referring to the advent of scientific realist explanations and their emerging application to evaluation. The central idea is of underlying causal mechanisms which cannot be understood by surface workings and measurement. Hence, 'events themselves are not the ultimate focus of scientific analysis . . . Reality consists not only of what we can see but also of the underlying causal entities that are not always discernible' (House, 1991b: 4). The underlying reality produces actual events, of which we have empirical experiences and sense impressions.

This is often described as a *generative* concept of causality:

> When we explain an outcome generatively we are not coming up with variables or correlates that associate with one another; rather we are trying to explain how the association itself comes about. The generative mechanisms thus actually *constitute* the outcome. (Pawson and Tilley, 1997b: 408)

The conventional concept of causation as regularities and associations is dismissed in favour of causal entities which have 'tendencies interacting with other tendencies in such a way that an observable event may or may not be produced' (House, 1991b: 5). House quotes Manicas and Secord saying that, 'For the standard view of science, the world is a determined concatenation of contingent events; for the realist, it is a contingent concatenation of real structures. And this difference is monumental' (House, 1991b: 5).

Hence, instead of merely documenting the sequence and association of events, the realist seeks to *explain* events. While this view of cause does not necessarily require a qualitative methodology, it does clearly lend itself to such methods. Causal accounts will be local and 'now-oriented' (Lofland and Lofland, 1995: 141). Miles and Huberman develop analytic methods which address causal attribution in both single and multiple case explanations. For example, they advocate the use of field research to map the 'local causal networks' which informants carry in their heads and to make connections with the evaluator's own emerging causal map of the setting. Such maps start from 'causal fragments' which lead on to linked building of logical chains of evidence. Such causal networks 'are not probabilistic, but specific and determinate, grounded in understanding of events over time in the concrete local context – *and* tied to a good conceptualization of each variable' (Miles and Huberman, 1994: 159).

Much of this reasoning was anticipated by Cronbach's arguments regarding causal models. Rejecting the idea of causation as events that can be predicted with a high degree of probability, Cronbach developed twin arguments. First, he argued that causes are contingent on local interactions of clusters of events. More than one cluster may be sufficient, but no one cluster is necessary. Second, he accepted that there are usually missing events or conditions that affect the outcome of a given programme, but about which we know little. He was the first theorist to produce a plausible explanation of contextual factors in evaluation. Hence he concludes that 'after the experimenter with his artificial constraint leaves the scene, the operating programme is sure to be adapted to local conditions' (Cronbach et al., 1980: 217). Furthermore, 'a programme evaluation is so dependent on its context that replication is only a figure of speech' (1980: 222).

Taken together, the experimental intervention is neither necessary nor sufficient for the predicted effect to occur. An experiment cannot provide a critical test for the effectiveness of a programme. The traditional formulation 'is not the world of social programmes and, in general, is not the social world at all' (House, 1993: 135).

Case studies in evaluation

> The case for case studies in qualitative evaluations rests on a confluence of their responsive political-value stance and their underlying interpretivist assumptions. (Greene, 1994: 538)

The serious criticisms of traditional experimental designs, and the developments in qualitative methodology which are able to incorporate a partial understanding of causal processes, have combined to place case studies centre stage as an evaluation design which offers a focus on evaluation outcomes linked to an appreciation of the contingent and constructivist nature of policies, programmes and practices.

Case studies in evaluation emerged in the 1970s in the education field: 'Case study was a metaphor that appealed to those who were looking for a way of integrating the comprehensive data requirements that emerged from the various critical reviews of the evaluation tradition' (Simon, 1987: 61–62). In the evaluation context case study was not simply a borrowing from existing social science traditions dating back to the Chicago School. For better or worse, evaluators were preoccupied with issues of audiences, time limits and power relationships, which produced a collaborative model of research. Many of the case studies conducted in this period 'lacked at least three key features of ethnographic research – immersion in the field, direct observation as the dominant technique, and an interpretive theory of the case by the ethnographer' (Simon, 1987: 79). Simon believes that evaluation case studies of the 1970s and 1980s were closer to oral history than to ethnography. The differences continue to the time of writing. A comparison, for example, of the texts on case studies by the evaluation theorist Stake (1995) and the methodologist Yin (1994) reveals extensive variations in emphasis, which reflect these differences.

Hakim remarks that, 'The case study is the social research equivalent of the spotlight or the microscope; its value depends crucially on how well the study is focused' (1988: 61). Case studies are flexible and multi-purpose. They may be descriptive, exploring and providing portraits of little known entities. They may also be selective, pursuing more richly detailed accounts of processes at work. They may also be designed to achieve a form of experimental isolation of selected social factors within a real life context. But whichever general purpose guides the adoption of case study evaluation, decisions about case study designs must address six issues. First, what will count as a 'case'? Second, what criteria should be applied to the decision whether or not a given programme or project should be evaluated? Third, will evaluation address a single case or multiple cases? Fourth, what will be the units of analysis? Fifth, what logic of generalization will be adopted? Finally, what is the intended relationship between practitioner values and evaluator values? We will briefly consider each of these.

First, what counts as a case? Stake says,

> The case is a special something to be studied, a student, a classroom, a committee, a program, perhaps, but not a problem, a relationship, or a theme. The case to be studied probably has problems and relationships, and the report of the case is likely to have a theme, but the case is an entity. The case, in some ways, has a unique life. (1995: 133)

We observed in the last chapter Atkinson and Delamont's overgeneralized and unduly heavy-handed criticisms of case study evaluators, but they are not always wide of the mark. For example, they complain of a tendency to looseness in talk of 'cases':

> What counts as a 'case' is ... much more problematic than 'case-study' researchers seem to allow for ... It is ... quite meaningless for authors of the case-study persuasion to write as if the world were populated by 'cases' whose status and existence were independent of methodological and theoretical concerns. (Atkinson and Delamont, 1993: 207)

Stake's hedge-betting definition exhibits some of this vagueness. Yet precedent suggests that case studies may be carried out with individuals, communities, social groups, organizations and institutions, and certain events, roles, relationships or interactions (Hakim, 1988).

Second, in reaching the decision whether or not a given programme or project should be evaluated, Cronbach places the reduction of uncertainty and information yield as the primary criteria: '*Leverage* is the bottom line. Leverage refers to the probability that the information – *if* believed – will change the course of events' (Cronbach et al., 1980: 265). This should not be read as an instrumentalist view of evaluation use because 'the questions with the greatest leverage are the ones that contribute to insight' (1980: 266). He suggests a rough algorithm:

1 Questions with high leverage and high uncertainty merit close attention.
2 Less – but some – leverage plus high uncertainty requires some investment.
3 In situations of high leverage and low uncertainty, low cost methods should be used.
4 In circumstances of low leverage and low uncertainty no evaluation should be undertaken.

However, matters of 'leverage' and 'uncertainty' will remain open to judgement.

Third, case studies may address either single or multiple cases. There are various rationales for focusing on a single case. Yin distinguishes critical cases (which allow the testing of a well-formulated theory), extreme or rare cases, and revelatory cases (a phenomenon hitherto inaccessible to scientific investigation). For example voluntary welfare agencies may set up projects which reflect a novel model of intervention which they wish to develop, local educational authorities may set up small numbers of innovative but relatively costly curriculum innovations, and government departments routinely introduce innovative or imported forms of dealing with offenders. Studies of critical or rare cases are possible in these cases. Changing public attitudes to the benefits or risks of a hitherto unimpeachable project may open up the possibility of revelatory case study evaluations in a previously no-go area of practice.

Innovations are frequently more widespread and therefore allow the possibility of multiple rather than single case studies. School innovations often fall into this category. By definition these are unlikely to be critical, rare or revelatory cases.

Multiple case studies can be achieved by setting up 'projects which are specifically designed as a series of ethnographic studies in different settings, selected on criteria developed from existing theory to provide the most significant dimensions for comparison' (Finch, 1986: 185). She suggests the advantage of a central team which provides a steer to the analytic themes and categories at the design stage, but does not dictate the research methods. Alternatively, multiple case studies could be done sequentially by planning cumulative comparative studies. While we should not expect this to yield an easy linear development of knowledge, it does provide opportunity for interdisciplinary evaluation, and would be a significant advance on most current case study evaluation.

EXAMPLE 7.3   MULTI-SITE CASE STUDY

Burgess and others (1994) report a multi-site case study of the introduction of records of achievement into high schools in an English Midlands county. A researcher (two years) and two seconded teachers (each for one year) each spent a term in one of the schools, working with teachers and pupils, and where possible participating in activities relating to the record of achievement process.

The four schools were 'illustrative of the range of schools which existed in the authority' (Burgess et al., 1994: 131), and enabled comparisons between urban and rural schools, selective and non-selective schools, schools serving predominantly working class and middle class populations, and all white and multi-ethnic schools. The schools also varied in the extent to which they had introduced the scheme. The authors claim that: 'Overall the strength of the study rested in its comparative nature. The research design facilitated the examination of a wide range of substantive educational issues in different contexts' (1994: 136).

Individual reports were written on each school, plus a thematic report. Thematic issues such as the significance of time, and school-specific issues were both addressed. They stress the interconnectedness of resources, selection of sites, and analysis, and also imply some dangers in placing too much weight on local context. For example, they argue that the possibility of cross-case analysis stemmed from posing similar themes to the schools at the commencement of the evaluation.

It is clear from this example that the authors were interested in the cases at more than one level. Part of their argument deals with holistic analyses of each school, but they are also apparently interested in differences of class, school admission policies, and rural or urban location. Yin uses the term embedded to describe case studies where there is more than one unit of analysis, and this is the fourth aspect of design decision that evaluators need to resolve.

The fifth case study design issue is the logic of generalization from case studies. The focus of the generalization problem will be different according to whether case studies have a primarily descriptive or explanatory purpose. Either way, Yin rightly warns against inappropriate borrowing of survey logic when planning case studies, and underlines the distinction between analytical generalization and statistical generalization. 'A fatal flaw in doing case studies is to conceive of statistical generalization as the method of generalizing the results of the case' (Yin, 1994: 31). External validity problems in case study evaluation, and in qualitative evaluation more generally, are confused by incorrect analogies to samples and populations. Therefore, when selecting multiple cases the logic is not that of sampling but of replication: 'Each case must be selected so that it either (a) predicts similar results (a *literal replication*) or (b) produces contrasting results but for predictable reasons (a *theoretical replication*)' (Yin, 1994: 46).

Yin's argument is sound. Yet we should note that models of statistical generalization have occasionally been used effectively with multiple case studies. Sinclair (1971) reported a large-scale study of hostels for young male offenders which utilized an impressive range of data to draw conclusions regarding the effect of hostel environments on offending. He went on to argue with others that:

> The comparison of a large number of institutions within a single study enables a serious weakness of descriptive case studies to be overcome. This is the difficulty of linking the precise features of the care provided with its immediate and long term effects. (Tizard et al., 1975: 3)

They report a series of studies of residential establishments which show variations of ideology, organization, staffing and resident response. The risk of such qualitative evaluations is to resort to superficial mini-ethnographies. There are too many accounts of case studies which rely on fieldwork lasting no more than two or three days. Yet, provided resources are adequate, multi-site case studies provide rich opportunities for theoretically informed qualitative evaluation.

Sixth, we noted Simon's observation that the emergence of case studies in educational evaluation included a preoccupation with power relationships, and encouraged the emergence of collaborative models of case studies. Democratic evaluation models in Britain and the United States developed in a political context which supported discovery approaches in education. This fostered the early recognition that case studies may have an emancipatory potential 'based on respect for the autonomy of the individual and a rationale of stimulated self-improvement' (Simon, 1987: 83). In other words, the case study was seen as having educational potential in itself. Educational case studies in Britain during the 1970s and 1980s included a belief that 'people own the facts of their lives', and led evaluators to 'seek to portray divergence rather than resolve it' (1987: 86). Case studies which are broadly emancipatory have also been developed in other fields.

EXAMPLE 7.4   CASE STUDY FOR PRACTITIONERS AND RESEARCHERS

Bogdan and Taylor (1994) report a multi-site case study evaluation of forty programmes that aim to promote the integration into the community of people with learning disabilities and multiple disabilities. They have aimed to develop a model of evaluation which partially resolves the conflicting orientations of practitioners and researchers, by combining appropriately sceptical rigour with research which will 'help conscientious practitioners – people who are leading the reforms in the direction of integration' (1994: 295).

They studied each of the forty projects through a rolling programme of eight brief case studies a year over five years. The sites were selected through purposive sampling methods which combined asking key informants to nominate good programmes, and then undertaking telephone interviews. They wished to identify innovative and exemplary programmes rather than build a probability sample: 'We consciously tried to find places that can teach us about how people with severe disabilities can be integrated into the community' (1994: 298). Consistent with their theoretical orientation, they started with a deliberately vague definition of integration.

> We treat the concept of integration as problematic, something to be investigated rather than assumed. We want to learn about how agencies . . . define and accomplish integration. (Bogdan and Taylor, 1994: 297)

Their approach has resulted in much easier access and ironically people are more candid about dilemmas of practice than they may otherwise have been. Short reports are produced in the professional press on each project, and when the reports focus on negative aspects of less than exemplary agencies, agencies are allowed the choice of whether or not their names will be mentioned.

They are interested in generalizing – 'patterns that transcend individual cases' (1994: 300). They are also interested in theorizing, and 'developing sensitizing concepts and grounded theory that transcend the commonsense ideas of the people we study' (1994: 300). They do not discuss how they think generalizing works, or offer any reflection on the relationship between lay and scientific concepts.

Action and participation

Action research 'as a way of generating knowledge about a social system whole, at the same time, trying to change it' (Elden and Chisholm, 1993: 121) has been associated with the work of Lewin and, in Britain, with the Tavistock Institute's focus on intra-organizational and work life problems. In the late 1960s action research came to have a quite separate association through the American Poverty Programme, the introduction of programmes of positive discrimination in education, and Community Development Projects through the Home Office in Britain. Evaluation was not regarded as primarily concerned with discipline development but was intended to be directly responsive to the needs and agenda set by the action programme. It represented in many, though not all, instances an instrumental, activist view of research as intrinsically a political enterprise.

The label has survived in health, welfare and education (Hart and Bond, 1995). In education it covers a range of activities from self-evaluation through to group collaborative research (Ebbutt, 1985; Kelly, 1985).

EXAMPLE 7.5   CRITICAL EDUCATIONAL SCIENCE

Carr and Kemmis (1986) argue for action research as 'critical educational science', and hence place it firmly within critical evaluation. They delineate five characteristics. First, it is based on a dialectical view of rationality. As such it involves the transformation of practices over time, and searching for correspondences and non-correspondences between practices and understandings; practices and situations; and understandings and situations. Action research is deliberately activist. They reject the 'determinism and physicalism' of objectivism, and the 'relativism and rationalist theory of action' of subjectivism (Carr and Kemmis, 1986: 184).

Second, it employs teachers' interpretative categories. Nonetheless, they strongly reject the idea that 'tacit theory' represents a variety of 'having a theory':

> It is a misuse of the notion of 'theory' to assert that it is something which one can hold 'implicitly' or unconsciously. Indeed, for the concept of 'theory' to have any power at all requires that it is something consciously held . . . , and that it is the product of reflection rather than mere habit, custom or coercion. (1986: 189)

Their aim is the 'informed, committed action' of praxis. 'Action research therefore cannot be other than research into one's own practice' (1986: 191).

Third, action research locates false consciousness. In doing so it also 'treats the actor as the bearer of ideology as well as the "victim"' (1986: 193). Fourth, action research will move from the organization of enlightenment to the organization of action, through the exposure of aspects of social order which frustrate change. In doing so, they emphasize the collective and collaborative dimensions of self-reflection and the dangers of the self-reflection of the lone subject.

Finally, action research unites theory and practice. They reject as 'irresponsible radicalism' the tendency of some critical theorists to suspect too great a practicality.

Carr and Kemmis give little explicit guidance on the design of action research. Research and evaluation of different forms of citizen involvement has crystallized several areas of good practice, based on the belief that 'there is, after all, rather glaring inconsistency in exploring involvement in an excluding and unparticipatory way' (Beresford, 1992: 18). Much of this good practice links with the terms of the fair evaluation agreement which were outlined earlier in this chapter in the discussion of justice as fairness. We can summarize this advice as follows.

First, clarify and mutually agree the *purpose of participation*. For example, it may be regarded by liberal agency managers as a means of improving service responsiveness, while service users may regard it as a means of user empowerment, 'to extend the capacity of users to participate in decisions about the design, management and review of services' (Barnes and Wistow, 1992: 4).

Second, be clear with each other regarding the different *kinds of 'users'* who may have an interest. Fisher, for example, suggests that much participatory evaluation is naïve in underplaying the differences between voluntary and 'captive' clients. 'A problem in the new voluntarist language of welfare consumerism is that too little recognition is given to users who are "captive"' (Fisher, 1992: 55). This leads to social workers wrongly assuming that an agreement exists with clients when no such agreement has been reached: 'It is part of the professional clothing to assume that the work is based on negotiation and agreement' (1992: 48). Such agreements tend to be coercive (it is voluntary as long as you agree); conditional (because aimed at some social work outcome); and constrained (through resource problems which limit genuine choice).

Fisher also underlines the significance of differences between short- and long-term service users, and current and potential users, and calls for care in recognizing organizational and resource issues which will place service users in competition with one another.

Third, establish genuine mechanisms for continued collaborative work. Verbal agreements are usually too non-specific, and are liable to chronic decay.

Fourth, seek agreement on whether the project or programme is evaluable. We considered this issue at the beginning of this chapter in discussing evaluability assessments. The particular problems that need underlining are the recurrent risks of intrusion and imposition: 'Whether intrusion into your life takes place in the name of "helping" or "researching" the experience, it seems, can feel all too similar if you are on the receiving end' (Davis, 1992: 37).

Finally, agree the harm to be avoided and the benefits to be gained by those who collaborate. In reflecting on an extensive project to involve carers in the processes of planning and review in an English local authority Social Services Department, Barnes and Wistow (1994) caution that there are dangers in giving insufficient thought to whether meeting the needs of the service planning system, and meeting the needs of users and carers who become involved in that system, are incompatible:

> Providers should be sensitive to the demands they are placing on people whose lives are already complex and demanding. They should be ready to ensure that people derive some direct benefits from participation, as well as ensuring that . . . participation is justified by the outcomes it achieves. (1994: 91)

We have explored the logics and values of qualitative evaluation, and the ways in which they shape decisions regarding evaluation design. We have considered different ways in which the evaluability of a project or programme may be assessed. Issues of consent and privacy provided the basis for a consideration of ethical problems surrounding evaluation design. We sketched in ways in which evaluators may take into account fresh thinking regarding the importance of social justice agendas.

Qualitative evaluation research can address outcome issues in evaluation, and the elaboration of this case has been a central argument in this chapter. Case studies can address such concerns among others, and we have reviewed the several issues which case study design must take on board. The chapter concluded with reflections on the design considerations raised by developments in participatory and action-oriented evaluation.

We open the next chapter with an introduction to the criteria which inform practical design decisions regarding data collection methods. Individual and group interviews, observation, life stories, official and life documents, and simulations are as much part of the repertoire of qualitative evaluation as of research. The evaluative purpose is, once more, what gives evaluation fieldwork its particular twist.

8

Evaluation in the field

CONTENTS

If we have been right in arguing throughout this book that inquiry is evaluative when it is marked by evaluative purpose, then the forms taken by evaluation fieldwork are likewise contingent on purpose. The methods will be neither entirely the same as nor completely different from those of qualitative research in general. For this reason I am reluctant to rule *any* methods of inquiry out of court. But I am equally unwilling to recommend the routine adoption of even the most apparently relevant methodological devices. Methodological automatism will produce awkward, clumsy evaluations, lacking both rigour and relevance.

Any good text on qualitative research methodology is translatable into the cluster of dialects that make up the purposes of evaluation. Some are written with a weather eye open to such translation (Bogdan and Taylor, 1994; Crabtree and Miller, 1992a; Holstein and Gubrium, 1995). Because they are less obviously prescriptive, these are at least as helpful for the evaluator as those written explicitly about either qualitative evaluation (Patton, 1990) or evaluation as a whole (Wholey, 1994).

My aim in this chapter is to provide an illustrative introduction to an evaluative perspective on fieldwork, rather than a potted inventory of field-work methods covered with greater depth elsewhere in the literature. In the main part of the chapter we will consider how evaluative purposes shape decisions to use interviews, observation methods, life stories, documents, focus group interviews and simulations. Whatever the method/s, there are recurring methodological fieldwork issues, and we turn to these in the latter part of the chapter. These include ongoing access issues, evaluating sensitive groups, evaluation of stakeholder and service user satisfaction, practitioner evaluation, and participatory evaluation for empowerment. We will conclude with a reminder of how ethical issues are raised not only at the commencement of qualitative evaluation, but throughout the fieldwork.

An illustration of the connection between method and evaluative perspective may help. Many evaluators are concerned with the *collaborative* aspects of their work. For example, Woods and Pollard point out that their case for synthesizing symbolic interactionism and education evaluation is not primarily based on a wish to forestall any particular method:

> Our point, rather, relates to purpose. Where this is to influence/change teacher practice and policy within schools, we are recommending an alternative model of research and teaching which involves working *with* the change agents with their own specifications more firmly in mind, rather than *on* them with our own purposes to the forefront. (1988: 15)

Similar 'working with' purposes have guided much of the work within approaches to evaluation which actively involve stakeholders. Weiss (1983a, 1983b), for example, makes the considered if relatively modest claims for stakeholder evaluation that it:

- improves the fairness of the evaluation
- marginally improves the range of information collected
- gives more say to local groups, and
- democratizes access to information.

However, she also concludes that it does not produce harmony or resolve conflicts among diverse groups. On the basis of these conclusions a researcher may negotiate a collaborative dimension to a given evaluation, but is unlikely to do so on strictly methodological grounds.

We saw in Chapter 6 that others advocate participatory or empowerment rather than simply collaborative models. Empowerment evaluators are generally mistrustful of methods, and wish to go 'beyond technique'.

However, the links between purpose and methods do not go away. Vanderplaat, the title of whose paper we have just quoted, believes that the emancipatory agenda in evaluation may be at odds with the available evaluation strategies. This lack of fit reveals itself in tenuous linkages between the discourse of empowerment and the practice of social programming. While she warns that a singular concern with technique can 'effectively stifle the practical and emancipatory knowledge to be gained from these efforts', she acknowledges that 'evaluation informed by critical concerns must neither ignore instrumental issues nor privilege them' (Vanderplaat, 1995: 94).

We will now apply this general argument about purpose to the uses of qualitative evaluation interviews, observation, life histories, personal texts and documents, and simulation methods. We steer our initial path by considering a methods choice decision that qualitative evaluators often make – should I use interviews, or observation, or some combination of both?

Evaluative fieldwork methods

One way in to deciding the relative benefits and limitations of using interviewing or observation methods within qualitative evaluation is to directly compare the gains and limitations of each.

EXAMPLE 8.1   EXPLORING PROFESSIONAL DECISION-MAKING

McKeganey and colleagues (1988) report such a comparison undertaken as part of a study of professional decision-making when people are to be offered a place in a home for the elderly. Their interests were in aspects of the micro-processes of decision-making, and to understand discretion and variations in such decisions. Table 8.1 summarizes the points of comparison and the weight that the research team attached to each of these in the context of their study.

TABLE 8.1   *Interviewing or observation for evaluating professional decision-making*

	Interviews	Observation
Data level	Individuals	Processes
Decision points	Multiple	Few
Triangulation of accounts	Strong	Less strong
Components of decisions	Formal	Informal
Routine decisions	Less strong	Strong
Non-decisions	Weak	Weak
Rationality/non-rationality of decisions	Overstate rationality	Strong on non-rationality
Disclosure of private accounts	Less strong	Adequate

Source: Based on McKeganey et al. (1988)

The researchers concluded that it was difficult to use observation to focus on individual decisions because decisions occur across several contexts. Interviews, by contrast, can cover every decision point. These researchers decided to target the contexts for their observation in the light of prior interview outcomes. Interviewing was also judged stronger as a means of triangulating accounts by different professionals. The notion of triangulation is a much used one, and often confusingly so, and we will have more to say on this issue in Chapter 9. For the moment, we should note that the problem of *weighing up* the different accounts may be mitigated but is not resolved by the decision to interview.

'There may be a tendency for interviewers and interviewees to concentrate on only the formal components of the decision-making process', whereas 'one of the benefits of observational work is precisely the capacity to focus attention upon the informal aspects of professionals' decision-making' (McKeganey et al., 1988: 16). This formal/informal aspect was also reflected in their judgement that taken for granted dimensions of decisions may be harder for people to articulate in interviews, and better accessed via observation.

Interviews may tend to recreate past decisions as if they were more rational than in fact they were. McKeganey and colleagues conclude that observational work can tap the more chaotic character of present decisions. Finally, they believe that professionals may use private decision categories that include moral or pejorative aspects – perhaps especially when the demand for a service outstrips the supply and they are obliged to ration. They concluded that interviews would be less likely to disclose these elements, and that observation would at least problematize the grounds of decision-making.

Two important caveats are in order following this example. First, method choices made as a consequence of any such comparison must not be treated as absolute but contextualized within the specific study. We cannot transfer the pros and cons of Table 8.1 lock, stock and barrel to all evaluations where a method choice of this kind is being made. There is no absolute reason, for example, why either interviews or observation methods cannot elicit non-decisions. These researchers have clearly contextualized their assessment of the two methods. Second, we have, of course, elided too much that is different in compressing interviews into a single, apparently homogeneous evaluation option.

Evaluative interviewing

Interviews range from the informal everyday talk that takes place in all kinds of research, through unstructured interviews which focus on a particular topic, semi-structured interviews using interview guides, through to structured interviews utilizing interview schedules. For reasons springing from the importance of local purpose, I am unwilling to say that interview approach X is generally best for evaluation, while interview approach Y should be eschewed. However, interviewing approaches that have been developed with methodological antennae attuned for evaluative applications repay efforts at translation. Holstein and Gubrium's advocacy of *active interviewing* is one such example, and applications of McCracken's exposition of the semi-structured *long interview* provide another (Holstein and Gubrium, 1995; McCracken, 1988).

Holstein and Gubrium's argument runs somewhat as follows. Older sociological perspectives treat the interview conversation as a pipeline for transmitting knowledge from the respondent to the interviewer. It has long been argued – with some success – that this entails a major oversight: 'Both parties to the interview are necessarily and unavoidably *active*. Each is involved in meaning-making work' (Holstein and Gubrium, 1995: 4). The work of constructivist, ethnographic and postmodern approaches has located the interactional procedures of knowledge production – the *how* of meaning making – centre stage. Holstein and Gubrium welcome this development, but believe that the centrality of the hows of social process has been achieved 'at the expense of the *whats* of lived experience' (1995: 5). They wish to reappropriate the significance of substance and content to studies of the social construction process.

We have already observed in Chapter 3 that relativist versions of social constructivism pose special difficulties for evaluation researchers committed to qualitative inquiry. Holstein and Gubrium appear to provide an approach which partially resolves such difficulties through a view of meaning as neither predetermined nor absolutely unique, and which therefore is not constantly formulated anew but reflects relatively enduring local conditions (1995: 16). They suggest that the interview should be framed as an occasion for narrative production, in which the respondent is envisioned as a story-teller of sorts. They describe and illustrate such interviewing, using examples from research on home carers for people with dementia, a community-based cancer control agency, involuntary commitment proceedings for persons allegedly mentally ill, and quality of life for nursing home residents.

Holstein and Gubrium's premise that the interview should aim to incite narrative production has several points of similarity with McCracken's development of qualitative, depth-interviewing which uses open, direct questions to elicit stories and case narratives. Miller and Crabtree applied it to an evaluation-related study of how family physicians and paired patients identify and understand their experiences of pain. Describing the interview as 'a dance of intimacy and distancing' (Miller and Crabtree, 1992: 203), they underscore the mutuality present in the interview discourse and the need for the interviewer to be open to the pain and uncertainty of self-discovery.

McCracken relates this aspect to the problem created by the dulling effects that deep and long-lived familiarity with a culture typically produces. His plea is for a detailed preliminary review of personal experience related to the topic of interest. Such a 'cultural review' calls for minute examination:

> The investigator must inventory and examine the associations, incidents and assumptions that surround the topic in his or her mind . . . The object is to draw out of one's experience the systematic properties of the topic. (McCracken, 1988: 32)

For Miller and Crabtree's study of the understanding and experience of pain, each member of the research team inventoried her or his own past pain incidents, associations and assumptions. They develop McCracken's original application in two ways, both of which may be useful in an evaluation context. First, they recommend that the discovery of cultural categories be expanded to include preliminary direct contact with individuals from the cultural group being studied. Second, in addition to the conceptualizing value of the exercise, they argue that 'the self-exploration also prepares a reservoir of empathy for the researcher when the respondent shares similar thoughts and emotions' (Miller and Crabtree, 1992: 199). Incorporating cultural reviews is not, of course, limited to interview-based evaluation.

EXAMPLE 8.2   CULTURAL REVIEW

Suppose I am preparing to interview a woman having difficulties coping with caring for her son of 25 who has serious learning disabilities and lives at home. A personal and cultural review will require me to do two things:

1   Make a list of the different topics that would need to be the focus of my self-inquiry for a cultural review.
2   Make a paragraph of notes on each of the topics in my list.

My list of topics might include

- Who have I cared for?
- My own feelings about being cared for by a close relative.
- My reaction to carrying out personal care tasks.
- My feelings about the boundaries between family time and work time.
- My definition and use of free time.
- How I view 'free time' compared with 'work time'.
- Satisfactions gained from caring.

- How do I react when there are restrictions on my time?
- Daytime caring and evening caring.
- Weekday caring and weekend caring.
- My ideal balance between time alone and time with family.

Having made my list of headings, the next stage is to make notes under each heading. For example, I have included *my feelings about being cared for* by a close relative or partner. If I resent the thought that I may at some time have to face physical dependency on a close relative, then this may make me unreasonably negative towards the person who is caring. I have also listed *my experience of caring*. In cases where male family members have forced a woman into a stereotypical caring role, she will be especially sensitive to the potential for discrimination that exists in the caring role in western societies.

There is, I suspect, a particular interviewing problem that is more likely to occur in evaluative research of the kind where insider stakeholders have a strong influence, than in conventional research. It can be best illustrated in the context of evaluation linked to occupations where interviewing is an established professional competence. For example, social work and some forms of psychiatry have on occasion been labelled the professions of the interview. Does it follow we can assume that these professionals possess good enough skills in the use of interviewing as a channel for evaluating? I am not persuaded. Interviews have been rightly developed as means of guaranteeing practice accountability, with the consequence that some styles of interviewing have become more common than others. In consequence, social work practitioners have perhaps been insufficiently sensitive to the essential interactive nature of all interviews. Cicourel (1964) long ago argued that we need to see the interview empirically, as one variation of interaction in everyday life, and as an example of encounters with strangers. Rees (1974) has suggested that social work interviews can be viewed in a similar light. 'Bias' and distortion should be viewed as normal, common-sense responses, and it will prove impossible to have a standardized interview presentation. The social typification of interviewer roles varying between culture and class, the constant interactive tension as one person tries to penetrate the private world of another, and the advantages and disadvantages of rapport, are dimensions of interviewing which may not be part of social workers' awareness.

Take, for instance, the issues raised by interviewing children (Shaw, 1996b). The work of Piaget and Kohlberg has been foremost in fostering an image of childhood as marked by a series of developmental stages. Qualitative work with children has consequently been viewed as finding age-appropriate ways for the 'knowing' adult to learn about children. The special nature of interviewing children is regarded as deriving from the limited extents to which children are able to comprehend language, articulate subjective experience and sustain affective relationships (Parker, 1984). This deficit model surfaces in the ways researchers worry aloud to their readers about such interviews. For example, Bierman and Schwartz's account of clinical interviews warns that pre-school children:

> *have trouble* holding more than one concept at a time in mind. Additionally, their conceptions are *limited* to ideas that can take concrete, observable forms. They are *unable* to consider alternative perspectives . . . They are *just learning* how to interpret others' emotions. (1986: 268; emphasis added)

This view of childhood as an unfolding of developmental stages has constrained the methods of many researchers, and led to a model of child interviewing which it is believed 'can help the clinician assess the developmental sophistication of the child's interpersonal style and social-emotional reasoning' (1986: 276).

There are disturbing consequences of a deficit model of this kind for the understanding of the cultures of children. Indeed, children are unlikely to be seen as having their own culture, or at most their culture will be seen according to its approximation to the culture and world of adults. One of the major forces initiating a welcome corrective to this research was the work of Cicourel on children's language, which presented a view of children as capable of having their own culture, generationally transmitted by children. On this very different view of children they are seen to possess interpretative competence equal to or even greater than adults, and as being potentially 'more creative, more honest, in short, in some ways more human than adults' (Goode, 1986: 84). Goode regards the model of children as tabula rasa, growing in developmental stages, as an ethnocentric 'adultism' in which researchers reveal themselves as parents writing slightly abstract versions of their own or other people's children.

Interviewing strategies in research with children and young people have developed from this position in two directions. First, there has been a welcome and quite widespread acceptance of children as persons who have similar rights to those of adults in regard to giving informed consent to research access. For example, Butler and Williamson (1994) gave children the choice as to how they wished to be interviewed – whether singly, in pairs or in groups. They had warm-up sessions with children and young people to convey this ethos and freedom to pursue a particular line of thought. They put them in control of both the tape-recorder and the length of interview. When conducting an individual interview they accepted that it 'does not lend itself to tight structures and defined sequences. Children jump around and researchers have to jump with them' (Butler and Williamson, 1994: 30). This often included responding to children's humour and recognizing their 'serious listening inside a funny shell' (1994: 46).

The second development in interviewing with children and young people is, if anything, more far reaching. At its heart it involves a major reversal of how we view the interview, so that it is seen not as a source of information from young informants, but as data in and of itself. For instance, talking to adolescents is not a means of gaining information about socialization processes but, from this perspective, is itself an instance of socialization. Baker's 'second look' at interviews with adolescents exemplifies this approach. She argues that 'the key to turning the interview into a resource is to view it as a real event in the real world – not only as a means of access to data but as data' (Baker, 1983: 501, 508). This allows her to see the way the interviews display their character as adult–young person social encounters in which adults are questioning adolescents. The questions contain an implicit adult theory of adolescence and answers contain an implicit adolescent theory of adulthood. Interviews are an occasion for the management of identity:

> Interviews are socialization sites. In these interviews adolescents are invited to show membership in the adult language community by making sense of the questions and developing the discourse with the interviewer. (Baker, 1983: 516–517)

Siegert similarly concludes that 'data from interviews which are conducted by an adult interviewer give us more insight into competences displayed by children in interaction with adults ... It is questionable, however, if these findings can be generalized to other contexts, especially to contexts of peer interaction' (Siegert, 1986: 373). Conclusions of this kind clearly have implications for the evaluation fieldwork encounter involving talk between adults and children in health, social work and educational settings.

Observation

Observation methods also need to be mediated through evaluative purpose (Tanner and Le Riche, 1999). To stay with children and young people, understanding the world of childhood pulls with both fascination and mystery. How many of us have delved into Iona and Peter Opie's books in order both to learn and to remember (Opie and Opie, 1959, 1969)? The problem with 'Kid Society' (the term is Glassner's) is their physical closeness and social distance: 'Our proximity to children may lead us to believe that we are closer to them than we really are – only differing in that ... children are still growing up ... and they are often wrong' (Fine and Sandstrom, 1988: 34). The value of participant observation is that we need to make these neighbours into strangers and by that route into peers if we are to get a sense of what it means to be a child, and be able to view the world 'through their hearts and minds' (1988: 12). In doing so we will struggle to mine our own experience, and be challenged to breech our own well-constructed defences.

Observational studies of children have fallen into three kinds. There are those which find that children are more mature or capable than we expect; observations that de-romanticize childhood and find they are more tendentious or rebellious; and finally inquiries that shed light on how the secret process of education, or socialization by peers, occurs. Fine and Sandstrom remark that 'we know of no study that has found that children are more "childish" than we have given them credit for' (1988: 72).

The challenge for evaluators who choose to observe with children is to 'capture the dynamics of children's interactions and to fit into children's interpretive acts without disturbing the flow' (Mandell, 1988: 464). Perhaps the single most important decision that an evaluator will take in deciding to observe with children is the nature of the observer role. This will range from the detached observer, through the 'special friend' role adopted by Corsaro (1985) in his excellent study of children in a nursery school, to the active, fully participating 'least adult role' practised by Mandell (1988) in observing two pre-school centres. Mandell advocates suspending all adult-like characteristics except physical size, and taking a role which minimizes social distance, suspends judgements on children's immaturities, engages in joint action with children, and risks being taken for a fool.

Life histories

There is a cluster of developments in life history work which are valuable for qualitative evaluation fieldwork. The study of the life story is an area where ethnography and clinical methods have at times been close (Martin, 1995, 1999). As Cohler puts it,

> Understood as . . . a presently recounted past, experienced present, and antici-
> pated future, the concept of narrative is central both to the systematic study of
> lives over time and to the effort to intervene in order to reduce the experience
> of personal distress. (1994: 167)

The proximity is well illustrated by Bowen's account in his paper 'The delights of learning to apply the life history method to school non-attenders' (Bowen, 1993). He had about twelve meetings with each of four people who had currently or recently experienced serious education problems, ending up with eight or nine hours of audio-taped conversations. Three of these people wrote autobiographies of between 5,000 and 12,000 words.

Empowerment evaluation has led to the development of critical life stories (Barone, 1992; Clifford, 1994). Barone describes the benefits he believes accrue from critical story-telling. The authors of such stories 'attempt to make palpable and comprehensible the pain and the cruelty of isolation inflicted on people' (Barone, 1992: 146). He identifies the phases through which such 'qualitative problem-solving' moves, and gives an example from a case study of Billy Charles Barnett, who was a potential school drop-out.

- A catalogue of incoherent snippets as 'phenomena flicker without discernible pattern' (1992: 144).
- Tentative relationship with 'structured fragments' (1992: 144).
- A single metaphor or pervasive quality emerges. In the case of Billy Barnett this was the idea of riskiness, and combating the relentlessly encroaching civilization of which school was a part. Billy becomes a symbol for all those 'endangered by educational institutions' (1992: 145).
- The selection of material and the final story.

Barone concludes, 'It is my hope that ever more of today's qualitative educational inquirers will use their privileges to tell stories that enable readers to locate the source of that pain' (1992: 146).

A rather different approach is that represented by the growth of interest in 'life course sociology'. Once again, it should be emphasized that such methods are not intrinsically 'evaluation' and have usually been developed by researchers who would not regard their work as evaluation. The cultivating and grafting of these methods on to evaluative purpose is a constant requirement. Life course analysis 'places change and development at the heart of the analysis and seeks to explore the inevitable temporal dimension of our lives and experiences' (Morgan, 1985: 177).

EXAMPLE 8.3 HOUSING BIOGRAPHIES

Clapham, Means and Munro point out that housing research has tended to rely on snapshot pictures with little idea of how people reach their present housing position. They advocate seeing old age, and housing in old age, as:

> stages in the life course which can only be understood by reference to previous experience and the attitudes and choices of people and the opportunities open to them during the whole life course. (Clapham et al., 1993: 133)

Researchers proceed by constructing a personal biography through in-depth qualitative interviews, to understand how they reached their present housing situation. The interview focus is on why certain options were chosen and others rejected. It incorporates a recognition that class, gender and ethnic differences do not disappear with old age. Unlike a purely biographical approach distinctions are made between the different types of time in which housing pathways are structured. These include individual time (age, state of health, etc.); family time (the stage of the family life cycle at which certain decisions were taken or imposed); and historical time (the prevailing economic, social and political conditions).

There are obvious potential benefits from sharing a story, including a sense of perspective, self-knowledge, creation of community, and a better sense of how someone wants their own story to end (Atkinson, 1998). However, Atkinson risks sentimentalizing the story-telling process. Selwyn, for example, records a study in which prospective adopters told her their stories of how they came to apply to adopt, and their response to being judged 'failed' applicants. The interviews depict not only their painful experience of rejection, but also served in some instances to reawaken partly contained feelings of anger, wasted lives, emptiness and anticipated years of loneliness (Selwyn, 1991, 1996).

Texts and documents

The experience, stories and texts of pupils, parents, patients, carers and service users, and the re-storying of these in the informal narratives of professional conversation, case records, inter-agency reports, and so on, make up a rich yet frequently enigmatic store of material relevant to evaluation. Much of the guidance in the literature can be read and taken on board without too much re-working. This includes discussion of distinctions between oral and written texts, the significance of the audiences for whom they were first and subsequently envisaged, the varying levels of access to such texts, and the criteria of authenticity, accuracy, sincerity, representativeness, and meaning against which they may be assessed (Scott, 1990).

Much of this has been routinely taken on board in the literature on evaluation methodology, and in reports of evaluation studies. Yet there remain several lacunae in the use of records in evaluation. For example, there is an almost exclusive reliance on official and quasi-official documents, usually those generated by the organization sponsoring the programme and facilitating the evaluation. Qualitative evaluators will be sensitive to the opportunities for using other forms of text, especially in evaluation depicting stakeholder interests, practitioner evaluation, and participatory or empowerment evaluation.

Clandinin and Connelly (1994) have provided an acute review of personal experience methods in qualitative research, drawing on their earlier research work carried out in school settings. They distinguish between annals and chronicles. *Annals* can be envisaged as a 'line' that schematizes an individual's life, divided into moments or segments by events, places, years or significant memories. This allows a sense of the whole, including highs and lows, and the rhythms people construct around their life cycle. *Chronicles* are an elaboration of a single point in the annal. Both together are 'a way to scaffold their oral histories' (1994: 420), and recollect their experiences. They are also a way to begin to hear a person's family stories. These stories about family members and events are handed down across generations. Through them people learn self identity, both internally and in the relation of the family to the world. Photographs, correspondence, trinkets and other artefacts mark times, events and persons, around which stories are constructed and reconstructed, often by women to children.

Journals provide a way of giving accounts of experience. Clandinin and Connelly quote a delightful analogy to the effect that journal entries were to one woman like tiny children's sweets which are so small that separately they are not worth eating, but which together provide a pattern of enjoyment. Children and adolescents often keep journals of their thoughts, activities and stories. Most of these remain private, and it is usually only the accident of history that brings to public view the childhood writings of an Anne Frank or the Brontë children. Text-based childhood memories are more often emotions recollected in the relative tranquillity of older years. But it is likely, for example, that some children and young people keep journals as attempts to make sense of their experiences – 'capturing fragments of experience in attempts to sort themselves out' (Clandinin and Connelly: 1994: 421). Adults speaking of their experiences as a child raise special difficulties for the hearer. Who is speaking?

> Is it the adult interpreting the childhood experience, in which case it is the adult speaking. Or is it the adult expressing the child's story as the child would have told the experience, in which case it is the child speaking. (1994: 424)

The texts of personal experience disclose the scene and plot, the dimensions of place and time. Plot, meaning and interpretation are far from straightforward. Today's meanings may become items in tomorrow's chronicle of events, as the participants change their understandings.

Focus groups

One of the more promising developments in applying qualitative and participatory evaluation has come through work on focus groups (Dean, 1994; Kitzinger, 1994; Kreuger, 1994; Morgan, 1993, 1997). Focus groups originate from market research, but also draw stimulus from the work of the American sociologist Robert Merton, on focused interviews. They take the form of group discussions organized to explore a specific set of issues: 'The group is *focused* in the sense that it involves some kind of collective activity – such as viewing a film, evaluating a single health education message or simply debating a particular set of questions' (Kitzinger, 1994: 159). The planning and design of focus groups hinges mainly on decisions about the role of the group moderator, the development of the group agenda, the balance of openness and pre-structuring, recruitment methods, and decisions about group composition. Current best practice is to work with homogeneous groups: 'Holding separate sessions with homogeneous but contrasting groups is believed to produce information in greater depth than would be the case with heterogeneous groups' (Knodel, 1993: 40).

Focus groups have three particular advantages for qualitative evaluation. First, the group interaction is itself the data – 'the interaction is the method' (Jarrett, 1993: 198). Kitzinger says in summary that the method 'enables the researcher to examine people's different perspectives as they operate within a social network and to explore how accounts are constructed, expressed, censored, opposed and changed through social interaction' (1994: 159).

Second, focus groups are a form of participatory evaluation. They are valuable when there is a power differential between participants and decision-makers, and hence have considerable potential for application within qualitative evaluation. Finally, they introduce a valuable approach to learning the extent of consensus on a particular issue: 'The co-participants act as co-researchers taking the research into new and often unexpected directions and engaging with each other in ways which are both complementary . . . and argumentative' (Kitzinger, 1994: 166).

The majority of writers in this field have opposed the application of focus groups to anything other than research or formal evaluation purposes. In my view this is an unhelpful generalization. Focus groups also have a particular contribution to make to practitioner and participatory evaluating. Exercises in problem setting, project development, anti-discriminatory practice, addressing projects that have become 'stuck', consumer feedback exercises, and evaluating sensitive topics, are all ways in which focus groups have something to offer to qualitative evaluating. Gibbs summarizes the case for focus groups:

> [They] are particularly useful when there are power differences between the participants and decision-makers or professionals, when the everyday use of language and culture of particular groups is of interest, and when one wants to explore the degree of consensus on a given topic. (1997)

Despite the promise of this method, focus groups should be used within their limitations. The current almost knee-jerk adoption of group interviews labelled focus groups, regardless of their mode of operation, is way too undiscriminating. Focus groups, for example, always rely on interaction within the group based on topics that are supplied by the researcher. There is little or no research evidence on the relative benefits of focus groups against interview methods (but see Kitzinger), and there are situations where focus groups probably should not be used. They should not be used if the practitioner's intention is to improve participants' communication or group skills. More generally, they should not be adopted for therapeutic purpose, or when the main purpose is to secure immediate action. If information, understanding or explanation is not central to the group's agenda, then other methods of intervention should be used. It may also be difficult for the researcher to clearly identify individual messages within the group. There are other practical constraints on focus group work. If personal views cannot readily be expressed in such a context, or if breaches of confidentiality are likely to be a problem, then the method should not be used. When group members know each other particularly well focus groups are also ill-advised. Finally, bearing in mind the benefits of homogeneous group membership, it is not advisable to run focus groups comprising both patients/pupils/carers and evaluators/professionals.

Simulations

Simulations have the potential to provide 'a unique and innovative tool that has not yet been widely applied' in evaluation (Turner and Zimmerman, 1994: 335). They have two main applications – first, as an evaluative test for service discrimination, and second, as a qualitative proxy for control within a natural setting.

The first application typically entails the use of paired role players (man/woman; white/black; able-bodied/with a disability). The pairs present themselves separately to a given service, and present themselves as similar in terms of eligibility and need. 'To date, paired role playing has been used principally to test for racial and ethnic discrimination in housing and employment' (Turner and Zimmerman, 1994: 332), but the method will work equally well in evaluating the allocation of a given scarce resource, where the elements of judgement and discretion are present. For example, a variant of the method using just one researcher has been planned whereby a professionally qualifying social work student with a sight disability will apply for advertised social work posts, and systematically vary whether the disability is disclosed, as a test of the operation of non-discriminatory employment policies.

The second application is of more recent development, and represents an advance on the use of vignettes in policy research. Those who evaluate the process of professional practice come face to face with the invisibility of practice. How may we learn the ways in which lawyers, accountants, general medical practitioners, or social workers practice? How would different professionals deal with the same case? The methods we have discussed hitherto do not directly address this problem. Wasoff and Dobash (1992, 1996) have however, used a promising innovatory method in their study of how a specific piece of law reform was incorporated into the practice of solicitors. The use of simulated clients in 'natural' settings allowed them to identify practice variations that could be ascribed with some confidence to differences between lawyers rather than the artefacts of differences between cases.

Suppose, for example, that one wishes to carry out a qualitative evaluation of decisions made by housing managers, medical staff and social workers regarding the allocation of care management packages. Evaluators using simulated clients would prepare a small number of detailed case histories designed to test the practice decisions under consideration. A researcher or evaluator takes on the role of the client in the case history. The housing manager, relevant medical staff and social workers each interview the 'client' within the 'natural' setting of their work.

The method is a development of role play methods, and yet it is rather different. Role play has been used almost entirely within training courses and much less so in evaluation practice. Also, role play has been used for skill development and not for understanding and evaluation. The administration of the exercise is also very different from role playing, in that the scenario is much more detailed, and the researcher acting as the client or patient is the only one who is in a role. The professional is playing it for real, and the setting is not constructed.

The use of simulated clients has several things going for it. First, some evaluators are likely to be familiar with the 'family' of methods from which it is drawn. Second, other methods are not always feasible for practical or ethical reasons. Simulated clients overcome the ethical problems of seeking the co-operation of genuine clients. Above all, thirdly, it makes practice visible. It will be clear from the brief description that the method could not be a tool for evaluating particular cases, but would focus on specific *kinds* of practice.

There are limitations to the application of simulation methods. The method needs additional resourcing to prepare the case material, perhaps to act the role of clients, and to reflect on the quite detailed material that results from transcriptions of the interviews. The cost is therefore likely to be relatively high, and it requires reasonably high levels of research skills. The discrimination-test version is best applied to service *entry* issues. It is much harder to utilize the method to test for discrimination at other organizational levels, because of the additional ethical issues of prolonged covert evaluation. Finally, the use of simulation for discrimination testing risks raising concerns regarding entrapment.

Themes and issues in qualitative evaluation fieldwork

The choice of specific methods cannot be considered unarticulated from the themes and issues discussed earlier in the book. These include initial and continuing access issues, the frequency with which evaluation involves contact with groups where inquiry raises sensitive issues, and problems arising from reaching estimates of pupil, patient, client or service user satisfaction. Fieldwork issues are also present in practitioner evaluation, and participatory or empowerment evaluation. Finally, there are ethical matters throughout the data-gathering phase of evaluative inquiry. We will point up the main aspects of these themes and issues in the following paragraphs.

Yin also recommends the creation of a case study database to include fieldnotes, documents and narratives, and to maintain a chain of evidence: 'The principle is to allow an external observer . . . to follow the derivation of any evidence from initial research questions to ultimate case study conclusions' (Yin, 1994: 98).

Access

Access is not simply a hermetically sealed set of negotiations that occurs at the design stage of evaluative research: 'The possible combinations of investigator, setting, and participant attributes generate an almost endless litany of discrete "access situations"' (Lofland and Lofland, 1995: 22). Much of the experience and guidance developed in the mainstream research literature transfers readily to evaluation and needs no repeating here (for a solidly practical discussion see Hornsby-Smith, 1993).

The relationship of the evaluator to the setting is perhaps the most frequently misunderstood problem in evaluative research. This stems from the recurring tendency of evaluators to overrate the value of commencing evaluation as an insider. This is not true of all evaluation theorists. We saw earlier in the book the lengths to which Scriven (1997) goes in damning insider research. There are sound grounds for caution. Insider status may in fact *limit* access in that while the ascribed status already held by the insider is likely to open up access to some parts of an organization, it is just as likely to close it to others. The problems of theoretical taken-for-grantedness are more obvious for insiders who are more likely to believe that they already 'know' how things really are, hence disrupting the potential for the anthropological strangeness of the incomer. Referring to teacher-researchers, Burgess believes:

> many teachers have found it difficult to question such everyday concepts as teaching, learning, and assessment and definitions of 'good' and 'bad' pupils. Furthermore several teachers have encountered difficulties in asking naïve questions about the aims and objectives of a school. (1980: 169)

The Loflands conclude:

> The moral is this: be neither discouraged nor overconfident about your relationship to your setting. Whatever that relationship, it is simultaneously an advantage and a drawback. (Lofland and Lofland, 1995: 23)

The issue almost always rears its head in practitioner evaluation. The teacher-researcher, for example, faces the dilemma of whether to engage in covert evaluation with the associated problems of limited access. Alternatively, should she engage in semi-covert research by informing her colleagues and pupils but not the headteacher? Or conversely, discuss the inquiry with the headteacher but no one else? Burgess believes that this last option is the most frequent strategy. However, it raises the further problem in that while it provides support the researcher may have taken on the role of the spy or collaborator: 'Pupils may view the teacher-researcher more as a teacher-spy than as a researcher' (Burgess, 1980: 168). The consequent ethical dilemmas are real: 'Teacher-researchers have found evidence in projects on homework of colleagues who do not set this work and pupils who spend little time on it' (1980: 168).

Davies and Kelly (1976) sensitively and honestly recounted some years ago the extent to which problems of access, and associated ethical and political concerns, can move centre-stage during an evaluation. They provide a retrospective account of a participant observation evaluation of a city centre project in the north of England, working with drifting and homeless young people. The Loflands (1995) suggest that the successful negotiation of factions of a kind similar to those faced by Davies and Kelly, depends on:

- The perception by the participants that the researcher is truly an outsider to the dispute.
- The continued perception of the researcher's impartiality relative to the dispute.
- The researcher's scrupulous honesty about the fact of studying both sides, combined with scrupulous confidentiality regarding the content of each side's private views and strategies (that is, not playing double agent).
- Possession of a great deal of accurate information about what each side knows of the other throughout the life of the conflict.

Evaluation and sensitive topics

I have deliberately drawn extensively on examples of evaluation involving children and young people during this chapter partly in order to make the point that qualitative evaluators will engage in evaluative research which is sensitive. Such sensitivity may inhere in the evaluative problem, the methodology, or the relationship between the interests of inquiry participants. We do not, of course, imagine we can make a prior decision as to whether or not a given evaluation will be 'sensitive'. *Any* evaluation will vary in how 'sensitive' it is, either to different participants or at different stages of the evaluation.

Evaluation does not raise problems of sensitivity which are materially different from those faced in qualitative research, and there has been a growing literature (Lee, 1993; Renzetti and Lee, 1992; Zeller, 1993). Unfortunately it has yet to find its way fully into the evaluation literature. McKeganey and Bloor (1991) remark on a neglected example, in their discussion of ways in which relations between participants are gendered. Reflecting on participatory research in therapeutic communities, an adolescent drugs unit, and in home help services, they concluded that there are two aspects of gendered relations that are likely to be given insufficient recognition. First, although cultural blindness to same sex relations made access to males easier for them as male researchers, the activities and conversations of within-gender relations were still markedly gendered.

Second, in cross-gender relations sexual interpretations may be made of which the researcher is not aware:

> In everyday life there is recurrent slippage between gendered relationships and relationships with a sexual component. Many everyday asexual relationships frequently become problematic or ambiguous for one or both participants, with one party considering a possible sexual interpretation of an utterance or action of another. (McKeganey and Bloor, 1991: 209)

Satisfaction

> The boys would have said they enjoyed it, and they would probably say it made them think. They would probably have less faith in its effectiveness than I did. A few of them were quite critical. 'Yeah, well it's fine you can sit and talk about those things in here, but it's not like that out in the real world.' (Probation Officer)

This British probation officer is reflecting on the problems which arise when satisfaction questions are asked. There is widespread evidence that satisfaction surveys produce a uniformly high proportion of positive answers. In consequence, it has usually not proved feasible to differentiate which service users are more or less likely to be satisfied, and satisfaction surveys often do not tell us what needs to be changed. A strategy which appears at first glance to promise empowerment for service users can too easily prove a prop for conservatism and inaction. The risk is created that 'through high levels of relatively meaningless expressions of satisfaction an illusion of consumerism is created which seldom does anything but endorse the status quo' (Williams, 1994: 515). To understand why this is the case, we have to explore what takes place when consumers are asked to evaluate service provision.

For example, citizens may believe they do not have any control over the outcomes of their involvement with public officials. Without this measure of influence the very idea of evaluation will probably seem alien and meaningless. Furthermore, if a service is seen as a favour rather than a benefit to which the person is entitled, or as a sanction (for offending behaviour, personal failure, or breakdown), then criticism will be seen as a high risk strategy with no obvious benefits. Advocates of consumerism too easily ignore power differentials between professionals and their assumed beneficiaries.

The more that people see themselves as powerless the more likely they are to adjust their aspirations regarding what they can reasonably expect to gain from the exchange. They may come to adopt what Fisher and his colleagues recognized, in their work on the experiences of children cared for by the local authority and their families, as a strong sense of fatalistic resignation – a passive acceptance especially by mothers, of the loss of parental rights over their children (Fisher, Marsh and Phillips, 1986). In a similar manner, the sick role occupied by hospital patients requires passivity on their part. In his helpful discussion of whether satisfaction is a valid concept, Williams aptly remarks that this passivity might make the very idea and legitimacy of evaluation unfounded: 'In such a scenario patient satisfaction could be said to be primarily a reflection of the role patients adopt in relation to health professionals irrespective of the quality of the care itself' (1994: 513). Because of this dependency relationship consumers may simultaneously feel both gratitude and dissatisfaction with a service, and the quality of care may be worse than surveys of satisfaction seem to indicate. In other words 'consumerism is dependent on a refusal to accept paternalism; it relies on the existence of consumers and not passive patients' (1994: 514).

A final problem stems from the appreciation that consumer evaluations 'are relative to context, to knowledge of services available, to expectations, to help received in past encounters, to help received from other sources, to perceptions of the "pleasantness" of the social worker' (Rees and Wallace, 1982: 72). The point is in no way restricted to social work. An expression of satisfaction with a given service is a relative judgement – a comparison between aspirations and perceived status and well-being following the receipt of a service. Decontextualized measures of satisfaction are not sufficient. Evaluators and practitioners also need to know the nature and level of a service user's level of aspiration and their self-assessed personal status and well-being. Unless such factors are taken into account 'we can never be sure whether the high rate of client satisfaction is related more to factors like lack of knowledge or limited expectations, than the actual helpfulness of social service contact' (Rees and Wallace, 1982: 77).

The conclusion from all this is not that consumer satisfaction judgements should be abandoned. Narrative inquiry approaches to obtaining satisfaction overcome some of these problems by enabling participants in the evaluation to avoid the context-stripping tendencies of survey estimates. But satisfaction measures are not a panacea. They are difficult to interpret and utilize, and may prove politically disempowering.

Satisfaction inquiries are often carried out on a small sale, insider basis, and are especially prone to the problems we have identified. Good evaluative practice for assessing satisfaction has been suggested by some writers (Pryce-Jones, 1993; Shaw, 1996a). For example, evaluators should not rely on global ratings of satisfaction. Satisfaction must always be understood in the light of contextualized *aspirations* and *expectations*. It may be helpful to distinguish between preferred (or ideal) expectations, and practical (or realistic) expectations. A general response saying 'satisfied' may mean any of the following:

- I've evaluated the service and I'm happy with it.
- I don't think I have the ability to evaluate but I do have confidence in the staff.
- The service was appalling but I don't like to criticize; after all they're doing their best.

A final word of caution is in order. Consumer satisfaction, without other evidence, should not normally be regarded as an indication of success. It is tempting and unfair to draw that conclusion simply because we have made people happy about their experience. Fisher goes as far as to conclude that:

> Ratings of satisfaction cannot . . . be taken as a guide to the success of the service in meeting either its own goals or those of the clients. Such measures relate primarily to the quality of the encounter between worker and client, not to its outcome. (1983: 42)

Practitioner and empowerment evaluation

We opened this chapter with an illustration of the interplay of method and purpose in participatory and empowerment evaluation. Rather than revisit that discussion, I want to try to move closer to practitioners as they talk about their evaluation. In the following paragraphs Searight is discussing her observation and analysis of her practice as a therapist. Miller is describing an extended project in which she worked with others to extend the concept of teacher as researcher into reciprocal and interactive forms. Searight has reservations about the wider usefulness of the model she followed, while Miller believes there are transformative possibilities in the work that she and her colleagues undertook.

EXAMPLE 8.4   SELF-EVALUATION OF FAMILY THERAPY WITH CHILDREN HAVING BEHAVIOUR DISORDERS

Searight (1988) used a form of participant observation, informal interviews, and a mix of audio and narrative recordings in her work with eleven families. Her concerns were: how contexts relate to self-evaluation; the significance of the therapist's participation in the client's world; the varying perspectives of practitioners, co-therapists and clients; and how the meanings held by these people give shape and character to self-evaluation.

She proceeded on the assumption that the researcher needs to participate in the subject's world of meanings, and that this does not necessarily entail participation in the client's environment. She observed direct therapy events, including observed events in homes and the community. She observed all therapy sessions over a period of sixteen months.

Her own perspective changed, although it was not until the analysis that she grasped some understanding of these changes. Indeed, a central issue was that 'the practitioner-evaluator could not focus on data collection and be a full participant in practice evaluations simultaneously' (Searight, 1988: 312). Her conclusions go still further. She conducted the majority of the analysis after she left the setting, and concludes 'the examination of context, especially agency and institutional, seems particularly difficult while remaining in the setting' (1988: 314).

However, the model has utility in that it obliges the practitioner to define practice as including not only skills but also contexts of practice. In addition to the analytic benefits of this approach it 'helps the worker to move away from over-personalizing practice' (1988: 328) and avoid an individualized blame approach when practice goes wrong: 'Contexts are at least as important as skills in practice evaluation' (1988: 330). This goes a small way to countering a recognized weakness of self-evaluation, that it frequently fails to ask critical questions or locate projects within broader societal frameworks.

The discourse of empowerment advocates the idea of people producing change within and to their environment, rather than they themselves being the object of change producing strategies. Miller and her collaborators record a persuasive instance of such inquiry which takes practitioner research into different territory (Miller, 1990, 1992; Miller and Martens, 1990).

EXAMPLE 8.5   TEACHERS COLLABORATING FOR EMPOWERMENT

Miller worked with a group of her former graduate students who all held school posts. The group worked together for at least six years. They kept transcripts of their meetings, and each group member agreed to keep a journal, hence 'disrupting totalizing narratives which dissolve difference and contradiction' (Miller and Martens, 1990: 47).

They had early misgivings about the term emancipatory research, as a kind of 'authoritative discourse' (Miller, 1990: 16) from someone else. There was a constant struggle 'not to impose the concept of empowerment upon others in the name of liberation' (1990: 18; Miller, 1992). There were three constraints on their collaboration. First, they needed determination and mutual support to find space and time to meet and keep journals. Second, they spent cycles of time working through 'layers of embedded expectation' (Miller, 1990: 70). The constant telling of their stories kept the group from being captured by a single narrative. Third, they had to live with uncertainty. The process provoked 'private yet unsettling discrepancies within their educator roles' (1990: 77) and a wish for the right answer. The recurring issues they faced included:

- The worry that there may be 'nothing there'.
- A constant re-surfacing of 'conceptualizations of knowledge determined by someone else's research' (1990: 71). The standard separation of research and practice 'confounded our efforts to conceive of research as *praxis*' (1990: 73).
- The uncertainty, in the words of one member, of 'are we doing this right?'
- No one to talk to outside the group who shared their assumptions about becoming creators rather than transmitters of objective knowledge. The typical school does not encourage or welcome inquiry and reflection on work. The irony of their inquiry was that they were part of an institution that perpetuated the technical rationality model of research and evaluation they wished to challenge.
- 'The halting and undulating nature of our quest to become challengers' (1990: 70).

The group addressed 'the tensions between our desire for community and support in these explorations and the dangers of a collective unity that might veil the differences among us' (1990: 150). They also reflected on the significance of 'small' changes. One member recorded:

> I realized that, finally, I didn't really care about the end product – the lesson plans – with the students. It was the process, the struggling with the mess, the naming of the discrepancies that I really wanted . . . I guess this seems like a small step, but it is such a big one for me, given my whole rootedness in prescription. (1990: 138–139)

The group was sceptical regarding the teacher as researcher solution: 'We wonder if the label, teacher-as-researcher, in fact contributes in subtle ways to those theoretical and practical distinctions that continue to obscure the ways in which teaching itself is a "quiet form of research"' (1990: 150). They were also concerned that teacher research provides little if any challenge to the often hierarchical nature of university-formulated research agendas and interpretations of classroom teachers' work (Miller and Martens, 1990). Miller later reflects on classroom teachers and administrators that,

> The primary modes of analysis and self-reflective inquiry for most of them are not lodged within academic discourses or qualitative research methodology or the written word, but rather within the daily teaching, administering and counselling they do in their respective school buildings. (Miller, 1992: 170)

Thus, when the group came to discuss power issues, they 'were not couched in direct attempts to address issues of power and authority within qualitative research. They were attempts to address situations of power and authority in schools' (1992: 171).

Heron follows the language of Neitzsche in distinguishing between Apollonian and Dionysian cultures of co-operative inquiry. The Apollonian inquiry follows a rational cycle of sequences and steps – plan, act, observe and reflect, then re-plan. The Dionysian inquiry takes a more 'imaginal, expressive, spiralling, diffuse, impromptu and tacit approach to the interplay between making sense and action' (Heron, 1996: 46). Heron places his own work in the Apollonian culture. The work of Miller and her colleagues is a valuable incentive to risk the emergent uncertainties of Dionysian collaborative evaluation. The success of this group in holding to a shared commitment, yet within a context of multiple uncertainties, is very impressive.

Fieldwork ethics

The two previous examples assume the pervasive character of ethical issues in fieldwork. Lofland and Lofland (1995) list the main ongoing ethical concerns likely to occur in qualitative research:

- Is it ethical to see a severe need for help and not respond to it directly?
- Is it ethical to take a calculated stance towards other human beings?
- Is it ethical to take sides or to avoid taking sides in a factionalized situation?
- Is it ethical to 'pay' people with trade-offs for access to their lives and minds?

Each of these problems finds particular expression in the evaluation relationship. Feminist work has accomplished more than any other development to bring these issues to the forefront (Acker, et al., 1983; Ellsworth, 1989; Stacey, 1988). The research of Acker, Barry and Esseveld was on the relation between changes in the labour market situation of women, and changes in consciousness. They tried three strategies to reduce unequal power and acknowledge the subjectivity of the participants, although they admit they did not solve this problem:

1 Encourage the interviewee to take the lead in deciding what to talk about. This did not always work. The women often wanted to be asked questions. However, the approach did work better for those women with whom they had more than one interview.
2 Establish reciprocity, by offering to tell women something of themselves. This was accepted and often invited, and 'we formed friendships with many of the women' (1983: 428):

> However, we recognized a usually unarticulated tension between friendship and the goal of research. The researcher's goal is always to gather information, thus ... attempting to create a more equal relationship can paradoxically become exploitation and use. (1983: 428)

3   Show their written material to the women. However, they did not do
so with all of them. They admit that they shared most with 'those who
identified themselves as consciously trying to change'. They were
therefore the women who 'most shared our worldview', and 'we have
to admit some reluctance to share our interpretations with those who,
we expected, would be upset by them' (1983: 428). This raises the issue
of whether the evaluator should share interpretations with those
whose explanations are radically different from their own. This is the

> tension between the goal of reducing the power differences between the
> researcher and the researched and the difficulties of carrying this out when
> there is a lack of agreement on the meaning of experiences. (1983: 429)

Ethical issues need contextualizing, regardless of where we stand on
issues of relativity and relativism. A concluding example illustrates the
form this may take. It is drawn from a round-table discussion of ethics
which took place at a symposium on homelessness and social exclusion
organized in 1996 by the Paris-based Conseil National de L'Information
Statistique. I have retained the round-table format in the following
example, without disclosing the identity of the participants.

EXAMPLE 8.6   ETHICS AND HOMELESSNESS RESEARCH

Chair. She summarized the ethical issues in this field as linked to:

1   The purpose of any inquiry.
2   The balance of the value of the inquiry against the degree of intrusion.
3   Who are the beneficiaries? Is the respondent a beneficiary?
4   How is the information obtained?
5   How will it be used? Issues of privacy, and potential misinter-
pretation of the findings.

Discussant 1 argued that ethical issues are not *greater* in homelessness research but they do need *more careful formulation*. He believed
that they include:

* The right of refusal at *the point of contact*. But this right cannot be
exercised on someone's behalf. He was against the right of any
group to make a collective decision on behalf of others not to participate.
* *The interview.* There is a need for privacy of space. This may be
a special difficulty in homelessness research.
* *The content of the interview.* The emphasis of such interviews is
frequently on negatives – the deficiencies of the responder.

- *Ending the interview.* Offering some trade-off is difficult due to the lack of an address, but it is a central issue.

Discussant 2 referred to possible payment of interviewees. This is very rare in French research. On the one hand it poses the problem of paternalism. Yet consent to be interviewed can result in people losing their turn at a soup kitchen or 'begging' time. Their solution was to give a telephone card at the end of the interview, but not to say in advance that this would happen. The card allows contact with family and friends, and cannot be used directly to harm themselves.

Discussant 3 was concerned with the ethics of longitudinal research carried out in America. He reported research in which 1,500 interviews were undertaken, from which 500 were followed through at two-monthly intervals over about sixteen months. The ethics issues he identified were:

- *Paying.* It is the American standard practice in research to pay for long interviews. He acknowledged there might be risks attached to giving money, but argued for a non-paternalist stance on payment.
- *Privacy.* There is a problem of knowing how the information will be used. For example, it could be damaging to a homeless person to ask a third party (perhaps an official) for information related to the individual's homelessness. It may jeopardize the likelihood that the agency supplying information will continue to offer 'service'. As a partial solution they gave a non-damaging title to the research. Instead of naming it 'The Course of Homelessness Study' they called it 'The Course of Housing Study'.
- Implications of *obligations* arising from long-term relationships with people.

Discussant 4, a street level social worker, distinguished those who are 'sentenced to give' (social workers), and those who are 'sentenced to receive'. 'People who are homeless have been made cuckolds by life.'

It is what happens *after* the research that matters. How can we give back to them the knowledge they gave us? Learning to receive is the key ethical issue. He acknowledged he had no real answer to this problem of giving back. He had been involved in the organization of an art exhibition for homeless people, where the money gained was kept for collective use. He remarked that we also give back by keeping the information in ourselves. Listening as well as answering is part of giving back. Sometimes the person cannot be contacted or may die – but we are to become 'watchful' in our own behaviour.

Discussant 1 argued that the interview does have benefit. It can enable people not to see life as fate (for example, by learning to read behind the figures). This should be part of our ethical concerns. Finally, we should not forget the collective benefits of research. Judgements of benefit do not have to be limited to the immediate beneficiary.

The central themes of this chapter have been the articulation of evaluation purpose and method, the local contextualization of decisions about specific methods, and the issues and themes which are raised by their use. The same twin themes apply to the analysis of evaluation evidence, and it is that to which we turn in the final chapter.

9

Analysis: establishing evaluative claims

CONTENTS

Data analysis is not a discrete element of the evaluation process which can neatly be bracketed off. Indeed, we have come almost full circle. In the opening chapter we reflected on the *evaluative* dimension of this book, and also on the sense in which it is about *qualitative* evaluation. This final chapter is about how we may provide grounding for qualitative evaluation claims. It may feel almost tedious if I say once more that I do not believe there is a single, coherent package deal into which we buy. Evaluation is distinguished by its identifying purposes, rather than by a distinct methodology. As for evaluation design and fieldwork, so the strategies of analysis will be shaped by these particular purposes.

The pool of strategies from which it draws are much the same as those that are available for qualitative research. For this reason, rather than search the shelves for specialist books which deal with the analysis of evaluation, prospective evaluators are better advised to start with recent texts on qualitative research analysis (Coffey and Atkinson, 1996; Lofland and Lofland, 1995; Miles and Huberman, 1994; Silverman, 1993), and then filter this reading in the light of their inquiry needs. We will reflect briefly on the analysis of qualitative interviews in the early part of this chapter, not because we believe they provide a proxy for *all* analysis, but as an illustration and way in to some analytic issues and processes.

The major part of the chapter deals with the themes and issues posed by qualitative evaluation analysis. We pick up a thread from Chapter 6 and note ways that *practitioner* and *participatory* evaluation shape the approach to analysis. Participatory analysis raises important questions of *analysis ethics*, and we consider these and other ethical considerations posed by analyzing and reporting on evaluation. This provides the context for considering the core question of the chapter – how evaluative claims may be grounded and supported. We take up the argument from Chapter 7 regarding the relevance of qualitative evaluation for tackling thorny questions of *causes*. We move from there to consider several claims that have been made for ways in which qualitative analysis can be made more plausible. These include the use of methods of *member validation, triangulation*, and methods of *synthesizing* and *meta-analysis*. Important and difficult as these questions may be, issues of *generalization* and the *external validity* of evaluation are probably more so. We outline and review the more widely canvassed options and approaches. We close with a final visit to some of the issues of evaluation *authorship*, *reporting* and *use* that we considered in more general terms in Chapter 4.

Evaluative claims

'The attempt to establish and maintain the defensibility of normative and empirical claims about some phenomena to clients and stakeholders' (Fournier and Smith, 1993: 316) is the heart of evaluation. However, formal deductive logic, based on unequivocal evidence, cannot provide the basis for such claims.

> Everyone agrees that information somehow informs decisions, but the relationship is not direct, not simple. Often the more important the decision, the more obscure the relationship seems to be. (House, 1980: 68)

House goes as far as to say that, 'subjected to serious scrutiny, evaluations always appear equivocal' (1980: 72). We have met previously his argument that evaluations can be no more than acts of persuasion: 'Evaluation persuades rather than convinces, argues rather than demonstrates, is credible rather than certain, is variably accepted rather than compelling' (1980: 73). Evaluators have too frequently underplayed the role of judgement and hence of argumentation. This has resulted in an unduly technical, methods-oriented analysis, an over-confidence in quantification, and a tendency to represent knowledge in an impersonal, objectified form. Those who fail to accept the 'compelling' conclusions drawn from the evaluation are dismissed as irrational. If results are unequivocal then those who fail to accept them are 'wrong'.

There have been several attempts to take a different approach to thinking through the reasoning process involved in constructing justified evaluative arguments (Fournier, 1995; Fournier and Smith, 1993; Scriven, 1997). These typically emphasize the complex connection between evidence and conclusions, and commence from the differences between formal and informal reasoning. Whereas formal reasoning assumes a tight fit between the premises and conclusions within an argument, informal logic 'deals with ordinary, everyday language, where rules of inference are less precise and more contextual' (Fournier and Smith, 1993: 317). Toulmin's *The Uses of Argument* (1958) has been perhaps the most influential text. In explicating the connection between claims and evidence, he gives a central role to 'warrants'. A warrant provides the grounds explaining how we get from evidence to claim, and hence legitimizes the inference we make. In the later stages of this chapter we will be considering some of the characteristic warrants on which qualitative evaluators draw.

This approach has several advantages. For example, rather than starting from theoretical arguments about how we ought to reason, our attention is directed to how practitioners of evaluation actually do reason in the field. Empirical studies of these processes would allow us to understand whether and how evaluation inferences differ according to different purposes, settings, methodologies, and so on. For example, the various writers whose work we introduced in Chapter 2 employ rather different warrants. The arguments of Fournier, Scriven and Smith best fit what we have called a multi-partisan value position. Eraut uses the argument in exactly this way (Eraut, 1984: 33). It is less compatible with either strong enlightenment views of evaluation use, or committed advocacy positions. However, the inductivist, empirically driven character of the approach offers a promising way forward. It provides evaluators with a series of critical questions by which to examine their practice:

> What kinds of claim(s) am I trying to make in this evaluation? What authority source does the warrant need to appeal to? How strong is the authority source in supporting inferences drawn from evidence? What conditions would undermine the warrant? How forceful is (or will be) the resulting conclusion? (Fournier, 1995: 28)

Qualitative warrants

Cronbach remarked some time ago that it is 'rationalist to the point of unreality' to proceed on the basis that evaluation starts from agreement on goals (Cronbach et al., 1980: 129). All social programmes, he argued, have broad and vague goals, even supposedly targeted programmes. This is not escapism, as the rationalists would argue, but reflects the nature of programmes as operating within a climate of political accommodation: 'The first rule of the successful political process is, "Don't force a specification of goals or ends"' (1980: 130).

The lesson has been hard learned. Silverman, in his study of HIV counselling, still finds justifiable grounds to complain of the ways in which what he calls the Explanatory Orthodoxy of counselling research leads to a focus on either the causes or consequences of counselling. This approach 'is so concerned to rush to an explanation that it fails to ask serious questions about what it is explaining' (Silverman, 1997a: 24), such that the phenomenon of counselling 'escapes'. Traditional formulations of causal inputs and outcomes need at the very least to be delayed until we have understood something of the 'how'. For sound evaluative reasons we will want to ask the explanatory 'why' questions: 'There is no reason not to, provided that we have first closely described how the phenomenon at hand is locally produced' (1997a: 35). A qualitative approach to evaluation analysis will start from the premise that 'the ends of the goals should emerge from the process, not the other way round' (Sherman, 1990: 152).

Yet for all the strengths of qualitative evaluation research, policy and practice decision-makers schooled in the dominant tradition will frequently raise criticisms on the grounds that:

- It is unduly small scale.
- It is not representative and hence not capable of generalization.
- In aiming for validity at the level of meaning it falls short at the level of causal adequacy (Finch, 1986).

There is no reason why qualitative evaluators should take such criticisms lying down. Finch is modest and uncontentious when she concludes that qualitative policy research offers the advantages of:

> Flexibility in the research process itself; studies which place social life in its natural context; a concern with process as well as outcome; explanations which are adequate at the level of meaning, but which are also aware of questions of causal adequacy, even if they cannot be fully resolved. (1986: 161–162)

Each of the fieldwork methods we sketched in the previous chapter can support these evaluative analysis agendas. These range from the analysis of micro-processes by means of such approaches as conversation analysis (Silverman, 1997a) or change process research (Reid, 1990), to the more broad-scale analysis associated with case studies (Burgess et al., 1994; Stake, 1995; Yin, 1994). In between lies, for example, emerging work on the analysis of focus groups (Frankland and Bloor, 1999). By way of illustration we will briefly browse through some of the analytic issues and processes involved in analyzing qualitative interviews.

Analyzing qualitative evaluation interviews

There is a rich literature on qualitative interview analysis (Crabtree and Miller, 1992a; Holstein and Gubrium, 1995; McCracken, 1988), and a variety of analytic styles. Analytic styles lie somewhere on a continuum from deductive to inductive. Basic *content analysis* takes a systematic, deductive approach, bringing a clear a priori theoretical sense of analytic problems to an analysis of the substantive content of the text. Reid's (1990) work on change process research as a means of development evaluation is an example of this approach. A second approach is to develop a prior coding system based on previous research and the evaluator's ideas and experience, in order to address the latent content of the text in a relatively systematic and deductive fashion. We illustrate this approach in the subsequent discussion of causal analysis approaches in evaluation. Third, there is what Crabtree and Miller describe as the 'editing style' (1992b: 211), which adopts an inductive, comparative approach to the establishment of themes and analytic theses. Finally, the most inductive approach to analysis involves the evaluator becoming immersed in the text with the purpose of crystallizing its core understanding, in an 'intuitive, and intensely data-driven' way (1992b: 212).

None of these approaches can be ruled out of court in evaluation. Even the solely inductive approach may be the preferred option in ethnographic, knowledge-building evaluation projects. A fairly brief depiction of the third approach may serve to illustrate the point.

The evaluator brings to the analysis:

- A sense of what the literature and one's own previous work tells us ought to be there in the data.
- A sense of how this topic is constituted in one's own experience.
- A 'glancing sense of what took place in the interview' (McCracken, 1988: 42).

Beginning by identifying key utterances in the text of a single interview, the analyst should be ready to 'glimpse and systematically reconstruct a view of the world that bears no relation' to their own view or that of the literature. This entails the cultivation of a 'mannered' reading of the text: 'Come to the text with a certain disingenuous wonder, refusing to supply the assumptions and understandings' (McCracken, 1988: 44). It will involve watching for whatever associations the text evokes in the reader, including those occasions when the evaluator recognizes what is being said, not because the utterance has been successfully decoded, but because a sudden act of recognition has taken place' (1988: 44).

The evaluative interviewer seeks to identify 'narrative linkages' – 'The active interview study has two key aims: to gather information about *what* the research project is about and to explicate *how* knowledge concerning that topic is narratively constructed' (Holstein and Gubrium, 1995: 56). Holstein and Gubrium emphasize the collaborative aspects of the construction of meaning within the interview. For example, they describe coding as an 'indigenous' activity which takes place and unfolds as an integral part of the interview process, not just beforehand or afterwards.

EXAMPLE 9.1   EMERGENT INDIGENOUS CODING

In an example of what Fournier (1995) would describe as 'warrant establishing' evaluation, a probation officer describes an example of her work which had not gone well. A man had been placed on probation for an offence of threatening to kill his wife, which involved holding a knife to her throat. Once on probation he seemed to be doing 'amazingly well'. The probation officer was 'all set to take [the order] back to the court to ask for it to be revoked because I felt we'd made such an enormous amount of progress . . . Then of course his ex-wife phoned me and . . . said that he'd never stopped drinking and bullying her.'

A question from the interviewer codes reality by asking the probation officer to think in terms of certain evaluative options. In response to a question from the interviewer the probation officer refers to various analytic 'codes' for understanding her work. Some of the key terms are italicized in the following extract.

Interviewer: What was it about this case that you think you weren't doing well?

Probation Officer: [Sigh] The evidence was that I'd taken what the man had said very much at *face value*. I'm still not sure in retrospect whether I should have made more effort to follow up with his ex-wife. I mean *at the time* I was [sigh], I felt that actually offering her the information was sufficient, given that they weren't currently married, he wasn't currently living with her and that she had her *right to privacy* and not to be involved. There was also an issue of *confidentiality* about what he told me during the interviews, that obviously I wasn't going to be able to share that with his ex-wife without his permission. So I was, I mean basically I felt like a total mug, certainly in terms of effectiveness, not only totally ineffective but also possibly *worsened a bad situation* by *colluding* with this man in the belief that everything was actually all right, and *wasted a great deal of time* in supposed counselling sessions [laugh].

In addition to indigenous codes of this kind, the interviewer also is seeking to promote the visibility of narrative linkages. Holstein and Gubrium go as far as to claim that 'the interviewer interpretively challenges the respondent to make sense of experience in relation to various subjective possibilities' (1995: 59). The question and answer sequence immediately following the exchange in Example 9.1 illustrates the form this may take.

EXAMPLE 9.2 PROMOTING VISIBLE NARRATIVE LINKAGES

Interviewer: Is part of the difficulty the difficulty itself of being able to interpret evidence, because what you said was there seemed to be lots of clues which you could reasonably be expected to interpret as meaning things are going well?
Probation Officer: Yes.
Interviewer: And suddenly one bit of evidence jeopardizes all those other bits of evidence?
Probation Officer: Yeah, I mean it's basically the one bit of evidence, the phone call from the ex-wife, put a completely different interpretation on everything else that had occurred.
Interviewer: Is that something generally about interpreting work, the problem of interpreting evidence?
Probation Officer: It's a difficulty in evaluating people's attitudes [laugh] because you're very much dependent on the information they volunteer and what they tell you. This guy chose for his own reasons to deliberately mislead. I mean needless to say he was impeccable about keeping his appointments, about being on time [laugh]. He worked very hard to present a certain picture. As I say on the evidence I had available, I made one assessment that turned out to be completely false because of the evidence I didn't have access to, i.e. what was actually going on when he was visiting his ex-wife.

There is, of course, much more to the analytic task than the flavouring we have inserted here. The steps from evidence to evaluative claim are, as we have noted, complex. Through the gradual emergence of analytic themes, the aim is to compare and contrast emergent categories and to transform them into broader categories or theses. Crabtree and Miller describe the outcome of a similar process in their analysis of a study comparing and contrasting physicians' and patients' perception of pain and pain management (1992b: 213–218). Their analytic thesis was as follows:

1 The physician and patient both have personal visions of pain derived from personal experience, and which support their personal identities.
2 Both also have a professional vision of pain, but these visions are from different sources.

3 The physician learns from within the profession and uses this vision to support a professional identity.
4 The patient learns from contact with professionals and uses this vision again to support her personal identity.

In summary, 'the physician has potentially conflicted identities, the patient harmonious identities' (1992b: 218).

To reiterate, these snippets of interview analysis should not be read as either exclusively evaluative, or a proxies for the whole of the analytic endeavour. They are suggested as evaluation-relevant examples of qualitative analysis, which make visible the concern of qualitative evaluation with the interplay of substance and constructive processes.

We change focus from this point to consider the connected issues and themes posed by establishing and grounding evaluative claims. These include issues of causal analysis, member validation, triangulation, generalization, and the writing and use of evaluation. But before considering these, we will make some comments regarding practitioner and participatory analysis, and ethical issues posed by analysis.

Practitioner and participatory analysis

Practitioner and participatory evaluation bring their own agenda to the construction of meaning from inquiry. Practice and inquiry are *not* one and the same, and we have grumbled earlier about the implausible claims often made to this effect. But this by no means denies the fruitfulness of comparing the two. Lang interestingly considers 'differences in the data-processing strategies of social work practice and qualitative research and . . . how the two might be integrated' (Lang, 1994: 265). This concern with 'the correspondences and disjunctures between the activities of the qualitative researcher and the social work practitioner' (1994: 266) is led by her concern 'to permit both knowing and doing to be derived from the same data' (1994: 274). She exemplifies the way in which practitioner evaluation is equally likely to be concerned with better practice as it is with better discrete evaluation. Lang, for instance, advocates a greater readiness on the part of social workers to remain in the inductive pattern of inquiry. In a plausible paradox she argues that 'existing theory must have a more provisional status, a less central locus . . . in order to open the possibility of theory building' (1994: 276).

I am not convinced by arguments to the effect that research is one thing and practice is another and they should be kept separate (Hammersley, 1992). They are not one and the same, but neither can they be neatly disentangled. Evaluative analysis that addresses the range of practitioner evaluation concerns explored in Chapter 6 will be shaped by the tension and creative interplay of diverse purposes.

A similar point applies to participatory approaches to analysis. Analysis usually has a low profile in participatory research and evaluation. The primacy of method is often challenged, and qualitative methodology is regarded with askance ambivalence. Tripp, for example, argues from a participatory understanding of the interview that 'The ideal research strategy should simultaneously develop the view and provide information to evaluate its significance to the interviewee'. He believes this should not always be a gentle inquiry, but will include 'oppositional debate as well as discussion' (Tripp, 1983: 34). 'The aim is to produce an agreed-upon account of the views of the participants rather than agreed-upon accounts of the discussion' (1983: 35). This is a radically different picture of both the status of interview participants, and the data that results: 'The "data" are not necessarily the actual words spoken during the interview and subsequently transcribed, but a document which is the negotiated outcome of two people's views at the time of writing' (1983: 37).

Tripp's position that data is 'what the interviewee is satisfied to have written about what was said' (1983: 35) fails to 'protect us from our own passions' (Lather, 1986a: 77). Heron has his own version of the purpose of evaluation. Thus, he does not limit the outcomes of co-operative inquiry to what he describes as 'propositional reports', but also includes:

- Transformations of personal being through engagement with the focus and process of the inquiry.
- Presentations of insights about the focus of inquiry through dance, drawing, drama and all other expressive modes.
- Practical skills which are (1) skills to do with transformative action within the inquiry domain, and (2) skills to do with various kinds of participative knowing and collaboration used in the inquiry process. (Heron, 1996: 104)

Once we concede that the purpose of evaluation includes 'to enact rather than simply state' (Lather, 1991: 123), then analysis will be part of the evaluator's endeavour to 'maximize the research process as a change-enhancing, reciprocally educative encounter' (1991: 72), in which the process is more important than the product.

Much feminist work in this field acknowledges that the emancipatory potential of participatory analysis can only partly be attained. Acker and her colleagues reflect on their study of the relation between women's attempts to move into the labour market, and changes in consciousness. We referred in the previous chapter to the difficulties they encountered in the research relationship. They met with corresponding problems in the analysis of their extensive work: 'We found that we had to assume the role of the people with the power to define' (Acker et al., 1983: 429). For example, when they asked women to read their manuscript the women typically wanted 'more of our own sociological analysis. They wanted us, the researchers, to interpret their experience to them' (1983: 429). They came to accept that:

Ultimately the researcher must objectify the experience of the researched, must translate that experience into more abstract and general terms if an analysis that links the individual to processes outside her immediate social world is to be achieved. (1983: 425)

The tension is not solved by Tripp's abdication of data to the processes of negotiation: 'If we were to fulfil the emancipatory aim for the people we were studying, we had to go beyond the faithful representation of their experience, beyond "letting them talk for themselves"' (Acker et al., 1983: 429).

Ethics and analysis

Naïvety about ethics is itself unethical. We should not allow a proper emphasis on diverse constructions of reality and the local contextual distinctiveness of the programme, project or practice to excuse a lapse into ethical indifference. Experience 'is the stories people live. People live stories, and in the telling of them reaffirm them, modify them and create new ones' (Clandinin and Connelly, 1994: 415). Ethical issues are raised by the fact that as we encourage service users to tell their stories, we become characters in those stories, and thus change those stories. This can be positive, and be one way of helping someone to reassess a problem. But it also carries risks and re-emphasizes that evaluating must be done with care and not as 'a raid on mislaid identities' (Dannie Abse's phrase, from his poem *Return to Cardiff*). I recall a woman in a South Wales valley's town talking at length about the experience of bringing up at home her son with serious learning difficulties, then in his early twenties. She reflected that this was the first time she had ever talked to someone about this experience.

Broader ethical issues can be illustrated through reflecting on how different notions of justice affect the conclusions we draw as to whether a particular project or programme is good or not. A *utilitarian* view of justice proceeds on the basis that practices are judged right or wrong depending on whether they produce happiness or satisfaction for the greatest number of people. Rawls's theory of social justice is based on justice as *fairness*. His famous Difference Principle states that social and economic inequalities are just only if they result in compensating benefits for everyone, in particular for the least advantaged members of society. Hence we may feel able to justify pay rises for doctors, or teachers, at a level higher than benefit rate rises, on the grounds that disadvantaged people may thus benefit. Holders of an *egalitarian* theory of justice would insist that the disadvantaged must always gain redistributive benefit until equality is achieved. Consider the following social work example.

Social workers run a group with the aim of lowering car-related crimes. Suppose the outcome is that the group is successful for *all* members but *less so* for those with lower literacy levels. The conclusions we draw are contingent on the underlying view of justice to which we adhere (see Table 9.1). It may be worth inspecting our tacit response to these 'outcomes'. We have been academically socialized to respond with a methodological bent. Were the differences significant? Was the programme adequately implemented? Did the design provide an adequate basis for such implied causal inferences? These questions may or may not be relevant. But the methodological twist with which we treat evaluative claims illustrates the way in which efficiency has been preferred over justice. Our instinctive response becomes part of the problem.

TABLE 9.1   *Justice and evaluation outcomes*

Justice approach	Is it a just programme?
Utilitarian	Yes
Justice as fairness	Yes if the disadvantaged gain advantage
Egalitarian	Not just – it promotes inequality

But this may seem rather abstract. Consider instead the ethical and political dilemmas about how evaluation material is used. These issues are sometimes sharper in qualitative evaluation than in quantitative work. This arises partly from the greater closeness and consequent trust that may develop between evaluator and participant. In quantitative research the greater distancing may make these issues less agonizing. The risk of betrayal is also increased because of the typical use of smaller samples, and the emphasis on the details of how people live their lives. Finch describes from her playgroups evaluative research her 'sense that I could potentially betray my informants as a group, not as individuals' (1986: 207). 'Where qualitative research is targeted upon social policy issues, there is the special dilemma that findings could be used to *worsen* the situation of the target population in some way' (Finch, 1985: 117).

EXAMPLE 9.3   PLAYGROUPS – WHOSE SIDE ARE WE ON?

Finch's particular interest was in what self-help playgroup provision would mean for working class women living in economically deprived areas. Over a three-year period, through observation and semi-structured interviewing, she was able to document the character of self-help playgroups in such areas:

> I uncovered situations where practice diverged wildly from bourgeois standards of child care and education which most policy makers and academics would take as the norm, and at times were downright dangerous. (1985: 117)

She was worried that the publication of her work would further reinforce 'those assumptions deeply embedded in our culture and political life that working class women (especially the urban poor) are inadequate mothers' (1985: 117). Those who had welcomed her for three years would thus be betrayed.

She had to work through these problems. Had she been guilty of taking a middle class norm and imposing it on these groups? Yet that norm *was* the one to which the women who ran the groups aspired. It was the participants' model and not simply hers. She eventually developed reasoning which avoided the 'deficit' model of explanation, and argued that to view working class mothers as incompetent is improper and naïve. She acknowledges she is not certain she has fully resolved the issues, and accepts that,

> To argue like this is to take a frankly moral stance, far removed from the model of the objective social scientist . . . It seems to me that qualitative research on social policy issues will lead inevitably to explicit moral stances of that sort, and that it can never simply provide the 'facts'. (1985: 119–120)

Causes and explanations

In common qualitative parlance, 'observational data are used for "generating hypotheses", or "describing process". Quantitative data are used to "analyze outcomes", or "verify hypotheses"' (Trend, 1979: 83). We explained in some detail in Chapter 7 why we agree that 'this division of labour is rigid and limiting' (1979: 83). Having said this, the division is reinforced by the frequent absence of discussions of cause in qualitative methodology and analysis texts (Coffey and Atkinson, 1996). Qualitative evaluation cannot resolve the problems of causal conclusions any more than quantitative evaluation, but it can assess causality 'as it actually plays out in a particular setting' (Miles and Huberman, 1994: 10). Cronbach argued to similar effect that we need causal explanatory knowledge, 'not knowledge of things that work on average under a set of diverse conditions' (Shadish et al., 1990: 363).

Qualitative evaluation shares with qualitative research the recognition of the irony of social causes and consequences. Much of the sociology of deviance was based on just this sense of irony, with its exploration of deviant roles as doing necessary 'dirty work'. In evaluative terms we may ask the question what functions are served by a particular practice that would not be served by its absence. In less functional terms we may ask what are the typical results of this phenomenon in this setting, and what ends are served thereby? Lofland and Lofland (1995) make the important observation that causal answers are by and large based on *passivist* conceptions of human nature. Qualitative inquiry has often steered away from causal accounts, not because the methodology is weak in that area but because of a commitment to an *activist* conception of human nature. The Loflands argue that an activist conception will lead to a focus on questions that address both structures and strategies. This will involve 'deciphering and depicting exactly what sort of situation the participants are facing' (Lofland and Lofland, 1995: 146), and understanding the 'incessantly fabricated' strategies people construct to deal with the situation.

Take for example, Silverman's work on HIV counselling. He is right to conclude that 'it is usually unnecessary to allow our research topics to be defined in terms of . . . the "causes" of "bad" counselling or the "consequences" of "bad" counselling' (Silverman, 1997a: 34), insofar as such topics reflect the conceptions of social problems as recognized by professional or community groups. Nonetheless, this does not require the abandonment of causal inquiry in qualitative evaluation. Inquiry into the ways in which professionals incessantly fabricate service forms and structures does promise a better way to understand causes.

Miles and Huberman (1994) have suggested practical advice on several ways in which causal analysis can be undertaken through qualitative methodology. For example, local informants have 'local causal maps' in their heads, and much evaluative fieldwork involves eliciting such maps and using them in the development of broader causal networks. Causal networks 'are not probabilistic, but specific and determinate, grounded in understanding of events over time in the concrete local context – *and* tied to a good understanding of each variable' (Miles and Huberman, 1994: 159). Computing software has had a major impact on the potential for such mapping.

Causal networks exist at the level of the individual case. Miles and Huberman also develop ways in which ordering and explaining can be tackled through cross-case displays of data. They are confident of the ability of qualitative inquiry to go beyond the problems of inferring from association ('the weasel word of quantitative researchers'; 1994: 222). They summarize the process as follows:

> *Cross-case causal networking* is a comparative analysis of all cases in a sample, using variables estimated to be the most influential in accounting for the outcome criterion. You look at each outcome measure and examine, for each case, the stream of variables leading to or 'determining' that outcome. Streams that are similar to or identical across cases, and that differ in some consistent way from other streams are extracted and interpreted. (1994: 228)

They spell out the steps to accomplishing this analysis, but suggest that it may not be feasible for either larger or very small samples.

EXAMPLE 9.4   CAUSAL MAPS: PARTICIPANT MODELS FOR A RURAL ACTIVITY CENTRE

Shaw and colleagues (1992) describe an evaluation of a rural activity centre for people with learning disabilities. They observed and interviewed project participants, parents, carers, management group members, key workers and other professionals. Project records were analyzed.

When describing and explaining the workings of the centre, the people who were interviewed appeared to draw on one or more of three different models of the scheme. These were a training for work model, a personal and social growth model, and an education for life model. These operated in part as causal maps which entailed an array of model-specific positions on the aims of the project, optimal target groups, desirable programme patterns, staffing requirements, future development strategies, and likely or desirable project outcomes.

TABLE 9.2   *Stakeholder models of a rural activity centre*

	Training for work	Personal/social growth	Education for life
Aims	Credible work skills for independent/ sheltered work	Personal and social growth	Alternative occupation to enhance the quality of life
Target group	Demonstrable ability to benefit; younger	Wide range of age and ability	Wide ability range; younger
Programme	Time limited stay; skill learning; assessment and review; contracts; move-one facility; integration into work	Open stay period; small project; small-group activities; counselling; liaison with carers and social work agencies	Loosely held time limits; the best learning context; interest-led contracts; community-based activities and outside links; craft work and home making skills
Staffing	Education and special needs employment skills; plus volunteers	Social and group work qualifications; expert consultants	Education and social work qualifications; plus volunteers
Outcome	Regular throughput; work placements; normalization of work patterns; skill learning	No clear distinction between programme and outcome	Wide range of social skills; integration into community networks; change of attitudes on the part of outside community members

Source: Shaw, Williamson and Parry-Langdon (1992).

Member validation and triangulation

In our discussion of participatory analysis we noted the extreme view of Tripp that data is what the interviewee is satisfied to have written about what was said. Shed of its eccentric view of the nature of the evaluation task, Tripp may seem to be assuming a fairly self-evident truth – if we want to know if we have adequately represented the views, attitudes and behaviour of those whom we have observed or spoken to, we should ask them. Miles and Huberman, for example, often reiterate their view that the basic tactic for testing the validity of our findings is 'getting feedback from informants' (1994: 165). Guba and Lincoln have also argued that taking data back to the sources is the backbone of satisfying the validity criterion. In addition to the ethical grounds in favour of this approach, support for this view can also be argued from the welcome awareness of continuities between the common-sense thinking of community members and 'scientific thinking'. Writers who hold this position sometimes require that the adequacy of scientific propositions should be tested according to whether members understand them.

Bloor (1983) describes two validation exercises in which he asked if members recognized, understood and accepted his description. He conducted a study of clinical practices of tonsillectomy consultants, following which each consultant was given a report of their clinic practices on the basis of which they were interviewed. He reports that, 'While my accounts were recognizable to members, they were not isomorphic with their commonsense knowledge of their work practices' (Bloor, 1983: 160). The exercise met with several problems:

- Some consultants read his report with only limited interest.
- There was a sense of artifice in that critical points were sometimes created by the interview.
- 'An interview is a species of conversation and, as such, it follows the implicit rules of polite conversation in which open disagreement is minimized' (1983: 162). Thus, when 'reality disjuncture' surfaces in the interview it leads to 'conversational repair work' through which both sides seek consensus.
- The member validation exercise was falsely premised on the assumption that surgeons' views were invariant rather than provisional, contingent and subject to change over time.

> In sum, the validation exercise fell foul of some major problems – an inadequate reading by some surgeons, a lack of strong interest, contextual influences on the interviews, the consensus oriented nature of the project, and the essentially provisional character of members' reactions. (Bloor, 1983: 164)

Emerson and Pollner (1988) report a member validation exercise which encountered comparable problems. Following their field research on psychiatric emergency duty teams they had lunchtime discussions with one member of the team, and also held a subsequent public presentation of their results to the County Mental Health Department. At a fairly basic level it was not clear in several instances whether their report was being confirmed, qualified or contradicted. In addition, the relational context in which they talked over lunch with a team member to whom they had been close, introduced 'an equivocality regarding the extent to which apparent expressions of agreement or disagreement are shaped by the member's desire to support a friend' (1988: 192). The organizational context also shaped the exercises. Members can, of course, envision a variety of ways in which supposedly 'neutral' research may be put to uses with far-reaching consequences for organization staff. Hence, 'expressions of support or, for that matter, hostility, are apt to be constructed in light of the research report's consequences for promoting one or another of the competing interests' (1988: 194).

Bloor is sceptical of the value of such exercises as part of validation. He concludes that 'the very methodological frailties that lead sociologists to search for validating evidence are also present in the generation of that validating evidence' (Bloor, 1997b: 49). Rather than validation of evidence we should regard such exercises as valuable additional evidence. 'Validation exercises are not tests, but opportunities for reflexive elaboration' (1997b: 49) – in Emerson and Pollner's words, 'less as moments which transcend the field setting and more as a source of material to be culled and considered as part and parcel of the setting' (1988: 190).

Much of this appears sound sense. But I am left with the sense that the conclusions of Bloor, and Emerson and Pollner may be unduly pessimistic and even smack of academic élitism. On the pessimism charge, while we may believe that practitioners' judgements involve 'no epistemological, moral or political privilege about this matter', 'the fact that the observer was there and/or that participants believe the account to be true are important sorts of evidence for the validity of the account' (Hammersley, 1992: 76, 52–53). Phillips suggests that the heart of the matter is the precise nature of the findings or account the credibility of which is being probed. If it is 'an account of the beliefs held by an individual or by a group of subjects ... then the appropriate criterion is whether or not these subjects agree that the researcher has indeed accurately recorded their beliefs' (Phillips, 1987a: 20). If the purpose of the evaluation goes beyond seeking an understanding of participants' perspectives, then credibility is an inappropriate surrogate for validity.

On the charge of élitism, negotiation of member agreement on meaning may be justified on other than strictly methodological grounds. Lather studied student resistance to the introduction of a liberatory curriculum, and concluded that, 'Member checks seemed to have the major effect of contributing to a growing sense of collaboration as opposed to a negotiated validation of the descriptive level' (1991: 77). Arguments for member checks of this kind are, of course, the only ground on which a relativist evaluator can proceed. Smith thus concludes: 'One might undertake member checks because it is the morally and ethically correct thing to do under the circumstances, not because they will lead to a more objective study' (1992: 103). Arguments for such exercises on moral grounds do not require a relativist stance, but neither do they lose their force simply because the empirical outcomes are volatile and contingent.

Much the same logic applies to application to evaluation data of ideas regarding *triangulation*. The most frequently used basic idea of triangulation refers to the combination of two or more different research strategies in the study of the same empirical phenomenon (Denzin, 1989). The idea has been utilized somewhat confusingly in popular discourse. On the one hand it is sometimes viewed as a metaphor for obtaining a geographical 'fix' on the true 'location' of evidence. On the other hand it is frequently viewed as a source of varying perspectives and constructions. The confusion is understandable, and echoes the shifts in epistemology within social science. Triangulation as a multi-method means of validation goes back to work by Campbell and Fiske on convergent and discriminant validation by what they called multitrait or multi-method approaches. This work was associated with a traditional understanding of validity as a means of separating bias from reality.

A simplistic view of triangulation does without doubt run the risk of being accused of naïve realism. It also supports the unhelpful notion that using multiple methods will lead to sounder, consensual conclusions in an easy, additive fashion. An astringent antidote to both of these failings can be gained from a reading of an early and classic account of problems in the reconciliation of quantitative and qualitative data (Trend, 1979). Trend was engaged in a major evaluation of social experiments undertaken by the US Department of Housing and Urban Development (HUD) designed to test the concept of using direct cash housing allowance payments to help low income families obtain decent housing in the open market. In one case study the quantitative data suggested that the programme was producing major improvements in the housing quality of people using that site. Yet all the qualitative, observational data indicated that the programme would be a failure. The assiduous pursuit of a plausible explanation fills the major part of Trend's paper. His conclusion is that different methods of inquiry will not always be compatible: '[T]he complementarity is not always apparent. Simply using different perspectives, with the expectation that they will validate each other, does not tell what to do if the pieces do not fit' (1979: 83).

Trend's own advice on what to do in such circumstances is salutary: 'I suggest that we give the different viewpoints the chance to arise, and postpone the immediate rejection of information or hypotheses that seem out of joint with the majority viewpoint' (1979: 84). He cites Paul Feyerabend in support of this, who says 'It seems that it is not the puzzle-solving activity that is responsible for the growth of our knowledge, but the active interplay of various tenaciously held views' (quoted in Trend, 1979: 84).

Syntheses and meta-analysis

Questions of consensus and complementarity of evaluation evidence touches on a wider issue that has received attention in the evaluation literature. How far is it possible and desirable to synthesize evaluative judgements into an overall assessment of the merit and worth of a particular programme, policy or project? Scriven has long been an advocate of drawing syntheses from evaluations. Chelimsky used her time at the US General Accounting Office to promote syntheses of multiple evaluation studies. Despite problems of data quality, she believes they may be a more effective shield against 'partisan slings and arrows' than single studies (Chelimsky, 1995). There is a distinction entailed here. Chelimsky focuses on *external synthesis* (in the sense of the integration of research studies which were completed as stand alone studies, but which addressed a common topic), whereas Scriven stresses *internal synthesis*, where the different criteria of merit in a given study are evaluated.

Qualitative evaluators have traditionally remained suspicious. Stake, for example, describes his career as one in which he has 'increasingly replaced realist presumption with constructivist hesitation'. This explains why, 'even as an evaluator believing it our responsibility to judge programme quality, I am reticent to pursue authoritative summary statements' (Stake, 1991: 81). He prefers to leave such judgements to the audience.

The debate has taken a new direction following the advocacy of synthesizing judgements by House. He is convinced that 'conflicting criteria and data do not prevent evaluators from arriving at all-things-considered judgements most of the time' (House, 1995: 35). The jury remains out on this issue, and we must await further examples of worked out judgements of this kind. My concerns are twofold. First, House appears to underplay the problems arising from conflict resolution in such instances. The evaluator will implicitly take sides. Second, summaries risk glossing over local contextual contingencies. It is local context and contingency that provides the basis for transferring explanatory knowledge.

Generalization

Summary conclusions and judgements are one means of seeking a wider applicability of evaluation findings. Qualitative researchers have rightly been wary of the conventional logic of generalization based on probability sampling. 'Local context and the human story . . . are the primary goals of qualitative research and not "generalizability"' (Miller and Crabtree, 1994: 348).

Our response to this scepticism is that it all depends. We have suggested in Chapter 7 ways in which qualitative evaluation designs such as multi-site case studies can take into account generalization requirements. We have also considered ways in which causal explanation can allow us to extrapolate. Yet all our thinking in this field needs the caution that generalization requires an extrapolation that can never be fully justified logically.

The process of generalization is present in all learning, and a grasp of issues of generalizing in evaluation will be stronger for an awareness of how we learn lessons in everyday life. Reflective approaches to practitioner evaluation have been aware of this issue. Eisner's case for extrapolating from his connoisseurship and educational criticism model rests almost entirely on such arguments. He distinguishes *generalizing* in the sense of the exact application of what was learned in situation A to situation B, from *transfer*, in which we recognize that all situations are different to some extent:

> Since no generalization can fit an individual context perfectly, modification is always necessary. This modification requires judgement on the part of intelligent practitioners. (Eisner, 1991a: 212)

The expression 'transfer of learning' captures exactly this implicit distinction.

Eisner poses the interesting question of where generalization is focused. He wants to allow for the idea of 'retrospective generalization' which occurs when we see our past in a new light, naming something so that we can find a new significance in an array of past experience. We 'find a fit between a general statement and our personal histories. New ideas can reconstruct our past' (1991a: 206).

These ideas find partial echoes in more formal notions of how generalization occurs in qualitative inquiry. There are three ways in which qualitative evaluation can address problems of extrapolation – by logic which approximates surveys; by analytic generalization; and by case to case transfer through detailed, 'thick' description of local instances. We comment briefly on each of these.

Survey logic

We mention the application of survey logic to qualitative extrapolation mainly to underline its limitations. We considered in Chapter 7 how the advocacy of multi-site case studies has sometimes been on the grounds of probability logic (Tizard et al., 1975). Yet the problems usually outweigh the gains. Conclusions based on probabilities are of limited utility in specific cases. While we might know that 'on average' a particular school, medical intervention, or correctional programme has a given chance of being successful, this does not help us to weigh the particular contingencies for a specific choice. We lose 'case identity'. Also, the typical situation facing practitioners, parents or programme managers is not one of exact generalization, but, to repeat Eisner's term, transfer to settings or interventions which are different to some degree. Cronbach, of course, argues his whole case for the importance of external validity on just this point.

Analytic generalization

We have referred once or twice to Atkinson and Delamont's heavy and unduly tendentious criticism of case study approaches in educational research. Where their criticisms stick, however, is when they complain of ways in which some representatives of case study research suggest that generalization is not a concern of qualitative studies of particular institutions. Their response is that this is founded on a misapprehension of how generalization might take place in such instances (Atkinson and Delamont, 1993). They explore an approach familiar within symbolic interactionist writing, of comparative analysis. This method is sometimes referred to as analytic induction. It proceeds by employing the notion of a 'generic problem', which is applied to an explicit and implicit comparison of institutions. The use of the constant comparative method, including the identification of critical and deviant cases, enables the identification of common features between institutions.

This approach to analysis illustrates the way in which a theoretical stance in evaluation proves essential. It also pushes us to look at diverse settings and evaluation contexts. The work of Goffman is a classic example of this approach through his formal concepts of stigma and total institution. There is all too little evaluation that proceeds in this way. Firestone has demonstrated how issues of generalization can be dealt with systematically while remaining in the analytic mode (Firestone, 1993). Stake and Trumbull's idea of naturalistic and vicarious generalization has important points of contact through its stress on general analytic categories, but it is more associated with the experiential and the private, and assumes a morally consensual framework. The worst case scenario is that if qualitative evaluators are unwilling to grapple with concepts and theories, 'they merely substitute one variety of atheoretical "findings" – based mainly on observation and interview – for another – based mainly on test scores' (Atkinson and Delamont, 1993: 218).

Case by case transfer and 'thick description'

We have implied the importance of extrapolation based on detailed narratives of process throughout the book, and do not need to expound it further. Listening to Geertz as he talks about anthropology may serve as sufficient final exhortation. What defines anthropology is the kind of intellectual effort it is – an elaborate venture in 'thick description'. So reasoned Geertz, in what has become a benchmark paper. While he has no apparent interest in evaluation, it is difficult to read a text on qualitative evaluation without running into the expression. It is his vision of the relationship between the obscure and the public, the small and the broadscale, which seems to appeal to evaluators and ethnographers alike. His argument is inspirational rather than didactic, and is constructed around a fieldwork account of Jews, Berbers and French in Morocco in 1912, and an elaborate story of sheep stealing. He stresses the microscopic character of ethnographic descriptions: 'The anthropologist characteristically approaches ... broader interpretations ... from the direction of exceedingly extended acquaintances with extremely small matters' (Geertz, 1973: 21). He confronts grand realities of Power, Faith, Oppression, Prestige, Status and Love, 'but he [sic] confronts them in contexts small enough to take the capital letters off' (1973: 21).

On the problem of how we may generalize from the local to the broadscape, Geertz rejects the idea that a given town or locale acts as a microcosm ('an idea which only someone too long in the bush could possibly entertain'; 1973: 22). Rather, 'what generality it contrives to achieve grows out of the delicacy of its distinctions, not the sweep of its abstractions' (1973: 25). In his eminently quotable phrase, 'small facts speak to large issues, winks to epistemology, or sheep raids to revolution' (1973: 23). Hence, 'The essential task of theory building ... is not to codify abstract regularities but to make thick description possible, not to generalize across cases, but to generalize within them' (1973: 26).

The argument for qualitative evaluation has never been that its claims for generalizability are outstandingly strong. Yet this brief overview of analytic approaches, linked to the discussion of evaluation design in Chapter 7, demonstrates that in any event qualitative methods should not be avoided because of the fear that their claims for wider relevance are especially weak. This is not the case.

Making evaluation relevant

How should evaluation be authored? Who should do it, and in what voice or voices should it speak? What responsibility, if any, does the evaluator have for the direct or longer-term uses to which evaluation may be put? None of these questions is easy. We noted in Chapter 4 the difference between descriptive and prescriptive stances taken by qualitative evaluators. We also recognized the difference between those who place primary emphasis on the instrumental value of evaluation, and those who rather see evaluation as having a less direct enlightenment value. We also devoted some space to looking at the widely different positions taken by evaluators on their political role.

Yet whatever our position is on these issues, all qualitative evaluators are likely to be influenced by what has been described as the fundamentally appreciative stance of ethnography, as part of what Finch calls the 'alternative tradition' within British policy research. Ethnographers do, of course, take a range of positions on the sense in which ethnography is and can be 'relevant'. Hammersley, for example, believes there are important questions about the capacity of ethnography to produce relevant results:

These stem from the fact that the situations studied by ethnographers rarely have intrinsic relevance. Rather, the findings have to be made relevant by appeal to empirical generalization or theoretical inference. (Hammersley, 1992: 77)

Evaluators should understandably respond by asserting the intrinsic relevance of some – though by no means all – of the problems they address. Yet, as we have already seen in Chapter 6, Hammersley's doubts remain. Writing regarding the teacher as researcher movement he suggests several grounds for believing that research cannot routinely solve teachers' problems (Hammersley, 1993a).

Hammersley is, I believe, too influenced by his concern to warn against developments that he fears will undermine the quality and credibility of research. Ethnographers can plausibly adopt a more sanguine position. We described for example in the closing paragraphs of Chapter 6 how Bloor and McKeganey demonstrate the potential practitioner relevance of ethnography. And Holstein and Gubrium provide a telling illustration of how their process of active interviewing can yield both research rigour and personal benefits to the respondent in their account of an interview with an 88 year old woman (1995: 59–65).

Co-authorship?

Should evaluators collaborate with participants in the writing of the final report? What form should that report take? How should evaluators handle the potential and pitfalls of advocacy in connection with the report?

Scriven, it may be recalled, regards participatory authorship of the final report as the sloppiest of all possible evaluation practices (1997: 486). Returning to Tripp's vision of co-authorship and negotiation, we may be surprised that he joins the ranks of those who regard co-authorship as less than rigorous. He advocates, we noted, the production of co-authored data. But he proceeds from there to make a firm distinction between data and the report. He refers to his own research in which he 'goaded' many of his respondents into agreeing 'frank, even provocative, statements' such that working relationships in the institution were jeopardized (Tripp, 1983: 38). Yet he insists that when participants have agreed to their statements 'they are held personally responsible and accountable to each other in a way that precludes any moderation of the impact' (1983: 38). Not only that, but he believes 'that the author of a research report should attempt to retain control over the hermeneutic understanding' (1983: 43) so that the researcher has rights of interpretation which are denied to the reader. One can only imagine the reactions of his participants to this *mélange* of democratic and authoritarian images of research knowledge and skills!

The problems we discussed under the rubric of member validation occur once more in connection with co-authoring of reports, along with other more practical difficulties.

EXAMPLE 9.5   DEMOCRATIC PRINCIPLES IN PRACTICE

Simon describes the SAFARI (Success and Failure and Recent Innovation) project, which was an evaluation of the impact of four curriculum projects at high school level in British education. These were in the fields of technology, geography, humanities and science.

In a meeting with heads of departments she stressed three points regarding the participatory ethos of the project:

> First, the participatory aspirations of the research. Second, the opportunity that shared control gave them to shape the study and determine the process and extent of release within and beyond the school. Thirdly, the responsibility I would like them to take in identifying my personal and professional biases ... It was 'their' study as much as mine. (Simon, 1987: 96–97)

The second of these is particularly relevant for co-authorship practices. She completed very brief ethnographic evaluations through three-day visits to each school and then allowed a further one or two days for clearing the data with staff. This became overtaken by a major problem surrounding the confidentiality of the data and points up how 'unfamiliar procedures for internal control of data, intended to protect participants, can easily be overtaken by traditional processes of complaint' (1987: 110). There were positive aspects to this, in that it raised the 'reality level' of the inquiry, but it shows how responsive evaluation can easily get out of 'logistical control'.

The time needed to carry out participatory evaluation became a major issue. She did at least three drafts of each of her five reports and eventually had to withdraw from the process: 'I had started something I could not finish' (1987: 125).

Presenting the findings

Debates regarding the presentation of evaluation findings often hide diverse agendas. Finch, for example, is concerned with the negative views which policy-makers and decision-makers hold regarding qualitative research. She therefore argues the need for evaluators to give enough information about the methodology of the study to enable the policy-maker to assess it, and to demonstrate that control over methods has been maintained throughout. If evaluation proceeds along the lines of participatory design and analysis, then evaluation will be presented in forms consistent with an emphasis on the process of the work as much as the outcome. Strong stakeholder versions of evaluation will typically go for diverse forms of reporting and feedback. These different positions on presenting reports are therefore contingent. The real issue is evaluative purpose, and the demand that we present the inquiry in ways that reinforce that purpose.

Yet we can say rather more than this. There has been extensive work on qualitative inquiry as a form of story-telling. Miller and Crabtree, in their account of clinical research, say that sharing the knowledge entails 'telling methodologically, rhetorically and clinically convincing stories' (1994: 348).

> Qualitative clinical research is convincing if the methods are appropriate for the question and the investigator's relationship with informants, data, and audience are clearly addressed; if the audience recognizes itself in the findings; and if the question and results matter to clinical participants. (1994: 349)

EXAMPLE 9.6   LEE CRONBACH ON TELLABLE STORIES

The evaluator faces a mild paradox. 'All research strives to reduce reality to a tellable story', but 'thorough study of a social problem makes it seem more complicated' (Cronbach et al., 1980: 184). Their resolution of this paradox lies in aphorism that comprehensive examination does not equal exhaustive reporting: 'When an avalanche of words and tables descends, everyone in its path dodges' (1980: 186).

The main criterion is the extent to which relevant people learn from the evaluator's communications. Therefore the evaluator should seek constant opportunity to communicate with the policy-shaping community throughout the research. They believe that 'much of the most significant communication is informal, not all of it is deliberate, and some of the largest effects are indirect' (1980: 174). Their recommendations are:

- Be around.
- Talk briefly and often.
- Tell stories. Always be prepared with a stock of anecdotes regarding the evaluation.
- Talk to the manager's sources.
- Use multiple models of presentation.
- Provide publicly defensible justifications for any recommended programme changes. These will be very different from scientific arguments.

Cronbach is strongly opposed to holding on until all the data are in and conclusions are firm. Influence and precision will be in constant tension, and if in doubt we should always go for influence. Live, informal, quick overviews, responsiveness to questions, the use of film and sound clips, and personal appearances, are the stuff of influence. The final report thus acts as an archival document:

> The impotence that comes with delay . . . can be a greater cost than the consequences of misjudgement. The political process is accustomed to vigorous advocacy . . . [and] is not going to be swept off its feet by an ill-considered assertion even from an evaluator. (1980: 179–180)

Handling advocacy

However *we* may describe our stance on advocacy: 'in the short term, good social research will often be greeted as a betrayal of one or other side of a particular controversy' (Rossi, 1987: 79). Rossi's chastened conclusion – slightly tongue in cheek – is that 'no good applied social research goes unpunished'.

Even committed advocacy evaluators may hesitate. We have few guidelines, Stake suggests, for distinguishing good and bad advocacies:

> I feel our stance should be to resist advocacy, to minimize advocacy, even though it is ever present, to help to recognize worthy and unworthy advocacies but to resist joining them. (1997: 474)

If our stance is one of multi-partisanship, then this gives us no excuse for quiescence. Multi-partisanship is an activist stance. It goes beyond the complacency of liberal pluralism manifested in some forms of responsive and interpretive evaluation. Eraut (1984), for example, pleads for what he describes as divergent evaluation which allows the evaluator to introduce values not heeded by respondents, albeit without giving them any special priority.

My own sympathies are for a reformist evaluation, which would have the evaluator seek out the data most likely to support programmes that benefit the dispossessed. I recognize the acute sense of dissonance that can stem from arguing for a rigorous evaluative methodology in one breath, and a reformist, partisan advocacy based on the evidence, in the next. But I stay with it for the present, and also with the conviction that, to reiterate Jennifer Greene's words:

> Absent an engaged, accountable position like scientific citizenship, I fear that qualitative evaluation will be relegated to the sidelines of important debates about pressing public issues ... No longer can we shroud our citizen-selves behind our scientific subjectivities. We must become scientific citizens. (1996: 286–287)

Appendix

Exercises

The exercises in the following pages give you the opportunity to explore the themes and methodology discussed in the book. Some of the exercises ask you to consolidate your learning. Others are more participatory, and ask you to engage in evaluation-related tasks, or to carry out a role play. I have linked each exercise to the chapter on which it most closely draws, but they should always be used flexibly and in terms of your own learning. Some are best carried out as individual exercises and others as group exercises, but once again I have aimed for flexibility.

Chapter 1   What makes a qualitative evaluation?

This observation exercise is in two stages. Each stage will take about an hour. It works best if the first stage is started a week before the second stage. Participants usually enjoy this exercise, and find it worth the time and effort taken to complete. It can, of course, be adapted to the requirements of a conventional methodology course.

Step 1

For not more than fifteen minutes observe a setting in which you regularly participate. It does not matter what kind of setting it is. It may be within your family, in your place of work, or among people you meet elsewhere.

Before you start the observation spend a few minutes thinking about the setting and deciding possible foci for your observation. It is impossible not to be selective and, given the short observation period, you will need to have some definite ideas about the kind of things you may look for. However, it is not a good idea to decide on a single focus for your observation, as you will need to be responsive to emergent aspects of the setting.

You will need to decide in advance how you will record the observation. You may record during the observation, or make notes and write them up as soon as possible after the observation. You will also need to decide whether you disclose what you are doing to the members of the setting.

As soon as possible after the observation, write three or four paragraphs in which you generate as many explanations as you can for the events you have described. You should spend about 45 minutes analyzing your observation in this way.

Step 2

Re-read the pages on the characteristics of *qualitative* evaluation in Chapter 1. Identify which typical characteristics of qualitative inquiry are reflected in your description and analysis. If you engage in sharing of observation work with others, this will take about an hour to complete.

Chapter 2   Persuasions and persuaders

Re-read the list of agenda items that closes Chapter 2.

1   Copy the list and note down which theorist/s have helped to focus attention on each issue.
2   Which three or four issues in this list do you think are the most fundamental for the development of qualitative evaluation in the setting with which you are most familiar? If you are working in a group, you should compare your lists of priorities for different settings.

Chapter 3   Paradigms and evaluation questions

Write brief notes on a scenario with which you are familiar. This may be a curriculum or welfare innovation, the implementation of legislation in your place of work, a housing scheme, a new university assessment scheme, and so on.

Imagine this scenario is to be evaluated. Write down three evaluation questions that would be uppermost in the minds of each of the following:

• A realist postpositivist.
• A critical evaluator.
• A constructivist evaluator.

Chapter 4   Partisanship and evaluation

Re-read the pages on 'Validity and values' in Chapter 4, pages 64–72.

Where do you stand on partisanship issues? Are you primarily a multi-partisan, a reformist or an openly ideological evaluator?

Playing devil's advocate with your own sympathies, what are the main *weaknesses* of the position you favour?

A useful added dimension to this exercise will be gained if you set up a forum in which you defend the results of your reflections to a small group of fellow students/evaluators.

Chapter 5   Assessing programme evaluations

In Chapter 5 I said that qualitative evaluators:

1   Will consider the *process* of programme activities and delivery prior to considering programme outcomes.
2   Will be mistrustful of programme delivery and evaluation that depends heavily on assumptions of *rational decision-making*.
3   Should not ignore the significance of *theorizing* about programmes.
4   Will be less enthusiastic about the value of *accountability* models of evaluation.
5   Include a range of positions on the place of programme evaluation in contributing to *social change*.

Choose a planned or published example of evaluation that includes qualitative methodology. Find out, by whatever means are appropriate (study review, group discussion, conversations with stakeholders, etc.), how far this evaluation reflects the points made in the first half of Chapter 5 regarding these five criteria.

Chapter 5   Information use

Carol Weiss and her colleagues interviewed 155 people who held high level positions in federal, state and local mental health agencies. Among the questions she asked were:

1   Do you consciously use the results of social science research in reaching decisions on your job?
2   In what ways do you use social science research on your job?
3   Do you seek out research information when you're considering policy or programme alternatives?
4   Under what circumstances do you seek research? (Weiss, 1980).

The first two questions ask about *conscious use* of research. The second two also ask about *active search*.

Arrange to interview a senior official (either known or not known to you), and ask this sequence of questions. Compare the results of this interview with the points made in the second half of Chapter 5, pages 92–95.

Chapter 6   Reflective evaluation through peer interviewing

You need to be a present or recent teacher, social worker, police officer, nurse, or similar, in order to carry out this exercise. The exercise requires you to work with one other person. Note that the exercise assumes that you will be the *respondent* rather than the interviewer. It is possible, however, to act as the interviewer. In that case you need to arrange to interview someone working in a service-delivery role to people. You will be part of a peer interview, which will last somewhere between 30 and 75 minutes.

The interviewer should be equipped with a good quality hand-held cassette recorder. Make sure you will not be interrupted during the interview. You should spend a few minutes (but not more) in thinking about the questions before you start, in particular to decide which two pieces of work you will talk about. This exercise works much better if you are able to work from a transcript of the interview. You should be warned that you need to allow approximately eight times the interview length to complete the transcribing. For example, an interview of 40 minutes will take just over five hours to transcribe. But the time is well spent. The 'debriefing' can be undertaken by yourself, although you will also need to be pushed by someone else to reflect on it. All participants must agree that the interview and the tape will not be used for any purpose other than those agreed by you in advance. The exercise can also be used in connection with the questions discussed in Chapter 8.

I have referred in the book to some results from studies of this kind. A similar sequence of questions was asked in the research reported in Shaw and Shaw (1997a, 1997b).

Interview questions

[Note for the interviewer: This interview is open-ended and only loosely structured. There will certainly be additional prompts you will wish to give, and the interview sequence will sometimes vary. However, the interview is for the benefit of the person doing the talking, and the interviewer must steadfastly resist pursuing his/her personal interests.]

I   When someone uses the word 'evaluation' what is your reaction? Pause for a moment and do a free association of words you think of.
II   The view increasingly has been expressed that people working in your field should evaluate their work. How do you react to that idea? Do you think evaluation genuinely matters or not? Do you try to evaluate your own practice?

In the next part of the interview I am going to ask you to talk about two recent examples of your work. I would like you to talk about one example of your work where you think you were doing the work well, and one example where you think you were practising less well. Please take a moment to decide in which order you wish to discuss these examples.

III   Could you start by very briefly describing the work, and especially what went well/less well?

IV   How did you know if you were doing this well/not well?

V   What was the evidence that you actually used in this instance? (Be specific to the example please.)

VI   If we were able to speak to the people on the receiving end of this example of your work, do you think they would have held similar views to yourself? Do you think they would use the same or different criteria in deciding whether the work had gone well or not?

VII   Were service users/managers/colleagues/carers/other professionals involved in evaluating in some way? If so, do you think they would have used the same or different criteria in deciding whether the work had gone well or not?

VIII Are you happy that your own yardsticks for judging whether you were doing well or not were the right ones in this particular instance?

Go through the same questions again for the second example of work done well or less well. Then ask:

IX   Is there anything else that these examples raise? For example, did they illustrate anything about your attitudes or views about evaluating?

Ask if there is anything they would like to clarify in what they have said.

When you have completed this, reflect on the implications of the results for the four kinds of practitioner evaluation discussed in Chapter 6.

Chapter 7   Evaluation design: a role play – 'Young people's involvement in prostitution'

Introduction and outline

This should be copied to the facilitators and presented verbally to the participants.

In this exercise you will spend most of the time in a role play, as a member of a Consultative Group which has met three times over the last six months to develop an agreed evaluation research proposal. The exercise is about research *design*, and so your focus will be mainly about the research *process* more than about what happens to the eventual outcomes of the research.

The exercise will last for one hour. You need eight 'players', with a minimum of seven and a maximum of ten. You also need one or two facilitators.

Remember throughout the exercise that the main purpose is not to explore group dynamics or to evaluate anyone's performance in their roles. The purpose is to learn about ways of managing research processes in such a way as to promote usable, relevant and participatory research.

[*Note*: The role briefs are not about actual agencies or organizations. However, you may decide to add a flavour of realism by agreeing names of agencies, for example for the various children's agencies.]

You have worked together very well at earlier meetings and have a good degree of consensus on what kind of inquiry is needed. There is a good level of trust among you. You are all committed to producing relevant, usable research, and also to agreeing a process that is strongly participatory. You have been able to collaborate despite the differences of perspective and agenda that exist between the agencies represented. The purpose of the role-played meeting of the Consultative Group is to reach agreement about specific ways in which the project will ensure these broad goals are met. This is the only item on the agenda.

Step 1   General briefing

Distribute the shared general briefing sheet (see pages 201–202) and spend *5 minutes* familiarizing yourself with the contents. The facilitator will act as a resource person for any clarification questions you have at this stage – and will make sure you keep to time during the role play! You are not in role as yet.

Facilitators may decide to distribute the briefing in advance of the role play to allow longer thinking time.

Step 2   Individual role briefing

Each member should take one of the *individual role briefing* envelopes (pages 202–205). This is your *personal* briefing. If there are only seven 'players' you should remove envelope 3 before opening envelopes. If there are more than eight 'players' then you should randomly choose players to act as observers with the brief of observing the meeting and helping to facilitate the feedback at Step 4.

While there will be some sharing of the contents of the envelopes during the exercise you should only do so as a planned part of your involvement in the role play. Do *not* start by immediately asking 'What's in *your* envelope?'!

Spend *5 minutes* on your own, getting into your role. This will involve careful reading of your briefing, and preparing for how you plan to play your role – remembering as you do so the information you have been given about the tone and content of previous meetings of the group. As soon as you feel sufficiently familiar with your role you should spend a *few minutes* in informal conversation with others in the group. You are now in your role and the purpose of this informal conversation is to make connections with your fellow group members following the several weeks' gap since the last meeting, and to make sure you know who has turned up to the meeting.

Step 3   Consultative group meeting

The chair will call you together to commence the meeting. The meeting will last for approximately *30 minutes*.

[Note: Ensure that you play to your role briefs. If you are an observer make sure that you in no way 'contaminate' the role play. This can happen, for example, by sitting too close to the role play, by laughing at amusing comments made in the role play, by non-verbal communication with participants, and of course by talking during the role play.]

Step 4   Debriefing

The two smaller groups reconvene and spend *15–20 minutes out of role* sharing the decisions made in each group. Refer back to the third paragraph of this introduction to remind yourself of the purpose of the exercise.
  You should:

- Make sure you do not relate to individuals in their role but as themselves.
- First, each individual should make a note of the decisions you believe were made by the meeting.
- Then discuss the extent to which you were all clear and in agreement regarding these decisions. If not, why and what are the consequences?
- Reflect on the extent to which each of you 'delivered' on your role brief. The point here is that if key agencies do not voice their stakeholder interests *in* the group then they will certainly voice them within their own constituency, with the result that genuine consent regarding the project is unlikely. This is partly a chair's role, but also, of course, the individuals' role.
- Identify the potential and pitfalls of planning usable, relevant and participatory research.

Step 4 will be led by the facilitator(s).

Consultative Group briefing

You have agreed at three previous meetings of the group that you want to support the academics in a bid to the research council for a research grant which will:

1   Estimate the scale of children and young people's involvement in prostitution in a large city.
2   Identify the routes children and young people take into and especially out of prostitution.
3   Make recommendations for policy and practice.

The research will combine both quantitative and qualitative methods, over a two-year period. The design of the study is summarized in the following *Scheme Outline*.

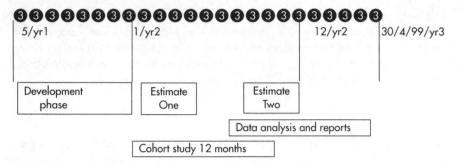

You are meeting in the offices of the Homeless Federation. Agencies represented at this or previous meetings have included:

- Homeless Federation – a federal network of the major homelessness agencies in the city.
- Several large homelessness agencies which provide services for homeless people and have also campaigned for the interests of homeless people.
- Senior managers from four different major children's agencies.
- Project leaders from street level projects working with particular groups, for example, young gay men, homeless young people, young women, HIV+ people with problems of shelter, people involved in prostitution.
- The Association of Chief Officers of Social Work (ACOSW) – a representative chief officer who chairs the ACOSW Children and Families Committee.
- Senior area police.
- Medical staff working in the field of prostitution.
- Two researchers from a university.

The meeting will be attended by the Chief Executive of Homeless Federation (who chairs the group), project leaders from a young woman's project and a young man's project, a research officer from a national children's agency, a senior manager of a large homelessness agency, a chief officer in his/her capacity as chair of a key committee for the Association of Chief Officers of Social Work, and one or both of the researchers. The other representatives have sent apologies.

Individual role briefings

Facilitators should give individual briefs in sealed envelopes to role holders.

1 The Chief Executive of the Homeless Federation

You have welcomed the research approach from the researchers, and been willing to act as link person for the homelessness agencies. You have an interest in the homelessness aspects of prostitution.

Your agency is a federal network that acts on behalf of a large number of homelessness agencies. You do not provide a direct service.

You are the Chair of the group. You have received apologies from the police, children's agency X (with a message to say they hope a strong policy on participatory research will be achieved), children's agency Y, the medical team member, CASH (City Action for Sexual Health), and New to City (one of the active Homeless Federation members). You will be concerned to ensure all agencies – including those which have sent apologies – are content with the decisions, though you have no serious anxieties on that score.

2 University Researcher (1)

You have taken the lead role and will be the main grant holder if the project is successful. You are very supportive of the idea of participatory research, though your university is based in another city and you are slightly concerned that an over-complex project management apparatus may jeopardize the success of the project. But you are ready to reach a compromise to keep the full consent of the end-users.

You are also keen to have an *expert panel* of academics to provide multi-disciplinary input at key points, and hope this can be achieved alongside whatever else is agreed.

Although you have your own views you are very aware that you cannot proceed with the research bid without the collective support of these key agencies. You will be supportive to the chair to facilitate a good outcome.

3 University Researcher (2)

You are not especially enthusiastic about participatory research. You feel most confident with the quantitative aspects of the research and want a 'quality' outcome to the design. But you are hoping you do not feel obliged to make an issue of this.

You have heard some agency people in previous meetings worry about the risk of creating expectations among young people that cannot be met once the project ends. You share these concerns, and hope the group will include a *policy on research ethics* that protects the young people involved. You have decided that you will speak for this.

4 Middlepoint Homeless Agency

You work as a fairly senior person in a large homelessness agency, which is committed to both service provision and campaigning. Your agency is one of the leading members of the Homeless Federation, and you regard the Chief Executive of the Federation as one of your key allies.

You have seen participatory research work very well before and want this to be a strong part of this project, which avoids tokenism. You have been impressed with the extent to which the group has held together on contentious issues. However, you nurse a lurking suspicion that the Association of Chief

Officers of Social Work (ACOSW) representative is too anxious to avoid criticism of social work departments for not protecting young people 'cared for' by them from exploitation by paedophile groups.

You want to see a standing *consultative group of young people*, which will work as a focus group throughout the project, though you have not worked out the details of how this could happen. You will argue for this in the meeting.

5   Street Project for Young Men

You are a project worker for a well established street agency which conducts outreach work with gay young men, some of whom are involved in drugs and a majority of whom are at risk of HIV, and involved in sex work. You have been very enthusiastic about the research project and think you have the ear of the researchers. You are, in fact, hoping a post as a researcher on the project will open up for you (you already have a master's degree and have done some small-scale research which has been strongly commended by the external examiner).

You think that some of the other voluntary agencies working in the city have not been as committed to usable and relevant research as they might be, so you are keen to capitalize on this opportunity. You think your own agency could play a strong role in guaranteeing a genuinely participatory project, and could provide premises for group meetings. You are convinced that the young people should be regarded as having a direct role as co-researchers.

In previous meetings you have voiced a worry about the risk of creating expectations among young people that cannot be met once the project ends. Your memory is that the second researcher supported you, though you are not sure he/she will be at the meeting. You will support the adoption of a *policy on research ethics* that protects the young people involved.

6   Research Officer for National Children's Agency A

Your agency is keen to take a lead among children's agencies in the research field and you have solid support from your senior managers for involvement in this group. You are still hoping that the project will have a strong emphasis on the needs and problems of younger people involved in prostitution (those aged 16 and under). If you were approached for funding to facilitate an appropriate involvement of young people in the research process you would back such a bid in your agency (but it would raise problems if your agency were asked to fund a group with older young people involved – those aged 18 and over). *You will raise this idea at an appropriate moment* in the discussion.

7   Project Worker with National Children's Agency B

Your project works with young women, including some who have absconded from care. You have been involved in setting up a safe house project. Your agency has a strong equal opportunities policy, which includes ensuring that any research involvement addresses issues of race and gender – a policy you fully consent to. You welcome the 'in principle' readiness of the other group members to acknowledge your position, though you are conscious that some group members may feel uncomfortable with your emphasis.

You know the person from Middlepoint Homeless Agency and gather that he/she will raise a proposal for a standing *consultative group of young people* who will work as a focus group throughout the project. You like the idea very much, so long as it is not made up only of white young men.

8   Representative of Association of Chief Officers of Social Work (ACOSW): Convenor of their Children and Families Committee

You have held a brief for ACOSW policy and practice in this field for some time, and want it to have a properly resourced part in service provision. You are concerned that the research should not be hijacked by people who will use it to hammer social work, but you have been happy with the attitudes of those on the group (but unsure of the positions of others in their agencies). You are just emerging from a period of frosty relationships with some of the major children's agencies, but have had fruitful collaboration with the police in developing a joint policy on child prostitution. You will want to make sure the group briefs the police fully on any decisions taken at today's meeting.

Your main concern is that the research should produce results that will be useful and will shape policy. Your main agenda in this meeting is to *make sure the issue of eventual dissemination of the research is properly planned for.* You will want clear decisions about eventual press releases, radio and TV interviews, and what kind of publications are agreed.

Chapter 8   Cultural review

In Chapter 8 (pages 148–149) I described and illustrated a cultural review. Re-read that part of the chapter, especially the example. Imagine you are planning to interview one of the following:

1   An elderly person who is reluctantly considering admission to a residential home.
2   A young woman who reports having been sexually harassed by her teacher at school.
3   A young man aged 16 who is to appear in court on a charge of demanding money with menaces from boys in his neighbourhood.
4   A woman who has had a recurrence of a depressive illness.
5   A woman having difficulties coping with caring for her son of 25 who has serious learning disabilities and lives at home.

• Make a list of the different topics that would need to be the focus of your self-inquiry for a personal and cultural review.

- Make a paragraph of notes on *two* of the topics in your list.

This exercise should take you 20–30 minutes.

Chapter 9   Evaluative interview analysis

Obtain the transcript of a qualitative interview that includes an evaluation dimension. You will sometimes find longer extracts from transcripts in published qualitative evaluation research. There is an interesting one, for example, in Pithouse and Atkinson (1988). Alternatively, staff or colleagues in any strong social science department of a university may be able to facilitate access to appropriate anonymized interview transcripts.

Re-read the section in Chapter 9 (pages 174–177) that discusses analyzing evaluation interviews, and make brief notes on your transcript regarding *indigenous coding* and *narrative linkages*.

References

Acker, J., Barry, K. and Esseveld, J. (1983) 'Objectivity and truth: problems in doing feminist research', *Women's Studies International Forum*, 6 (4): 423–435.

Altheide, D. and Johnson, J. (1994) 'Criteria for assessing interpretive validity in qualitative research', in Denzin, N. and Lincoln, Y. (eds), *Handbook of Qualitative Research*. Thousand Oaks: Sage.

Altheide, D. and Johnson, J. (1997) 'Ethnography and justice', in Miller, G. and Dingwall, R. (eds), *Context and Method in Qualitative Research*. London: Sage.

Anderson, G. (1989) 'Critical ethnography in education: origins, current status, and new directions', *Review of Educational Research*, 59 (3): 249–270.

Atkinson, P. (1995) *Medical Talk*. London: Sage.

Atkinson, P. and Delamont, S. (1993) 'Bread and dreams or bread and circuses? A critique of case study research in evaluation', in Hammersley, M. (ed.), *Controversies in the Classroom*. Buckingham: Open University Press.

Atkinson, P., Delamont, S. and Hammersley, M. (1988) 'Qualitative research traditions: a British response to Jacob', *Review of Educational Research*, 58 (2): 231–250.

Atkinson, R. (1998) *The Life Story Interview*. Thousand Oaks: Sage.

Baker, C., (1983) 'A second look at interviews with adolescents', *Journal of Youth and Adolescence*, 12 (6): 501–519.

Barnes, M. and Wistow, G. (eds) (1992) *Researching User Involvement*. Leeds: Nuffield Institute for Health Services Studies, University of Leeds.

Barnes, M. and Wistow, G. (1994) 'Involving carers in planning and review', in Connor, A. and Black, S. (eds), *Performance, Review and Quality in Social Care*. London: Jessica Kingsley.

Barone, T.E. (1992), 'Beyond theory and method: a case of critical story telling', *Theory into Practice*, 31 (2): 142–146.

Bassey, M. (1986) 'Does action research require sophisticated research methods?', in Hustler, D., Cassidy, A. and Cuff, E. (eds), *Action Research in Classrooms and Schools*. London: Allen and Unwin.

Becker, H. (1970) *Sociological Work*. Chicago: Aldine Publishing Company.

Becker, H. (1993) 'Theory: the necessary evil', in Flinders, D. and Mills, G. (eds), *Theory and Concepts in Qualitative Research: Perspectives from the Field*. New York: Teachers College, Columbia University Press.

Beresford, P. (1992) 'Researching citizen involvement: a collaborative or colonising enterprise?', in Barnes, M. and Wistow, G. (eds), *Researching User Involvement*. Leeds: Nuffield Institute for Health Services Studies, University of Leeds.

Bernstein, R. (1976) *The Restructuring of Social and Political Theory*. Oxford: Blackwell.

Best, J. (1989) *Images of Issues: Typifying Contemporary Social Problems*. New York: Aldine de Gruyter.

Bierman, K. and Schwartz, L. (1986) 'Clinical child interviews: approaches and development consideration', *Child and Adolescent Psychiatry*, 3 (4): 309–325.

Bloom, M. (1999) 'Single-system evaluation', in Shaw, I. and Lishman, J. (eds), *Evaluation and Social Work Practice*. London: Sage.

Bloor, M. (1978) 'On the routinised nature of work in people-processing agencies: the case of adeno-tonsillectomy assessments in ENT outpatient clinics', in Davis, A. (ed.), *Relationships Between Doctors and Patients*. Farnborough: Saxon House.

Bloor, M. (1983) 'Notes on member validation', in Emerson, R. (ed.), *Contemporary Trends in Field Research*. Boston: Little, Brown.

Bloor, M. (1997a) 'Addressing social problems through qualitative research', in Silverman, D. (ed.), *Qualitative Research: Theory, Method and Practice*. London: Sage.

Bloor, M. (1997b) 'Techniques of validation in qualitative research', in Miller, G. and Dingwall, R. (eds), *Context and Method in Qualitative Research*. London: Sage.

Bloor, M. and McKeganey, N. (1987) 'Outstanding practices: evaluative aspects of a descriptive study of eight therapeutic communities', *International Journal of Therapeutic Communities*, 8 (3): 273–285.

Bloor, M. and McKeganey, N. (1989) 'Ethnography addressing the practitioner', in Gubrium, J. and Silverman, D. (eds), *The Politics of Field Research: Sociology Beyond Enlightenment*. Newbury Park: Sage.

Blumer, H. (1969) *Symbolic Interactionism: Perspective and Method*. Englewood Cliffs, NJ: Prentice-Hall.

Bogdan, R. and Taylor, S. (1994) 'A positive approach to qualitative evaluation and policy research in social work', in Sherman, E. and Reid, W. (eds), *Qualitative Research in Social Work*. New York: Columbia University Press.

Booth, D. (ed.) (1994) *Rethinking Social Development*. Harlow: Longman.

Bowen, D. (1993) 'The delights of learning to apply the life history method to school non-attenders', in Broad, B. and Fletcher, C. (eds), *Practitioner Social Work Research in Action*. London: Whiting and Birch.

Brody, S. (1976) *The Effectiveness of Sentencing*. London: HMSO.

Bulmer, M. (1982) *The Uses of Research*. London: Allen and Unwin.

Bull, R. and Shaw, I. (1992) 'Constructing causal accounts in social work', *Sociology*, 26 (4): 635–649.

Burgess, R. (1980) 'Some fieldwork problems in teacher-based research', *British Educational Research Journal*, 6 (2): 165–173.

Burgess, R., Pole, C., Evans, K. and Priestley, C. (1994) 'Four studies from one or one study from four? Multi-site case study research', in Bryman, A. and Burgess, R. (eds), *Analysing Qualitative Data*. London: Routledge.

Butler, I. and Williamson, H. (1994) *Children Speak: Children, Trauma and Social Work*. Harlow: Longman.

Campbell, D. (1964) 'Distinguishing differences of perception from failures of communication in cross-cultural studies', in Northrop, F. and Livingston, H. (eds), *Cross-Cultural Understanding: Epistemology in Anthropology*. New York: Harper and Row.

Campbell, D. (1978) 'Qualitative knowing in action research', in Brenner, M. and Marsh, P. (eds), *The Social Context of Methods*. London: Croom Helm.

Campbell, D. (1979) 'Degrees of freedom and the case study', in Cook, T. and Reichardt, C. (eds), *Qualitative and Quantitative Methods in Evaluation Research*. Beverly Hills: Sage.

Campbell, D. (1994) 'Foreword' in Yin, R.K., *Case Study Research*. Thousand Oaks: Sage.

Campbell, D. (1996) 'Can we overcome worldview incommensurability/relativity in trying to understand the other?', in Jessor, R., Colby, A. and Shweder, R. (eds), *Ethnography and Human Development*. Chicago: University of Chicago Press.

Campbell, D. and Stanley, J. (1966) *Experimental and Quasi-experimental Designs for Research*. Chicago: Rand McNally.

Cancian, F. and Armstead, C. (1992) 'Participatory research', in Borgatta, E.F. and Borgatta, M. (eds), *Encyclopaedia of Sociology*. New York: Macmillan.

Carr, W. and Kemmis, S. (1986) *Becoming Critical: Education, Knowledge and Action Research.* London: Falmer Press.

Chambers, R. (1983) *Rural Development: Putting the Last First.* Harlow: Longman.

Cheetham, J. (1998) 'The evaluation of social work: priorities, problems and possibilities', in Cheetham, J. and Kazi, M. (eds), *The Working of Social Work.* London: Jessica Kingsley Publishers.

Chelimsky, E. (1995) 'Politics, policy and research synthesis', *Evaluation,* 1 (1): 97–104.

Chelimsky, E. (1997) 'Thoughts for a new Evaluation Society', *Evaluation,* 3 (1): 97–118.

Cicourel, A. (1964) *Method and Measurement in Sociology.* New York: Free Press.

Clandinin, J. and Connelly, F.M. (1994) 'Personal experience methods', in Denzin, N. and Lincoln, Y. (eds), *Handbook of Qualitative Methods.* Thousand Oaks: Sage.

Clapham, D., Means, R. and Munro, M. (1993) 'Housing, the life course and older people', in Arber S. and Evandrou, M. (eds), *Ageing, Independence and the Life Course.* London: Jessica Kingsley.

Clarke, R. and Cornish, D. (1972) *The Controlled Trial in Institutional Research.* London: HMSO.

Clifford, D. (1994) 'Critical life histories: key anti-oppressive research methods and processes, in Humphries, B. and Truman, C. (eds), *Rethinking Social Research: Anti-Discriminatory Approaches in Research Methodology.* Aldershot: Avebury.

Cochran-Smith, M. and Lytle, S. (1990) 'Research on teaching and teacher research: the issues that divide', *Educational Researcher,* 19 (2): 2–22.

Coffey, A. and Atkinson, P. (1996) *Making Sense of Qualitative Data.* London: Sage.

Cohler, B. (1994) 'The human services, the life story, and clinical research', in Sherman, E. and Reid, W. (eds), *Qualitative Research in Social Work.* New York: Columbia University Press.

Comstock, D. (1982) 'A method for critical research', in Bredo, F. and Feinburg, W. (eds), *Knowledge and Values in Educational Research.* Philadelphia: Temple University Press.

Cook, T. (1985) 'Postpositivist critical multiplism', in Shotland, R. and Mark, M. (eds), *Social Science and Social Policy.* Beverly Hills: Sage.

Cook, T. and Campbell, D. (1979) *Quasi-Experimentation.* Chicago: Rand McNally.

Corsaro, W. (1985) *Friendship and Peer Culture in the Early Years.* New Jersey: Ablex, Norwood.

Crabtree, B. and Miller, W. (1992a) *Doing Qualitative Research.* Newbury Park: Sage.

Crabtree, W. and Miller, W. (1992b) 'The analysis of narratives from a long interview', in Stewart, M., Tudiver, F., Bass, M., Dunn, E. and Norton, P. (eds), *Tools for Primary Care Research.* Newbury Park: Sage.

Cronbach, L. (1982) *Designing Evaluations of Educational and Social Programs.* San Francisco: Jossey-Bass.

Cronbach, L. (1986) 'Social inquiry by and for earthlings', in Fiske, D. and Shweder, R. (eds), *Metatheory in Social Science: Pluralisms and Subjectivities.* Chicago: University of Chicago Press.

Cronbach, L., Ambron, S., Dornbusch, S., Hess, R., Hornik, R., Phillips, D. Walker, D. and Weiner, S. (1980) *Toward Reform of Program Evaluation.* San Francisco: Jossey-Bass.

Davies, M. and Kelly, E. (1976) 'The social worker, the client and the social anthropologist', *British Journal of Social Work,* 6 (2): 213–231.

Davis, A. (1992) 'Who needs user research? Service users as research subjects or participants', in Barnes, M. and Wistow, G. (eds), *Researching User Involvement.* Leeds: Nuffield Institute for Health Services Studies, University of Leeds.

Dean, R. (1994) 'How good are you?', *Voluntary Housing,* January.

Denzin, N. (1989) *The Research Act.* New York: McGraw Hill.

Dullea, K. and Mullender, A. (1999) 'Evaluation and empowerment', in Shaw, I. and Lishman, J. (eds), *Evaluation and Social Work Practice*. London: Sage.

Ebbutt, D. (1985) 'Educational action research: some general concerns and specific quibbles', in Burgess, R.G. (ed.), *Issues in Educational Research: Qualitative Methods*. London: Falmer Press.

Edwards, M. (1989) 'The irrelevance of development studies', *Third World Quarterly*, 11 (1): 116–135.

Edwards, M. (1994) 'Rethinking social development: the search for relevance' in Booth, D. (ed.), *Rethinking Social Development*. Harlow: Longman.

Eisner, E. (1988) 'Educational connoisseurship and criticism: their form and functions in educational evaluation', in Fetterman, D.M. (ed.), *Qualitative Approaches to Evaluation in Education*. New York: Praeger.

Eisner, E. (1990) 'The meaning of alternative paradigms for practice', in Guba, E. (ed.), *The Paradigm Dialog*. Newbury Park: Sage.

Eisner, E. (1991a) *The Enlightened Eye: Qualitative Inquiry and the Enhancement of Educational Practice*. New York: Macmillan.

Eisner, E. (1991b) 'Taking a second look: educational connoisseurship revisited', in McLaughlin, M.W., and Phillips, D., *Evaluation and Education at Quarter Century*. Chicago: University of Chicago Press.

Elden, M. and Chisholm, R. (1993) 'Emerging varieties of action research', *Human Relation*, 46 (2): 121–141.

Elks, M. and Kirkhart, K. (1993) 'Evaluating effectiveness from the practitioner's perspective', *Social Work*, 38 (5): 554–563.

Elliott, J. (1991) 'Changing contexts of educational evaluation: the challenge for methodology', *Studies in Education*, 17: 215–238.

Ellsworth, E. (1989) 'Why doesn't this feel empowering? Working through the myths of critical pedagogy', *Harvard Educational Review*, 59 (3): 297–324.

Emerson, R. and Pollner, M. (1988) 'On the uses of members' responses to researchers' accounts', *Human Organisation*, 47 (3): 189–198.

England, H. (1986) *Social Work as Art*. London: Allen and Unwin.

Epstein, L. (1996) 'The trouble with the researcher-practitioner idea', *Social Work Research*, 20 (2): 113–118.

Eraut, M. (1984) 'Handling value issues', in Adelman, C. (ed.), *The Politics and Ethics of Evaluation*. London: Croom Helm.

Erikson, E. (1959) 'The nature of clinical inference', in Lerner, D. (ed.), *Evidence and Inference*. Illinois: Free Press.

Everitt, A., and Hardiker, P. (1996) *Evaluating for Good Practice*. London: Macmillan.

Everitt, A., Hardiker, P., Littlewood, J. and Mullender, A. (1992) *Applied Research for Better Practice*. London: Macmillan.

Filstead, W. (1979) 'Qualitative methods – a needed perspective in evaluation research', in Cook, T. and Reichardt, C. (eds), *Qualitative and Quantitative Methods in Evaluation Research*. Beverley Hills: Sage.

Finch, J. (1985) 'Social policy and education: problems and possibilities of using qualitative research', in Burgess, R. (ed.), *Issues in Educational Research: Qualitative Methods*. London: Falmer Press.

Finch, J. (1986) *Research and Policy: the Uses of Qualitative Methods in Social and Educational Research*. London: Falmer Press.

Fine, G. and Sandstrom, K. (1988) *Knowing Children: Participant Observation with Minors*. Newbury Park: Sage.

Firestone, W. (1993) 'Alternative arguments for generalising from data as applied to qualitative research', in *Educational Researcher*, 22 (4): 16–23.

Fisher, M. (1983) *Speaking of Clients*. Sheffield: University of Sheffield Joint Unit for Social Services Research.

Fisher, M. (1992) 'Users' experiences of agreements in social care', in Barnes, M. and Wistow, G. (eds), *Researching User Involvement*. Leeds: Nuffield Institute for Health Services Studies, University of Leeds.

Fisher, M. (1997) 'Research, knowledge and practice in community care', *Issues in Social Work Education*, 17 (2): 17–30.

Fisher, M., Marsh, P., Phillips, D. with Sainsbury, E. (1986) *In and Out of Care: The Experiences of Children, Parents and Social Workers*. London: Batsford.

Fook, J. (ed.) (1996) *The Reflective Researcher: Social Workers' Theories of Practice Research*. St Leonards, NSW: Allen and Unwin.

Fortune, A. (1994) 'Ethnography in social work', in Sherman, E. and Reid, W. (eds), *Qualitative Research in Social Work*. New York: Columbia University Press.

Fournier, D. (ed.) (1995) *Reasoning in Evaluation: Inferential Links and Leaps*. San Francisco: American Evaluation Association/Jossey-Bass.

Fournier, D. and Smith, N. (1993) 'Clarifying the merits of argument in evaluation practice', *Evaluation and Program Planning*, 16 (4): 315–323.

Frankland, J. and Bloor, M. (1999) 'Some issues arising in the systematic analysis of focus group materials', in Barbour, R. and Kitzinger, J. (eds), *Developing Focus Group Research: Politics, Theory and Practice*. London: Sage.

Fuller, R. and Petch, A. (1995) *Practitioner Research: the Reflexive Social Worker*. Buckingham: Open University Press.

Gage, N. (1989) 'The paradigm wars and their aftermath', *Educational Researcher*, 18 (7): 4–10.

Garrison, J. (1988) 'The impossibility of atheoretical research', *Journal of Educational Thought*, 22 (1): 21–25.

Garrison, J. (1994) 'Realism, Dewey and pragmatism', *Educational Researcher*, 21 (1): 5–14.

Geertz, C. (1973) *The Interpretation of Cultures*. New York: Basic Books.

Geertz, C. (1983) *Local Knowledge*. New York: Basic Books.

Gelsthorpe, L. (1992) 'Response to Martin Hammersley's paper on feminist methodology', in *Sociology*, 26 (2): 213–218.

Gibbs, A. (1997) *Focus Groups*. Social Research Update, no. 19, Department of Sociology, University of Surrey.

Gibbs, L., Gambrill, E., Blakemore, J., Begun, A., Keniston, A., Peden, A. and Lefcowitz, J. (1995) 'A measure of critical thinking about practice', *Research on Social Work Practice*, 5 (2): 193–204.

Goldstein, H. (1994) 'Ethnography, critical inquiry and social work practice', in Sherman, E. and Reid, W. (eds), *Qualitative Research in Social Work*. New York: Columbia University Press.

Goode, D. (1986) 'Kids, culture and innocents', *Human Relations*, 9 (1): 83–106.

Gould, N. (1999) 'Qualitative practice evaluation', in Shaw, I. and Lishman, J. (eds), *Evaluation and Social Work Practice*. London: Sage.

Gould, N. and Taylor, I. (eds) (1996) *Reflective Learning for Social Work*. Aldershot: Ashgate.

Greene, J. (1990) 'Three views on the nature and role of knowledge in social science', in Guba, E. (ed.), *The Paradigm Dialog*. Newbury Park: Sage.

Greene, J. (1992) 'The practitioner's perspective', *Curriculum Inquiry*, 21 (1): 39–45.

Greene, J. (1993) 'The role of theory in qualitative program evaluation', in Flinders, J. and Mills, G. (eds), *Theory and Concepts in Qualitative Research*. New York: Teachers College Press.

Greene, J. (1994) 'Qualitative program evaluation: practice and promise', in Denzin, N. and Lincoln, Y. (eds), *Handbook of Qualitative Research*. Thousand Oaks: Sage.

Greene, J. (1996) 'Qualitative evaluation and scientific citizenship', *Evaluation*, 2 (3): 277–289.

Greene, J. and McClintock, C. (1991) 'The evolution of evaluation methodology', *Theory into Practice*, 30 (1): 13–21.

Guba, E. (1990) 'The alternative paradigm dialog', in Guba, E. (ed.), *The Paradigm Dialog*. Newbury Park: Sage.

Guba, E. and Lincoln, Y. (1989) *Fourth Generation Evaluation.* Newbury Park: Sage.

Hakim, C. (1988) *Research Design.* London: Allen and Unwin.

Hall, B. (1979) 'Participatory research: an approach for change', *Convergence,* 8 (2): 24–31.

Hammersley, M. (1992) *What's Wrong With Ethnography?* London: Routledge.

Hammersley, M. (1993a) 'On the teacher as researcher', *Educational Action Research,* 1 (3): 425–445.

Hammersley, M. (1993b) 'On methodological purism', *British Educational Research Journal,* 19 (4): 339–341.

Hammersley, M. (1993c) 'On practitioner ethnography', in Hammersley, M. (ed.), *Controversies in Classroom Research.* Buckingham: Open University Press.

Hammersley, M. (1994) 'Ethnography, policy making and practice in education', in Halpin, D. and Troyna, B. (eds), *Researching Education Policy: Ethical and Methodological Issues.* London: Falmer Press.

Hammersley, M. (1995) *The Politics of Social Research.* London: Sage.

Hammersley, M. and Gomm, R. (1997) 'Bias in social research', *Sociological Research Online,* 2, 1. *<http: //www.socresonline.org.uk/socresonline/2/1/2.html>*

Hart, E. and Bond, M. (1995) *Action Research for Health and Social Care.* Buckingham: Open University Press.

Harvey, L. (1990) *Critical Social Research.* London: Unwin Hyman.

Hawkesworth, M. (1989) 'Knowers, knowing, known: feminist theory and claims of truth', *Signs: Journal of Women in Culture and Society,* 14 (3): 533–555.

Heap, J. (1995) 'Constructionism in the rhetoric and practice of fourth generation evaluation', *Evaluation and Program Planning,* 18 (1): 51–61.

Hedrick, T. (1988) 'The interaction of politics and evaluation', *Evaluation Practice,* 9 (1): 5–14.

Heron, J. (1996) *Co-operative Inquiry: Research into the Human Condition.* London: Sage.

Holman, B. (1987) 'Research from the underside', *British Journal of Social Work,* 17 (6): 669–683.

Holstein, J. and Gubrium, J. (1995) *The Active Interview.* Thousand Oaks: Sage.

Hornsby-Smith, M. (1993) 'Gaining access', in Gilbert, N. (ed.), *Researching Social Life.* London: Sage.

House, E. (1980) *Evaluating With Validity.* Beverly Hills: Sage.

House, E. (1991a) 'Evaluation and social justice: where are we now?', in McLaughlin, M. and Phillips, D. (eds), *Evaluation and Education: at Quarter Century.* Chicago: Chicago University Press.

House, E. (1991b) 'Realism in research', *Educational Researcher,* 20 (6): 2–9.

House, E. (1993) *Professional Evaluation.* Newbury Park: Sage.

House, E. (1995) 'Putting things together coherently: logic and justice', in Fournier, D. (ed.), *Reasoning in Evaluation: Inferential Links and Leaps.* San Francisco: American Evaluation Association/Jossey-Bass.

Humphrey, C. and Pease, K. (1992) 'Effectiveness measurement in the Probation Service: a view from the troops', *Howard Journal,* 31 (2): 31–52.

Humphreys, L. (1975) *Tearoom Trade.* Chicago: Aldine.

Humphries, B. (1997) 'From critical thought to emancipatory action: contradictory research goals?', *Sociological Research Online:* <http: //www.socresonline.org.uk/socresonline/2/1/3.html>

Humphries, B. (1999) 'Feminist evaluation', in Shaw, I. and Lishman, J. (eds), *Evaluation and Social Work Practice.* London: Sage.

Jacob, E. (1987) 'Qualitative research traditions: a review', *Review of Educational Research,* 57 (1): 1–50.

Jarrett, R. (1993) 'Focus group interviewing with low income minority populations', in Morgan, D. (ed.), *Successful Focus Groups: Advancing the State of the Art.* Newbury Park: Sage.

Johnson, J. (1995) 'In dispraise of justice', *Symbolic Interaction*, 18 (2): 191–205.

Kelly, A. (1985) 'Action research: what is it and what can it do?', in Burgess, R. (ed.), *Issues in Educational Research*. London: Falmer Press.

Kirkhart, K. (1995) 'Seeking multicultural validity: a postcard from the road', *Evaluation Practice*, 16 (1): 1–12.

Kirkpatrick, I. and Lucio, M. (eds) (1995) *The Politics of Quality*. London: Routledge.

Kitzinger, J. (1994) 'Focus groups: method or madness?', in Boulton, M. (ed.), *Challenge and Innovation: Methodological Advances in Social Research on HIV/AIDS*. London: Taylor and Francis.

Knodel, J. (1993) 'The design and analysis of focus group studies: a practical approach', in Morgan, D. (ed.), *Successful Focus Groups*. Newbury Park: Sage.

Kreuger, R. (1994) *Focus Groups: a Practical Guide for Applied Research*. Thousand Oaks: Sage.

Kushner, S. (1997) 'Consumers and heroes: a critical review of some recent writings of Michael Scriven', *Evaluation*, 5 (3): 363–374.

Lakatos, I. (1970) 'Falsification and the methodology of scientific research programmes', in Lakatos, I. and Musgrave, A. (eds), *Criticism and the Growth of Knowledge*. Cambridge: Cambridge University Press.

Lang, N. (1994) 'Integrating the data processing of qualitative research and social work practice to advance the practitioner as knowledge builder: tools for knowing and doing', in Sherman, E. and Reid, W. (eds), *Qualitative Research in Social Work*. New York: Columbia University Press.

Lather, P. (1986a) 'Issues of validity in openly ideological research', *Interchange*, 17 (4): 63–84.

Lather, P. (1986b) 'Research as praxis', *Harvard Educational Review*, 56 (3): 257–277.

Lather, P. (1991) *Getting Smart: Feminist Research and Pedagogy with/in the Postmodern*. New York: Routledge.

Lather, P. (1992) 'Critical frames in educational research: feminist and post-structural perspectives', *Theory Into Practice*, 31 (2): 87–99.

Lee, R. (1993) *Doing Research on Sensitive Topics*. London: Sage.

Leplin, J. (ed.) (1984) *Scientific Realism*. Berkeley: University of California Press.

Lerner, D. (ed.) (1959) *Evidence and Inference*. New York: Free Press.

Lewis, H. (1988) 'Ethics and the managing of service effectiveness in social welfare', in Patti, R., Poertner, J. and Rapp, C. (eds), *Managing for Service Effectiveness in Social Welfare Organisations*. New York: Haworth.

Lincoln, Y. (1990) 'The making of a constructivist: a remembrance of transformations past', in Guba, E. (ed.), *The Paradigm Dialog*. Newbury Park: Sage.

Lincoln, Y. and Guba, E. (1986a) 'But is it rigorous? Trustworthiness and authenticity in naturalistic evaluation', in Williams, D.D. (ed.), *Naturalistic Evaluation*. New Directions in Program Evaluation, No. 30, San Francisco: Jossey-Bass.

Lincoln, Y. and Guba, E. (1986b) 'Research, evaluation and policy analysis: heuristics and disciplined inquiry', *Policy Studies Review*, 5 (3): 546–565.

Lincoln, Y. and Guba, E. (1989) 'Ethics: the failure of positivist science', *Review of Higher Education*, 12 (3): 221–240.

Lofland, J. and Lofland, L. (1995) *Analysing Social Settings*. Belmont: Wadsworth.

Lyman, S. and Scott, M. (1970) *A Sociology of the Absurd*. New York: Appleton-Century-Crofts.

Mandell, N. (1988) 'The least adult role in studying children', *Journal of Contemporary Ethnography*, 16 (4): 433–467.

Martin, M. (1994) 'Developing a feminist participative research framework', in Humphries, B. and Truman, C. (eds), *Rethinking Social Research: Anti-Discriminatory Approaches in Research Methodology*. Aldershot: Avebury.

Martin, M. (1996) 'Issues of power in the participatory research process', in de Koning, K. and Martin, M. (eds), *Participatory Research in Health*. London: Zed Books.

Martin, R. (1995) *Oral History in Social Work*. Thousand Oaks: Sage.

Martin, R. (1999) 'Histories in social work', in Shaw, I. and Lishman, J. (eds), *Evaluation and Social Work Practice*. London: Sage.

Mayer, J. and Timms, N. (1970) *The Client Speaks*. London: Routledge and Kegan Paul.

McCracken, G. (1988) *The Long Interview*. Newbury Park: Sage.

McKeganey, N. and Bloor, M. (1991) 'Spotting the invisible man: the influence of male gender on fieldwork relations', *British Journal of Sociology*, 42 (2): 195–210.

McKeganey, N., MacPherson, I. and Hunter, D. (1988) 'How "they" decide: exploring professional decision making', *Research, Policy and Planning*, 6 (1): 15–19.

McLennan, G. (1995) 'Feminism, epistemology and postmodernism: reflections on current ambivalence', *Sociology*, 29 (2): 391–409.

McNamara, D. (1980) 'The outsider's arrogance: the failure of participant observers to understand classroom events', *British Educational Research Journal*, 6 (2): 113–125.

Miles, M. and Huberman, A. (1994) *Qualitative Data Analysis: an Expanded Sourcebook*. Thousand Oaks: Sage.

Miller, J. (1990) *Creating Spaces and Finding Voices: Teachers Collaborating for Empowerment*. New York: State University of New York Press.

Miller, J. (1992) 'Exploring power and authority issues in a collaborative research project', *Theory into Practice*, 21 (2): 165–172.

Miller, J. and Martens, M. (1990) 'Hierarchy and imposition in collaborative inquiry: Teacher-researchers' reflections on recurrent dilemmas', *Educational Foundations*, 4 (4): 41–59.

Miller, W. and Crabtree, B. (1992) 'Depth interviewing: the long interview approach', in Stewart, M., Tudiver, F., Bass, M., Dunn, E. and Norton, P. (eds), *Tools for Primary Care Research*. Newbury Park: Sage.

Miller, W. and Crabtree, B. (1994) 'Clinical research', in Denzin, N. and Lincoln, Y. (eds), *Handbook of Qualitative Methods*. Thousand Oaks: Sage.

Morgan, D. (1985) *The Family: Politics and Social Theory*. London: Routledge.

Morgan, D.L. (ed.) (1993) *Successful Focus Groups: Advancing the State of the Art*. Newbury Park: Sage.

Morgan, D.L. (1997) *Focus Groups as Qualitative Research*. Newbury Park: Sage.

Oliver, M. (1992) 'Changing the social relations of research production?', *Disability, Handicap and Society*, 7 (2) 101–114.

Opie, I. and Opie, P. (1959) *The Lore and Language of Schoolchildren*. Oxford: Oxford University Press.

Opie, I. and Opie, P. (1969) *Children's Games of Street and Playground*. Oxford: Oxford University Press.

Outhwaite, W. (1987) *New Philosophies of Social Science*. London: Macmillan.

Palumbo, D. (1987) 'Politics and evaluation' in Palumbo, D. (ed.) *The Politics of Program Evaluation*. Newbury Park, CA: Sage.

Parker, W. (1984) 'Interviewing children: problems and promise', *Journal of Negro Education*, 53 (1): 18–28.

Parlett, M. and Hamilton, D. (1972) *Evaluation as Illumination*. Edinburgh: Centre for Research in the Educational Sciences.

Patton, M. (1988a) 'The evaluator's responsibility for utilization', *Evaluation Practice*, 9 (1): 5–24.

Patton, M. (1988b) 'Paradigms and pragmatism', in Fetterman, D. (ed.), *Qualitative Approaches to Evaluation in Education*. New York: Praeger.

Patton, M. (1990) *Qualitative Evaluation*. Newbury Park: Sage.

Pawson, R. and Tilley, N. (1997a) *Realistic Evaluation*. London: Sage.

Pawson, R. and Tilley, N. (1997b) 'An introduction to scientific realist evaluation', in Chelimsky, E. and Shadish, W. (eds), *Evaluation for the 21st Century*. Thousand Oaks: Sage.

Payne, G. and Cuff, E. (eds) (1982) *Doing Teaching: the Practical Management of Class-rooms*. London: Batsford.

Phillips, D. (1987a) *Philosophy, Science and Social Inquiry*, New York: Pergamon.

Phillips, D. (1987b) 'Validity in qualitative research', *Education and Urban Society*, 20 (1): 9–24.

Phillips, D. (1990a) 'Postpositivistic science: myths and realities', in Guba, E. (ed.), *The Paradigm Dialog*. Newbury Park: Sage.

Phillips, D. (1990b) 'Subjectivity and objectivity: an objective inquiry', in Eisner, E. and Peshkin, A. (eds), *Qualitative Inquiry in Education*. New York: Teachers College, Columbia University.

Pithouse, A. (1998) *Social Work as an Invisible Trade*. Aldershot (England): Avebury.

Pithouse, A. and Atkinson, P. (1988) 'Telling the case: occupational narrative in a social work office', in Coupland, N. (ed.), *Styles of Discourse*. London: Croom Helm.

Pitman, M. and Maxwell, J. (1992) 'Qualitative approaches to evaluation: models and methods', in LeCompte, M. and Preissle, J. (eds), *The Handbook of Qualitative Research in Education*. San Diego: Academic Press.

Plaut, T., Landis, S. and Trevor, J. (1993) 'Focus groups and community mobilisation', in Morgan, D.L. (ed.), *Successful Focus Groups: Advancing the State of the Art*. Newbury Park: Sage.

Popkewitz, T. (1990) 'Whose future? Whose past?', in Guba, E. (ed.), *The Paradigm Dialog*. Newbury Park: Sage.

Popper, K. (1966) *The Open Society and Its Enemies* (II). London: Routledge and Kegan Paul.

Popper, K. (1989) *Conjectures and Refutations: the Growth of Scientific Knowledge*. London: Routledge.

Pryce-Jones, M. (1993) 'Critical incident technique as a method of assessing patient satisfaction', in Fitzpatrick, R. and Hopkins, A. (eds), *Measurement of Patients' Satisfaction with their Care*. London: Royal College of Physicians.

Pulice, R. (1994) 'Qualitative evaluation methods in the public sector: under-standing and working with constituency groups in the evaluation process', in Sherman, E. and Reid, W. (eds), *Qualitative Research in Social Work*. New York: Columbia University Press.

Reason, P. (ed.) (1994a) *Participation in Human Inquiry*. London: Sage.

Reason, P. (1994b) 'Three approaches to participative inquiry', in Denzin, N. and Lincoln, Y. (eds), *Handbook of Qualitative Research*. Thousand Oaks: Sage.

Reason, P. and Rowan, J. (eds) (1981) *Human Inquiry: a Sourcebook of New Paradigm Research*. Chichester: John Wiley.

Rees, S. (1974) 'No more than contact', *British Journal of Social Work*, 4 (3): 255–279.

Rees, S. and Wallace, A. (1982) *Verdicts on Social Work*. London: Edward Arnold.

Reichardt, C. and Cook, T. (1979) 'Beyond qualitative *versus* quantitative methods', in Cook, T. and Reichardt, C. (eds), *Qualitative and Quantitative Methods in Evaluation Research*. Beverly Hills: Sage.

Reid, W. (1988) 'Service effectiveness and the social agency', in Patti, R., Poertner, J. and Rapp, C. (eds), *Managing for Effectiveness in Social Welfare Organizations*. New York: Haworth.

Reid, W. (1990) 'Change-process research: a new paradigm?', in Videka-Sherman, L. and Reid, W. (eds), *Advances in Clinical Social Work Research*. Silver Spring, MD: NASW Press.

Reid, W. (1994a) 'Reframing the epistemological debate', in Sherman, E. and Reid, W. (eds), *Qualitative Research in Social Work*. New York: Columbia University Press.

Reid, W. (1994b) 'Field testing and data gathering on innovative practice inter-ventions in early development', in Rothman, J. and Thomas, E. (eds), *Intervention Research: Design and Development of Human Service*. New York: Haworth Press.

Reid, W. (1994c) 'The empirical practice movement', *Social Service Review*, 68 (2): 165–184.

Reid, W. (1997) 'Research on task-centred practice', *Social Work Research*, 21 (3): 132–137.

Reid, W. and Hanrahan, P. (1982) 'Recent evaluations of social work: grounds for optimism', *Social Work*, 27: 328–340.

Reid, W. and Shyne, A. (1969) *Brief and Extended Casework*. New York: Columbia University Press.

Reid, W. and Zettergren, P. (1999) 'A perspective on empirical practice', in Shaw, I. and Lishman, J. (eds), *Evaluation and Social Work Practice*. London: Sage.

Renzetti, C. and Lee, R. (eds) (1992) *Researching Sensitive Topics*. Newbury Park: Sage.

Rist, R. (1994) 'Influencing the policy process with qualitative research', in Denzin, N. and Lincoln, Y. (eds), *Handbook of Qualitative Research*. Thousand Oaks: Sage.

Rodwell, M. and Woody, D. (1994) 'Constructivist evaluation: the policy/practice context', in Sherman, E. and Reid, W. (eds), *Qualitative Research in Social Work*. New York: Columbia University Press.

Rorty, R. (1979) *Philosophy and the Mirror of Nature*. Princeton NJ: Princeton University Press.

Rorty, R. (1991) 'Feminism and pragmatism', *Radical Philosophy*, 59, 3–14.

Rossi, P. (1987) 'No good applied social research goes unpunished', *Society*, 25, November/December: 74–79.

Rothschild Report (1971) *A Framework for Government Research and Development*. Cmnd 4814, London: HMSO.

Ruckdeschel, R. (1999) 'Qualitative clinical research and evaluation: obstacles, opportunities and issues', in Shaw, I. and Lishman, J. (eds), *Evaluation and Social Work Practice*. London: Sage.

Ruckdeschel, R., Earnshaw, P. and Firrek, A. (1994) 'The qualitative case study and evaluation: Issues, methods and examples', in Sherman, E. and Reid, W. (eds), *Qualitative Research in Social Work*. New York: Columbia University Press.

Sackett, D. and Rosenberg, T. (1995) 'On the need for evidenced based medicine', *Health Economist*, 4 (2): 249–254.

Schon, D. (1983) *The Reflective Practitioner: How Professionals Think in Action*. New York: Basic Books.

Schon, D. (1992) 'The crisis of professional knowledge and the pursuit of an epistemology of practice', *Journal of Interprofessional Care*, 6 (1): 49–63.

Schon, D. (1995) 'Reflective inquiry in social work practice', in Hess, P. and Mullen, E. (eds), *Practitioner–Researcher Partnerships*. Washington, DC: NASW Press.

Schwab, J. (1969) 'The practical: a language for curriculum', *School Review*, November: 1–23.

Schwandt, T. (1993) 'Theory for the social sciences: crisis of identity and purpose', in Flinders, D. and Mills, G. (eds), *Theory and Concepts in Qualitative Research: Perspectives from the Field*. New York: Teachers College Press.

Schwandt, T. (1997) 'Evaluation as practical hermeneutics', *Evaluation*, 3 (1): 69–83.

Scott, D. (1990) 'Practice wisdom: the neglected source of practice research', *Social Work*, 35 (6): 564–568.

Scriven, M. (1972) 'Objectivity and subjectivity in educational research', in Thomas, L. (ed.), *Philosophical Redirection of Educational Research*. Washington: National Society for the Study of Education.

Scriven, M. (1986) 'New frontiers of evaluation', *Evaluation Practice*, 7 (1): 7–44.

Scriven, M. (1995) 'The logic of evaluation and evaluation practice', in Fournier, D. (ed.), *Reasoning in Evaluation: Inferential Links and Leaps*. San Francisco: American Evaluation Association/Jossey-Bass.

Scriven, M. (1996) 'The theory behind practical evaluation', *Evaluation*, 2 (4): 393–404.

Scriven, M. (1997) 'Truth and objectivity in evaluation', in Chelimsky, E. and Shadish, W. (eds), *Evaluation for the 21st Century*. Thousand Oaks: Sage.

Searight, P. (1988) *Utilizing Qualitative Research to Self-Evaluate Direct Practice*. Doctoral Dissertation, Saint Louis University.

Selwyn, J. (1991) 'Applying to adopt: the experience of rejection', *Adoption and Fostering*, 15 (3): 26–29.

Selwyn, J. (1996) '"Mirror, mirror on the wall. Who is the fairest of them all?" Involuntary childlessness and identity', in Butler, I. and Shaw, I. (eds) *A Case of Neglect? Children's Experiences and the Sociology and Childhood*. Aldershot (England): Avebury.

Shadish, W. (1995) 'Philosophy of science and quantitative-qualitative debates: thirteen common errors', *Evaluation and Program Planning*, 18 (1): 63–75.

Shadish, W., Cook, T. and Leviton, L. (1990) *Foundations of Program Evaluation: Theories of Practice*. Newbury Park: Sage.

Shaw, I. (1996a) *Evaluating in Practice*. Aldershot (England): Ashgate.

Shaw, I. (1996b) 'Unbroken voices: children, young people and qualitative methods', in Butler, I. and Shaw, I. (eds), *A Case of Neglect? Children's Experiences and the Sociology of Childhood*. Aldershot (England): Avebury.

Shaw, I. (1997) *Be Your Own Evaluator: a Guide to Reflective and Enabling Evaluating*. Wrexham (Wales): Prospects Publishing.

Shaw, I. (1998) 'Practising evaluation', in Cheetham, J. and Kazi, M. (eds), *The Working of Social Work*. London: Jessica Kingsley Publishers.

Shaw, I. (1999) 'Seeing the trees for the wood: the politics of evaluating in practice', in Broad, B. (ed.), *The Politics of Research and Evaluation*. Birmingham (England): Venture Press.

Shaw, I. and Lishman, J. (eds) (1999) *Evaluation and Social Work Practice*. London: Sage.

Shaw, I. and Shaw, A. (1997a) 'Game plans, buzzes and sheer luck: doing well in social work', *Social Work Research*, 21 (2): 69–79.

Shaw, I. and Shaw, A. (1997b) 'Keeping social work honest: evaluating as profession and practice', *British Journal of Social Work*, 27 (6): 847–869.

Shaw, I., Williamson, H. and Parry-Langdon, N. (1992) 'Developing models for day services', *Social Policy and Administration*, 26 (1): 73–86.

Sheldon, B. and Macdonald, G. (1989–90) 'Implications for practice of recent social work effectiveness research', *Practice*, 6 (3): 211–218.

Sherman, E. (1990) 'Change process research: no new paradigm but a necessary complement to the old paradigm', in Videka-Sherman, L. and Reid, W.J. (eds), *Advances in Clinical Social Work Research*. Silver Spring, MD: NASW Press.

Sherman, E. and Reid, W. (eds) (1994) *Qualitative Research and Social Work*. New York: Columbia University Press.

Siegert, M. (1986) 'Adult elicited child behaviour: the paradox of measuring social competence through interviewing', in Cook-Gumperz, J., Corsaro, W. and Streeck, J. (eds), *Children's Worlds and Children's Language*. Berlin: Mouton de Gruyter.

Silverman, D. (1993) *Interpreting Qualitative Data: Methods for Analyzing Talk, Text and Interaction*. London: Sage.

Silverman, D. (1997a) *Discourses of Counselling: HIV Counselling as Social Interaction*. London: Sage.

Silverman, D. (1997b) 'The logics of qualitative research', in Miller, G. and Dingwall, R. (eds), *Context and Method in Qualitative Research*. London: Sage.

Simon, H. (1987) *Getting to Know Schools in a Democracy*. London: Falmer Press.

Sinclair, I. (1971) *Hostels for Probationers.*. London: HMSO.

Smith, J. (1992) 'Interpretive inquiry: a practical and moral activity', *Theory into Practice*, 31 (2): 100–106.

Smith, J. (1993) 'Hermeneutics and qualitative inquiry', in Flinders, D. and Mills,

Name index

Subject index